THE LIFE

OF

REV. DAVID BRAINERD,

CHIEFLY EXTRACTED FROM HIS DIARY

BY PRESIDENT EDWARDS

SOMEWHAT ABRIDGED

EMBRACING, IN THE CHRONOLOGICAL ORDER,

BRAINERD'S PUBLIC JOURNAL

OF THE MOST SUCCESSFUL YEAR OF HIS

Missionary Labors

BAKER BOOK HOUSE
Grand Rapids, Michigan

Paperback edition issued 1978
by Baker Book House
from the edition issued by
the American Tract Society

ISBN: 0-8010-0726-7

Second printing, June 1978

Printed in the United States of America

CONTENTS

THERE is one thing, easily discernible in the life of BRAIN-ERD, which by many may be considered an objection to the extraordinary evidences of his religion and devotion, viz. that he was, *by his constitution and natural temper, so prone to melancholy and dejection of Spirit.* There are some who think that all religion is a melancholy thing; and that what is called Christian experience is little else beside melancholy, disturbing the brain, and exciting enthusiastic imaginations. But that Brainerd's temper or constitution inclined him to despondency, is no just ground for supposing that his extraordinary *devotion* was only the fruit of a warm imagination. Notwithstanding this inclination to despondency, he was evidently one of those who usually are the farthest from a teeming imagination; being of a penetrating genius, of clear thought, of close reasoning, and a very exact judgment; as was apparent to all who knew him. As he had a great insight into human nature, and was very discerning and judicious in general; so he excelled in his judgment and knowledge in divinity, but especially in experimental religion. He most accurately distinguished between real, solid piety, and enthusiasm; between those affections that are rational and scriptural, having their foundation in light and judgment, and those that are founded in whimsical conceits, strong impressions on the imagination, and vehement emotions of the animal spirits. He was exceedingly sensible of men's exposure to these things; how extensively they had prevailed, and what multitudes had been deceived by them; of their pernicious consequences, and the fearful mischief they had done in the Christian world. He had no confidence in such a religion, and was abundant in bearing testimony against it, living and dying; and was quick to discern when any thing of that nature arose, though in its first buddings, and appearing under the most fair and plausible disguises. He had a talent, which I scarcely ever knew equalled, for describing the various workings of this *imaginary enthusiastic* religion, evincing its falseness and vanity, and demonstrating the great difference between this and true *spiritual* devotion.

His judiciousness did not only appear in distinguishing among the experiences of *others*, but also among the various exercises of *his own mind;* particularly in discerning what within himself was to be laid to the score of *melancholy;* in which he exceeded all melancholy persons that ever I was acquainted with. This was doubtless owing to a peculiar strength in his *judgment;* for it is a rare thing indeed, that persons under the influence of melancholy are sensible of their own disease, and convinced that such things are to be ascribed to it, as are its genuine operations and fruits. Brainerd did not obtain that degree of skill at once, but gradually; as the reader may discern by the following account of his life. In the *former* part of his religious course, he imputed much of that kind of gloominess of mind to spiritual *desertion*, which in the latter part of his life he was abundantly sensible was owing to the disease of *melancholy;* accordingly he often expressly speaks of it in his diary, as arising from this cause. He often in conversation spoke of the difference between melancholy and godly sorrow; between true humiliation and spiritual desertion; and the great danger of mistaking the one for the other, and the very hurtful nature of melancholy; discoursing with great judgment upon it, and doubtless much more judiciously for what he knew by his own experience.

Another imperfection in Brainerd, which may be observed in the following account of his life, was his being *excessive in his labors ;* not taking due care to proportion his fatigues to his strength. Indeed, the seeming calls of Providence were very often such as made it extremely difficult for him to avoid laboring beyond his strength; yea, his circumstances, and the business of his mission among the Indians, were such, that great fatigues and hardships were altogether inevitable. However, he was finally convinced that he had erred in this matter, and that he ought to have taken more thorough care, and been more resolute to withstand temptations to such degrees of labor as injured his health; and accordingly he warned his brother, who succeeded him in his mission, to be careful to avoid this error.

Besides the imperfections already mentioned, it is readily allowed that there were some imperfections which ran through his whole life, and were mixed with all his religious affections and exercises; some mixture of what was natural, with that which was spiritual; as it evermore is in the best saints in this world. Doubtless, natural temper had some influence in the religious exercises of Brainerd, as it most apparently had in those of the devout David, and the Apostles Peter, John, and Paul. There was undoubtedly very often some mixture of melancholy with true godly sorrow and real Christian humility; some mixture of the natural fire of youth, with his holy zeal for God; and some influence of natural principles, mixed with grace in various other respects, as it ever was and ever will be with the saints, while on this side heaven. Perhaps none were more sensible of Brainerd's imperfections than himself; or could distinguish more accurately than he, between what was natural and what was spiritual. It is easy for the judicious reader to observe that his

graces ripened, that the religious exercises of his heart be
came more and more pure, and he more and more distin
guishing in his judgment, the longer he lived. He had much
to teach and purify him, and he failed not to profit thereby.

Notwithstanding all these imperfections, every pious and
judicious reader will readily acknowledge that what is here
set before him is a remarkable instance of true and eminent
piety, in heart and practice—tending greatly to confirm the
reality of vital religion, and the power of godliness; that it is
most worthy of imitation, and in many ways calculated to
promote the spiritual benefit of the careful observer.

The reader should be aware that what Brainerd wrote in
his *diary*, out of which the following account of his life is
chiefly taken, was written only for his own private use; and
not to obtain honor and applause in the world, nor with any
design that the world should ever see it, either while he lived,
or after his death; except a few things which he wrote in a
dying state, after he had been persuaded, with difficulty, not
entirely to suppress all his private writings. He showed himself almost invincibly averse to the publishing of any part of
his *diary* after his death; and when he was thought to be dying at Boston, gave the most strict, peremptory orders to the
contrary. But being by some of his friends there, prevailed
upon to withdraw so strict and absolute a prohibition, he was
finally pleased to yield so far, as that " his papers should be
left in my hands, that I might dispose of them as I thought
would be most for God's glory and the interest of religion."

JONATHAN EDWARDS

LIFE

OF

REV. DAVID BRAINERD

CHAPTER I

From his birth to the time when he began to study for the Ministry—containing his own narrative of his conversion, his connection with Yale-College, and the grounds of his expulsion.

April 20, 1718--Feb. 1741

DAVID BRAINERD was born April 20, 1718, at Haddam, Connecticut. His father was Hezekiah Brainerd, Esq. and his mother, Dorothy Hobart, daughter of the Rev. Jeremiah Hobart.

He was the third son of his parents, who had five sons and four daughters. The oldest son was a respectable citizen of Haddam; the second was Rev. Nehemiah Brainerd, a worthy minister in Eastbury, in Connecticut; the fourth, Mr. John Brainerd, who succeeded his brother David as missionary to the Indians, and pastor of the same church of Christian Indians in New-Jersey; and the fifth was Israel, lately student at Yale-College, who died soon after his brother David. Their mother, having lived about five years a widow, died when the subject of this memoir was about fourteen

years of age; so that in his youth he was left both
fatherless and motherless. The following is the account he has himself given of the first twenty-three
years of his life.

"I was from my youth somewhat sober, and inclined
to melancholy; but do not remember any thing of conviction of sin, worthy of remark, till I was, I believe,
about seven or eight years of age. Then I became
concerned for my soul, and terrified at the thoughts of
death; and was driven to the performance of religious
duties: but it appeared a melancholy business that destroyed my eagerness for play. And though, alas! this
religious concern was but short-lived, I sometimes attended secret prayer; and thus lived "without God in
the world," and without much concern, as I remember,
till I was above thirteen years of age. In the winter
of 1732 I was roused out of this carnal security by, I
scarce know what means at first; but was much excited by the prevalence of a mortal sickness in Haddam. I was frequent, constant, and somewhat fervent
in prayer; and took delight in reading, especially Mr.
JANEWAY's *Token for Children*. I felt sometimes much
melted in the duties of religion, took great delight in
the performance of them, and sometimes hoped that I
was converted, or at least in a good and hopeful way
for heaven and happiness; not knowing what conversion was. The Spirit of God at this time proceeded
far with me. I was remarkably dead to the world; my
thoughts were almost wholly employed about my soul's
concerns; and I may indeed say, "Almost I was persuaded to be a Christian." I was also exceedingly distressed and melancholy at the death of my mother, in
March, 1732. But afterward my religious concern
began to decline, and by degrees I fell back into a con-

siderable degree of security, though I still attended secret prayer.

"About the 15th of April, 1733, I removed from my father's house to East-Haddam, where I spent four years; but still "without God in the world," though, for the most part, I went a round of secret duty. I was not much addicted to the company and the amusements of the young; but this I know, that when I did go into such company I never returned with so good a conscience as when I went. It always added new guilt, made me afraid to come to the throne of grace, and spoiled those good frames with which I was wont sometimes to please myself. But, alas! all my good frames were but self-righteousness, not founded on a desire for the glory of God.

"About the end of April, 1737, being full nineteen years of age, I removed to Durham, to work on my farm, and continued about one year; frequently longing after a liberal education. When about twenty years of age I applied myself to study; and was now engaged more than ever in the duties of religion. I became very strict, and watchful over my thoughts, words, and actions; concluded that I must be sober indeed, because I designed to devote myself to the ministry; and *imagined* that I *did* dedicate myself to the Lord.

"Sometime in April, 1738, I went to live with Rev. Mr. Fiske, of Haddam, and continued with him during his life. I remember he advised me wholly to abandon young company, and associate myself with grave elderly people; which counsel I followed. My manner of life was now wholly regular, and full of religion, such as it was; for I read my bible more than twice through in less than a year, spent much time every day in prayer and other secret duties, gave great attention to the word preached, and endeavored to my utmost to retain it. So much concerned was I about religion, that I agreed with some young persons to meet privately on Sabbath evenings for religious exercises, and thought myself *sincere* in these duties; and after our meeting was ended I used to repeat the discourses of the day to myself; recollecting what I could, though sometimes very late at night. I used occasionally on Monday mornings to recollect the same sermons; had sometimes pleasure in religious exercises, and had many thoughts of joining the church. In short, I had a very good *outside*, and rested entirely on my duties, though I was not sensible of it.

" After Mr. Fiske's death I proceeded in my studies with my brother; was still very constant in religious duties, often wondered at the levity of professors, and lamented their carelessness in religion.—Thus I proceeded a considerable length on a *self-righteous* foundation; and should have been entirely lost and undone, had not the mere mercy of God prevented.

"Sometime in the beginning of winter, 1738, it pleased God, one Sabbath morning, as I was walking out for secret duties, to give me on a sudden such a sense of my danger, and the wrath of God, that I stood amazed, and my former good frames presently vanished. From the view which I had of my sin and vileness, I was much distressed all that day, fearing that the vengeance of God would soon overtake me. I was much dejected; kept much alone; and sometimes envied the birds and beasts their happiness, because they were not exposed to eternal misery, as I evidently saw that I was. Thus I lived from day to day, being frequently in great distress: sometimes there appeared mountains before me to obstruct my hopes of mercy; and the work of conversion appeared so great, that I thought I should never be the subject of it. I used, however, to pray and cry to God, and perform other duties with great earnestness; and thus hoped by some means to make the case better.

"Hundreds of times I renounced all pretences of any worth in my duties, as I thought, even while performing them; and often confessed to God that I deserved nothing for the very best of them, but eternal condemnation; yet still I had a secret hope of *recommending* myself to God by my religious duties. When I prayed affectionately, and my heart seemed in some measure to melt, I hoped that God would be thereby moved to pity me. There was, then, some appearance of *goodness* in my prayers, and I seemed to *mourn* for sin. I could in some measure venture on the mercy of God in Christ, as I thought; though the preponderating thought, the foundation of my hope was some imagination of goodness in my meltings of heart, the warmth of my affections, and my extraordinary enlargements in prayer. Though at times the gate appeared so very strait that it looked next to impossible to enter; yet, at other times I flattered myself that it was not so very difficult, and hoped I should by diligence and watchfulness soon gain the point. Sometimes after enlargement in duty and considerable affection, I hoped I had made a *good step* toward heaven, and imagined that God was affected as I was, and would hear such *sincere cries*, as I called them. And so sometimes, when I withdrew for secret prayer in great distress, I returned comfortable; and thus healed myself with my duties.

"In February, 1739, I set apart a day for secret fasting and prayer, and spent the day in almost incessant cries to God for mercy, that he would open my eyes to see the evil of sin, and the way of life by Jesus Christ. God was pleased that day to make considerable discoveries of my heart to me. Still I *trusted* in all the duties I performed, though there was no manner of goodness in them; there being in them no respect to the glory of God, nor any such principle in my heart. Yet God was pleased to make my endeavors, that day, a means to show me my helplessness in some measure.

"Sometimes I was greatly encouraged, and imagined that God loved me and was pleased with me, and thought I should soon be fully reconciled to God. But the whole was founded on mere presumption, arising from enlargement in duty, or warmth of affections, or some good resolutions, or the like.   And when, at times, great distress began to arise on a sight of my vileness and inability to deliver myself from a sovereign God, I used to put off the discovery, as what I could not bear. Once, I remember, a terrible pang of distress seized me; and the thought of renouncing myself, and standing naked before God, stripped of all goodness, was so dreadful to me that I was ready to say to it, as Felix to Paul, "Go thy way for this time." Thus, though I daily longed for greater conviction of sin; supposing that I must see more of my dreadful state in order to a remedy; yet, when the discoveries of my vile, wicked heart were made to me, the sight was so dreadful, and showed me so plainly my exposedness to damnation, that I could not endure it. I constantly strove after whatever *qualifications* I imagined others obtained before the reception of Christ, in order to *recommend* me to his favor. Sometimes I felt the power of a hard heart, and supposed it must be softened before Christ would accept of me; and when I felt any meltings of heart, I hoped now the work was almost done. Hence, when my distress still remained I was wont to murmur at God's dealings with me; and thought, when others felt their hearts softened, God showed them mercy; but my distress remained still.

"At times I grew remiss and sluggish, without any great convictions of sin, for a considerable time together; but after such a season convictions sometimes seized me more violently. One night I remember in particular, when I was walking solitarily abroad, I had opened to me such a view of my sin that I feared the ground would cleave asunder under my feet, and become my grave; and send my soul quick into hell, before I could get home. Though I was forced to go to bed, lest my distress should be discovered by others, which I much feared; yet I scarcely durst sleep at all, for I thought it would be a great wonder if I should be out of hell in the morning. And though my distress was sometimes thus great, yet I greatly dreaded the loss of *convictions*, and returning back to a state of carnal security, and to my former insensibility of impending wrath; which made me exceedingly exact in my behaviour, lest I should stifle the motions of God's Holy Spirit. When at any time I took a view of my convictions, and thought the degree of them to be considerable, I was wont to trust in them; but this confidence, and the hope of soon making some notable advances toward deliverance, would ease my mind, and I soon became more senseless and remiss. Again, when I discerned my convictions to grow languid, and thought them about to leave me, this immediately alarmed and distressed me. Sometimes I expected to take a large step, and get very far toward conversion, by some particular opportunity or means I had in view.

"The many disappointments, the great distress and perplexity which I experienced, put me into a most horrible frame of contesting with the almighty; with inward vehemence and virulence finding fault with his ways of dealing with mankind. My wicked heart often wished for some other way of salvation than by Jesus Christ. Being like the troubled sea, my thoughts confused, I used to contrive to escape the wrath of God by some other means. I had strange projects, full of Atheism, contriving to disappoint God's designs and decrees concerning me, or to escape his notice and hide myself from him. But when upon reflection I saw these projects were vain, and would not serve me, and that I could contrive nothing for my own relief, this would throw my mind into the most horrid frame, to wish there was no God, or to wish there was some *other* God that could control him. These thoughts and desires were the secret inclinations of my heart, frequently acting before I was aware; but, alas! they were *mine*, although I was frightened when I came to reflect on them. When I considered, it distressed me to think that my heart was so full of enmity against God; and it made me tremble, lest his vengeance should suddenly fall upon me. I used before to imagine that my heart was not so bad as the Scriptures and some other books represented it. Sometimes I used to take much pains to work it up into a good frame, a humble submissive disposition; and hoped there was *then* some goodness in me. But, on a sudden, the thoughts of the strictness of the law, or the sovereignty of God, would so irritate the corruption of my heart that I had so watched over and hoped I had brought to a good frame, that it would break over all bounds, and burst forth on all sides, like floods of waters when they break down their dam.

"Being sensible of the necessity of deep humiliation in order to a saving close with Christ, I used to set myself to produce in my own heart the *convictions* requisite in such a humiliation: as, a conviction that God would be just, if he cast me off for ever; that if ever God should bestow mercy on me, it would be mere grace, though I should be in distress many years first, and be never so much engaged in duty; and that God was not in the least obliged to pity me the more for all past duties, cries, and tears. I strove to my utmost to bring myself to a firm belief of these things and a hearty assent to them; and hoped that now I was brought off from *myself*, truly humbled, and that I bowed to the divine sovereignty. I was wont to tell God in my prayers, that now I had those very dispositions of soul which he required, and on which he showed mercy to others, and thereupon to beg and plead for mercy to me. But when I found no relief, and was still oppressed with guilt and fears of wrath, my soul was in a tumult, and my heart rose against God, as dealing hardly with me. Yet *then* my conscience flew in my face, putting me in mind of my late confession to God of his *justice* in my condemnation. This, giving me a sight of the badness of my heart, threw me again into distress; and I wished that I had watched my heart more narrowly, to keep it from breaking out against God's dealings with me. I even wished that I had not pleaded for mercy on account of my humiliation; because thereby I had lost all my seeming goodness. Thus, scores of times I vainly imagined myself humbled and prepared for saving mercy. While

I was in this distressed, bewildered, and tumultuous
state of mind, the corruption of my heart was especially *irritated* with the following things.

1. " The *strictness* of the divine *law.*   For I found
it was impossible for me, after my utmost pains, to answer its demands.   I often made new resolutions, and
as often broke them.   I imputed the whole to carelessness, and the want of being more watchful, and used
to call myself a fool for my negligence.   But when,
upon a stronger resolution, and greater endeavors, and
close application to fasting and prayer, I found all attempts fail; then I quarrelled with the law of God, as
unreasonably rigid.   I thought, if it extended only to
my *outward* actions and behavior, that I could bear
with it; but I found that it condemned me for my evil
thoughts, and sins of my *heart,* which I could not possibly prevent.   I was extremely loth to own my utter
helplessness in this matter: but after repeated disappointments, thought that rather than perish I could do
a little more still; especially if such and such circumstances might but attend my endeavors and strivings.
I hoped that I should strive more earnestly than ever,
if the matter came to extremity, though I never could
find the time to do my utmost in the manner I intended.   This hope of future more favorable circumstances,
and of doing something great hereafter, kept me from
utter despair in myself, and from seeing myself fallen
into the hands of a sovereign God, and dependent on
nothing but free and boundless grace.

2. "Another point that irritated me was, *that faith
alone was the condition of salvation;* that God would
not come down to lower terms; and that he would not
promise life and salvation upon my sincere and hearty

prayers and endeavors.   That word, Mark 16: 16, " He
that believeth not shall be damned," cut off all hope
there. I found that faith was the sovereign gift of God ;
that I could not get it as of myself; and could not oblige
God to bestow it upon me by any of my performances.
Eph. 2 : 1, 8.   " This," I was ready to say, "is a
hard saying, who can hear it ? " I could not bear that
all I had done should stand for mere nothing ; as
I had been very conscientious in duty, had been very
religious a great while, and had, as I thought, done
much more than many others who had obtained mercy. I confessed indeed the vileness of my duties; but
then what made them at that time seem vile, was my
wandering thoughts in them, rather than because I was
all over defiled like a devil, and the principle corrupt
from whence they flowed, so that I could not possibly
do any thing that was good. Hence I called what I did
by the name of *honest faithful endeavors ;* and could not
bear it, that God had made no promises of salvation
to them.

3."I could not find out *what* faith was; or *what* it
was to believe and come to Christ. I read the calls of
Christ to the *weary* and *heavy laden;* but could find no
way in which he directed them to come. I thought I
would gladly come, if I knew how; though the path
of duty were never so difficult. I read Stoddard's
Guide to Christ, (which I trust was, in the hand of God,
the happy means of my conversion,) and my heart rose
against the author; for though he told me my very
heart all along under convictions, and seemed to be
very beneficial to me in his directions; yet here he
seemed to me to fail: he did not tell me any thing I
could do that would bring me to Christ, but left me as
it were with a great gulph between me and Christ, without any direction how to get through.   For I was not

yet effectually and experimentally taught, that there
could be no way prescribed, whereby a natural man
could, of his own strength, obtain that which is supernatural, and which the highest angel cannot give.

4. " Another point was the *sovereignty* of God. I
could not bear that it should be wholly at God's pleasure, to save or damn me, just as he would. That passage, Rom. 9 : 11–23, was a constant vexation to me,
especially verse 21. Reading or meditating on this, always destroyed my seeming good frames; for when I
thought I was almost humbled, and almost resigned,
this passage would make my enmity against God appear. When I came to reflect on the inward enmity
and blasphemy which arose on this occasion, I was
the more afraid of God, and driven further from any
hopes of reconciliation with him. It gave me a dreadful view of myself; I dreaded more than ever to see
myself in God's hands, and it made me more opposite
than ever to submit to his sovereignty; for I thought
He designed my damnation.

" All this time the Spirit of God was powerfully at
work with me; and I was inwardly pressed to relinquish all *self-confidence*, all hope of ever helping myself by any means whatsoever. The conviction of my
lost estate was sometimes so clear and manifest before
my eyes that it was as if it had been declared to me in
so many words, " It is done, it is done, it is for ever
impossible to deliver yourself." For about three or
four days my soul was thus greatly distressed. At
some turns, for a few moments, I seemed to myself
lost and undone; but then would shrink back immediately from the sight, because I dared not venture myself into the hands of God, as wholly helpless, and at

the disposal of his sovereign pleasure. I dared not see that important truth concerning myself, that I was "dead in trespasses and sins." But when I had, as it were, thrust away these views of myself at any time, I felt distressed to have the same discoveries of myself again; for I greatly feared being given over of God to final stupidity. When I thought of putting it off to a more "convenient season," the conviction was so close and powerful, that the *present* time was the best, and probably the *only* time, that I dared not put it off.

"It was the sight of truth concerning myself, truth respecting my state, as a creature fallen and alienated from God, and that consequently could make no demands on God for mercy, but was at his absolute disposal, from which my soul shrank away, and which I trembled to think of beholding. Thus, he that doeth evil, as all unregenerate men continually do, hates the light of truth, neither cares to come to it, because it will reprove his deeds, and show him his just deserts. John, 3 : 20. Sometime before, I had taken much pains, as I thought, to submit to the sovereignty of God; yet I mistook the thing, and did not once imagine, that seeing and being made experimentally sensible of this truth, which my soul now so much dreaded and trembled at, was the frame of soul which I had so earnestly desired. I had ever hoped that when I had attained to that *humiliation* which I supposed necessary to precede faith, then it would not be fair for God to *cast me off;* but now I saw it was so far from any goodness in me, to own myself spiritually dead and destitute of all goodness, that on the contrary, my mouth world be for ever stopped by it; and it looked as dreadful to me, to see myself, and the relation I stood in to God—I a sinner and criminal, and he a great Judge and Sovereign—as it would be to a poor trembling creature to venture off some high precipice. Hence I put it off for a minute or two, and tried for better circumstances to do it in: either I must read a passage or two, or pray first, or something of the like nature; or else put off my submission to God with an objection, that I did not know how to submit. But the truth was, I could see no safety in owning myself in the hands of a sovereign God, and could lay no claim to any thing better than damnation.

"After a considerable time spent in similar exercises and distress, one morning, while I was walking in a solitary place, as usual, I at once saw that all my contrivances and projects to effect or procure deliverance and salvation for myself were utterly in vain; I was brought quite to a stand, as finding myself totally lost. I had thought many times before, that the difficulties in my way were very great; but now I saw, in another and very different light, that it was for ever impossible for me to do any thing toward helping or delivering myself. I then thought of blaming myself, that I had not done more, and been more engaged, while I had opportunity—for it seemed now as if the season of doing was for ever over and gone—but I instantly saw, that let me have done what I would, it would no more have tended to my helping myself, than what I had done; that I had made all the pleas I ever could have made to all eternity; and that all my pleas were vain. The tumult that had been before in my mind was now quieted; and I was somewhat eased of that distress which I felt while struggling against a sight of myself, and of the divine sovereignty. I had the greatest certainty that my state was for ever miserable, for all that I could do; and wondered that I had never been sensible of it before.

"While I remained in this state my notions respecting my duties were quite different from what I had ever entertained in times past. Before this, the more I did in duty, the more hard I thought it would be for God to cast me off; though at the same time I confessed, and thought I saw, that there was no goodness or merit in my duties; but now, the more I did in prayer or any other duty, the more I saw that I was indebted to God for allowing me to ask for mercy; for I saw that self interest had led me to pray, and that I had never once prayed from any respect to the glory of God. Now I saw that there was no necessary connection between my prayers and the bestowment of divine mercy; that they laid not the least obligation upon God to bestow his grace upon me; and that there was no more virtue or goodness in them than there would be in my *paddling with my hand in the water*, (which was the comparison I had then in my mind;) and this because they were not performed from any love or regard to God. I saw that I had been heaping up my devotions before God, fasting, praying, &c. pretending, and indeed really thinking sometimes, that I was aiming at the glory of God; whereas I never once truly intended it, l ut only my own happiness. I saw that as I had never done any thing for God, I had no claim on any thing from him, but perdition, on account of my hypocrisy and mockery. Oh, how different did my duties now appear from what they used to do! I used to charge them with sin and imperfection; but this was only on account of the wandering and vain thoughts attending them, and not because I had no regard to God in them; for this I thought I had. But when I saw evidently that I had had regard to nothing but self-interest; then they appeared a vile

mockery of God, self-worship, and a continued course
of lies. I saw that something worse had attended my
duties than barely a few wanderings; for the whole
was nothing but self-worship, and an horrid abuse
of God.

"I continued, as I remember, in this state of mind
from Friday morning till the Sabbath evening following, (July 12, 1739,) when I was walking again in the
same solitary place where I was brought to see myself
lost and helpless, as before mentioned. Here, in a
mournful melancholy state, I was attempting to pray,
but found no heart to engage in prayer or any
other duty. My former concern, exercise, and religious affections were now gone. I thought that the
Spirit of God had quite left me; but still was not distressed; yet disconsolate, as if there was nothing in
heaven or earth could make me happy. Having been
thus endeavoring to pray—though, as I thought, very
stupid and senseless—for near half an hour; then, as I
was walking in a dark thick grove, *unspeakable glory*
seemed to open to the view and apprehension of my
soul. I do not mean any *external* brightness, for I
saw no such thing; nor do I intend any imagination of
a body of light, somewhere in the third heavens, or
any thing of that nature; but it was a new inward apprehension or view that I had of God, such as I never
had before, nor any thing which had the least resemblance of it. I stood still, wondered, and admired! I
knew that I never had seen before any thing compara-
ble to it for excellency and beauty; it was widely different from all the conceptions that ever I had of God,
or things divine. I had no particular apprehension of
any one person in the Trinity, either the Father, the
Son, or the Holy Ghost; but it appeared to be *Divine*

glory that I then beheld. My soul rejoiced with joy unspeakable, to see such a God, such a glorious divine Being; and I was inwardly pleased and satisfied, that he should be God over all for ever and ever. My soul was so captivated and delighted with the excellency, loveliness, greatness, and other perfections of God, that I was even swallowed up in him; at least to that degree that I had no thought, as I remember, *at first*, about my own salvation, and scarce reflected that there was such a creature as myself.

"Thus God, I trust, brought me to a hearty disposition to *exalt him*, and set him on the throne, and principally and ultimately to aim at his honor and glory, as King of the universe. I continued in this state of inward joy, peace and astonishment, till near dark, without any sensible abatement; and then began to think and examine what I had seen; and felt sweetly composed in my mind all the evening following. I felt myself in a new world, and every thing about me appeared with a different aspect from what it was wont to do.

"At this time the *way of salvation* opened to me with such infinite wisdom, suitableness, and excellency, that I wondered I should ever think of any other way of salvation; I was amazed that I had not dropped my own contrivances and complied with this lovely, blessed, and excellent way before. If I could have been saved by my own duties, or any other way that I had formerly contrived, my whole soul would now have refused. I wondered that all the world did not see and comply with this way of salvation, entirely by the *righteousness of Christ*.

"The sweet relish of what I then felt continued with me for several days, almost constantly, in a greater or

less degree. I could not but sweetly rejoice in God,
lying down and rising up. The next Lord's day I felt
something of the same kind, though not so powerful
as before. But not long after, I was again involved in
darkness, and in great distress; yet not of the same kind
with my distress under convictions. I was guilty,
afraid, and ashamed to come before God; and exceedingly pressed with a sense of guilt; but it was not long
before I felt, I trust, true repentance and joy in God.

"In the beginning of September I went to Yale College, and entered there; but with some degree of reluctance, lest I should not be able to lead a life of strict
religion in the midst of so many temptations. After
this, in the vacation, before I went to tarry at college,
it pleased God to visit my soul with clearer manifesta-
tions of himself and his grace. I was spending some
time in prayer and self-examination, when the Lord,
by his grace, so shined into my heart, that I enjoyed
full assurance of his favor, for that time; and my soul
was unspeakably refreshed with divine and heavenly
enjoyments. At this time especially, as well as some
others, sundry passages of God's word opened to my
soul with divine clearness, power, and sweetness, so
as to appear exceeding precious, and with clear and
certain evidence of its being *the word of God*. I enjoyed considerable sweetness in religion all the winter
following.

"In Jan. 1740, the measles spread much in college,
and I, having taken the distemper, went home to Haddam. But some days before I was taken sick I seemed to be greatly deserted, and my soul mourned the
absence of the Comforter exceedingly. It seemed to
me that all comfort was for ever gone. I prayed and
cried to God for help, yet found no present comfort or

relief. But through divine goodness, a night or two
before I was taken ill, while I was walking alone in a
very retired place, and engaged in meditation and prayer,
I enjoyed a sweet refreshing visit, as I trust, from above;
so that my soul was raised far above the fears of death.
Indeed, I rather longed for death, than feared it. Oh,
how much more refreshing this one season was, than
all the pleasures and delights that earth can afford.
After a day or two I was taken with the measles, and
was very ill indeed, so that I almost despaired of life;
but had no distressing fears of death. Through divine
goodness I soon recovered; yet, owing to hard study,
and to my being much exposed to interruptions on account of my *freshmanship*, I had but little time for spiritual duties, and my soul often mourned for want of
more time and opportunity to be alone with God. In
the spring and summer following I had better advantages for retirement, and enjoyed more comfort in religion, though my ambition in my studies greatly
wronged the activity and vigor of my spiritual life. It
was, however, usually the case with me, that, "in the
multitude of my thoughts within me, God's comforts
principally delighted my soul." These were my greatest consolations day by day.

"One day, I think it was in June, 1740, I walked to
a considerable distance from college, in the fields alone,
at noon, and in prayer found such unspeakable sweetness and delight in God, that I thought, if I must continue in this evil world, I wanted always to be there, to
behold God's glory. My soul dearly loved all mankind,
and longed exceedingly that they should enjoy what I
enjoyed. It seemed to be a little resemblance of heaven.

"Some time in August following I became so reduced in health by too close application to my studies,

that I was advised by my tutor to go home, and disengage my mind from study as much as I could; for I was grown so weak that I began to raise blood. I took his advice, and endeavored to lay aside my studies. But being brought very low, I looked death in the face more steadfastly; and the Lord was pleased to give me renewedly a sweet sense and relish of divine things; and particularly October 13, I found divine help and consolation in the precious duties of secret prayer and self-examination, and my soul took delight in the blessed God:—so likewise on the 17th of October.

Oct. 18. "In my morning devotions my soul was exceedingly melted, and bitterly mourned over my great *sinfulness* and *vileness*. I never before had felt so pungent and deep a sense of the odious nature of sin, as at this time. My soul was then unusually carried forth in love to God, and had a lively sense of God's love to me. And this love and hope, at that time cast out fear.

Lord's day, Oct. 19. "In the morning I felt my soul hungering and thirsting after righteousness. While I was looking on the elements of the Lord's Supper, and thinking that Jesus Christ was now "set forth crucified before me," my soul was filled with light and love, so that I was almost in an ecstacy; my body was so weak I could scarcely stand. I felt at the same time an exceeding tenderness and most fervent love toward all mankind; so that my soul and all its powers seemed, as it were, to melt into softness and sweetness. But during the communion there was some abatement of this life and fervor. This love and joy cast out fear; and my soul longed for perfect grace and glory. This frame continued till the evening, when my soul was sweetly spiritual in secret duties.

Oct. 20. "I again found the assistance of the Holy Spirit in secret duties, both morning and evening, and life and comfort in religion through the whole day.

Oct. 21. "I had likewise experience of the goodness of God in 'shedding abroad his love in my heart,' and giving me delight and consolation in religious duties; and all the remaining part of the week my soul seemed to be taken up with divine things. I now so longed after God, and to be freed from sin, that, when I felt myself recovering, and thought I must return to college again, which had proved so hurtful to my spiritual interests the year past, I could not but be grieved, and thought I had much rather die; for it distressed me to think of getting away from God. But before I went I enjoyed several other sweet and precious seasons of communion with God, (particularly Oct. 30, and Nov. 4,) wherein my soul enjoyed unspeakable comfort.

"I returned to college about Nov. 6, and, through the goodness of God, felt the power of religion almost daily, for the space of six weeks.

Nov. 28. "In my evening devotion I enjoyed precious discoveries of God, and was unspeakably refreshed with that passage, Heb. 12:22–24. My soul longed to wing away to the paradise of God; I longed to be conformed to God in all things.—A day or two after I enjoyed much of the light of God's countenance, most of the day; and my soul rested in God.

Dec. 9. "I was in a comfortable frame of soul most of the day; but especially in evening devotions, when God was pleased wonderfully to assist and strengthen me; so that I thought nothing should ever move me from the love of God in Christ Jesus my Lord. Oh! *one hour with God* infinitely exceeds all the pleasures and delights of this lower world.

"Toward the latter part of January, 1741, I grew more cold and dull in religion, by means of my old temptation, ambition in my studies. But through divine goodness, a great and general *awakening* spread itself over the college, about the end of February, in which I was much quickened, and more abundantly engaged in religion."

This awakening was at the beginning of that extraordinary religious commotion which then prevailed through the land, and in which the college shared largely. For thirteen months from this time BRAINERD kept a constant diary containing a very particular account of what passed from day to day, making two volumes of manuscripts; but when he lay on his death bed he gave orders (unknown to me till after his death) that these two volumes should be destroyed, inserting a notice, at the beginning of the succeeding manuscripts, that a specimen of his manner of living during that entire period would be found in the first thirty pages next following, (ending with June 15, 1742,) except that he was now more "refined from some imprudences and indecent heats" than before.

A circumstance in the life of BRAINERD, which gave great offence to the rulers of the College, and occasioned his expulsion, it is necessary should be here particularly related. During the awakening in College, there were several religious students who associated together for mutual conversation and assistance in spiritual things. These were wont freely to open themselves one to another, as special and intimate friends: BRAINERD was one of this company. And it once happened, that he and two or three more of these intimate friends were in the hall together, after Mr.

Whittlesey, one of the tutors, had engaged in prayer with the scholars; no other person now remaining in the hall but Brainerd and his companions. Mr. Whittlesey having been unusually pathetic in his prayer, one of Brainerd's friends on this occasion asked him what he thought of Mr. Whittlesey; he made answer, "He has no more grace than this chair." One of the freshmen happening at that time to be near the hall, (though not in the room,) over-heard these words; and though he heard no name mentioned, and knew not who was thus censured, informed a certain woman in the town, withal telling her his own suspicion, that Brainerd said this of some one of the rulers of the College. Whereupon she informed the Rector, who sent for this freshman and examined him. He told the Rector the words which he heard Brainerd utter; and informed him who were in the room with him at that time. Upon this the Rector sent for them. They were very backward to inform against their friend respecting what they looked upon as private conversation; especially as none but they had heard or knew of whom he had uttered those words: yet the Rector compelled them to declare what he said, and of whom he said it. Brainerd looked on himself as very ill used in the management of this affair; and thought that it was injuriously extorted from his friends, and then injuriously required of him—as if he had been guilty of some open, notorious crime—to make a *public* confession, and to humble himself before the whole College in the hall, for what he had said only in private conversation. He not complying with this demand, and having gone once to the Separate meeting at New-Haven, when forbidden by the Rector; and also having been accused by one person of saying concerning the Rector, " that he wondered he did not expect to drop down dead for fining the scholars who followed Mr. Tennent to Milford, though there was *no proof* of it ; (and Brainerd ever professed that he did not remember saying any thing to that purpose,) for these things he was *expelled* the college.

How far the circumstances and exigencies of that day might justify such great severity in the governors of the college, I will not undertake to determine; it being my aim, not to bring reproach on the authority of the college, but only to do justice to the memory of a person who was, I think, eminently one of those whose *memory is blessed.*—The reader will see, in the sequel, (particularly under date of Septemper 14, 15, 1743,) in how christian a manner Brainerd conducted himself with respect to this affair; though he ever, as long as he lived, supposed himself ill used in the management of it, and in what he suffered.—His expulsion was in the winter, 1742, while in his third year at college.

CHAPTER II

From about the time when he began the study of Theology, till he was licensed to preach.

April 1, 1742—July 29, 1742

In the spring of 1742 Brainerd went to live with the Rev. Mr. Mills of Ripton, to pursue his studies with him for the work of the ministry. Here he spent the greater part of the time until he was licensed to preach; but frequently rode to visit the neighboring ministers, particularly Mr. Cooke of Stratford. Mr.

Graham of Southbury, and Mr. Bellamy of Bethlehem. The following are extracts from his diary at this period.

April 1, 1742.—" I seem to be declining, with respect to my life and warmth in divine things; have not had so free access to God in prayer to-day as usual of late. Oh that God would humble me deeply in the dust before him! I deserve hell every day, for not loving my Lord more, who has, I trust, "loved me and given himself for me;" and every time I am enabled to exercise any grace renewedly, I am renewedly indebted to the God of all grace for special assistance. " Where then is boasting?" Surely "it is excluded," when we think how we are dependent on God for the existence and every act of grace. O if ever I get to heaven, it will be because God pleases, and nothing else; for I never did any thing of myself but get away from God! My soul will be astonished at the unsearchable riches of divine grace when I arrive at the mansions which the blessed Savior is gone before to prepare.

April 2.—" In the afternoon I felt, in secret prayer, much resigned, calm and serene. What are all the storms of this lower world if *Jesus*, by his Spirit, does but come *walking on the seas!*—Sometime past I had much pleasure in the prospect of the Heathen being brought home to Christ, and desired that the Lord would employ *me* in that work; but now my soul more frequently desires to die, *to be with Christ*. Oh that my soul were wrapt up in divine love, and my longing desires after God increased! In the evening was refreshed in prayer, with the hopes of the advancement of Christ's kingdom in the world.

Lord's day, *April* 4.—" My heart was wandering

and lifeless. In the evening God gave me faith in prayer, made my soul melt in some measure, and gave me to taste a divine sweetness. O my blessed God! Let me climb up near to him, and love, and long, and plead, and wrestle, and stretch after him, and for deliverance from the body of sin and death. Alas! my soul mourned to think I should ever lose sight of its beloved again. "O come, Lord Jesus, Amen."

April 6.—" I walked out this morning; had an affecting sense of my own vileness; and cried to God to cleanse me, to give me repentance and pardon. I then began to find it sweet to pray; and could think of undergoing the greatest sufferings in the cause of Christ, with pleasure; and found myself willing, if God should so order it, to suffer banishment from my native land, among the heathen, that I might do something for their salvation, in distresses and deaths of any kind. Then God gave me to wrestle earnestly for others, for the kingdom of Christ in the world, and for dear Christian friends.

April 8.—" Had raised hopes to-day respecting the heathen. Oh that God would bring in great numbers of them to Jesus Christ! I cannot but hope that I shall see that glorious day. Every thing in this world seems exceeding vile and little to me: I appear so to myself. I had some little dawn of comfort to-day in prayer; but especially to-night, I think I had some faith and *power* of intercession with God. I was enabled to plead with God for the growth of grace in myself; and many of the dear children of God then lay with weight upon my soul. Blessed be the Lord! It is good to wrestle for divine blessings.

April 9.—" Most of my time in morning devotion was spent without sensible sweetness; yet I had one delightful prospect of arriving at the heavenly world. I am more amazed than ever at such thoughts; for I see myself infinitely vile and unworthy. No poor creature stands in need of divine grace more than I, and none abuse it more than I have done, and still do.

Lord's day, April 11.—" In the morning I felt but little life; yet my heart was somewhat drawn out in thankfulness to God for his amazing grace and condescension to me, in past influences and assistances of his Spirit. Afterward, I had some sweetness in the thoughts of arriving at the *heavenly world.* O for the happy day! After public worship, God gave me special assistance in prayer; I wrestled with my dear Lord, and intercession was made a delightful employment to me. In the evening, as I was viewing the light in the north, I was delighted in the contemplation of the glorious morning of the resurrection.

April 12.—" This morning the Lord was pleased to lift up the light of his countenance upon me in secret prayer, and made the season very precious to my soul. Though I have been so depressed of late, respecting my hopes of future serviceableness in the cause of God; yet now I had much encouragement. I was especially assisted to intercede and plead for poor souls, and for the enlargement of Christ's kingdom in the world, and for *special grace* for myself, to fit me for *special services.* My faith lifted me above the world, and removed all those mountains over which of late I could not look. I wanted not the favor of man to lean upon; for I knew that Christ's favor was infinitely better, and that it was no matter *when* nor *where,* nor *how* Christ should send me, nor what trials he should still exercise me with, if I might be prepared for his work and will.

April 14.—" My soul longed for communion with

Christ, and for the mortification of indwelling corruption, especially spiritual pride. O, there is a sweet day coming, wherein "the weary will be at rest!" My soul has enjoyed much sweetness this day, in the hope of its speedy arrival.

April 15.—" My desires apparently centered in God and I found a sensible attraction of soul after him sundry times to-day. I know that *I long for God*, and a conformity to his will, in inward purity and holiness, ten thousand times more than for any thing here below.

Lord's day, April 18.—" I retired early this morning into the woods for prayer; had the assistance of God's Spirt, and faith in exercise; and was enabled to plead with fervency for the advancement of Christ's kingdom in the world, and to intercede for dear, absent friends. At noon, God enabled me to wrestle with him, and to feel, as I trust, the power of divine love in prayer. At night, I saw myself infinitely indebted to God, and had a view of my failures in duty. It seemed to me that I had done, as it were, nothing for God, and that I had *lived to him* but a few hours of my life.

April 19.—" I set apart this day for fasting and prayer to God for his grace; especially to prepare me for the work of the *ministry ;* to give me divine aid and direction, in my preparations for that great work; and in his own time *to send me into his harvest.* Accordingly, in the morning I endeavored to plead for the divine presence for the day, and not without some life. In the forenoon I felt the power of intercession for precious, immortal souls; for the advancement of the kingdom of my dear Lord and Savior in the world; and withal, a most sweet resignation, and even consolation and joy, in the thoughts of suffering hardships, distresses, and even death itself, in the promotion of it; and had special enlargement in pleading for the enlightening and conversion of the poor heathen. In the afternoon God was with me of a truth. O, it was blessed company indeed! God enabled me so to agonize in prayer, that I was quite wet with sweat, though in the shade and the cool wind. My soul was drawn out very much for the world; I grasped for *multitudes* of souls. I think I had more enlargement for sinners than for the children of God; though I felt as if I could spend my life in cries for both. I had great enjoyment in communion with my dear Savior. I think I never in my life felt such an entire weanedness from this world, and so much resigned to God in every thing. O that I may always live to and upon my blessed God! Amen, Amen.

April 20.—" This day I am twenty-four years of age. O how much mercy have I received the year past! How often has God " caused his goodness to pass before me !" And how poorly have I answered the vows I made one year since, to be wholly the Lord's, to be for ever devoted to his service! The Lord help me to live more to his glory for the time to come. This has been a sweet, a happy day to me; blessed be God. I think my soul was never so drawn out in intercession for others, as it has been this night. Had a most fervent wrestle with the Lord to-night, for my enemies; and I hardly ever so longed to live to God, and to be altogether devoted to him ; I wanted to wear out my life in his service, and for his glory.

April 21. "Felt much calmness and resignation ; and God again enabled me to wrestle for numbers of souls, and gave me fervency in the sweet duty of in tercession. I enjoy of late more sweetness in intercession for others, than in any other part of prayer. My blessed Lord really let me come near to him, and plead with him.

Lord's day, April 25. "This morning I spent about two hours in secret duties, and was enabled, more than ordinarily, to agonize for immortal souls. At night I was exceedingly melted with divine love, and had some feeling sense of the blessedness of the upper world. Those words hung upon me with much divine sweetness. Psa. 84:7. "They go from strength to strength, every one of them in Zion appeareth before God." O the near access that God sometimes gives us in our addresses to him! This may well be termed "appearing before God:" it is so indeed, in the true spiritual sense, and in the sweetest sense. I think that I have not had such power of intercession these many months, both for God's children, and for dead sinners, as I have had this evening. I wished and longed for the coming of my dear Lord: I longed to join the angelic hosts in praises, wholly free from imperfection. O, the blessed moment hastens! All I want is to be more holy, more like my dear Lord. Oh for sanctification! My very soul pants for the complete restoration of the blessed image of my Savior; that I may be fit for the blessed enjoyments and employments of the heavenly world.

"Farewell, vain world; my soul can bid Adieu
"My Savior taught me to abandon you.
"Your charms may gratify a sensual mind;
"But cannot please a soul for God design'd.
"Forbear t' entice; cease then my soul to call;
"'Tis fixed through grace; my God shall be my all.
"While he thus lets me heavenly glories view,
"Your beauties fade, my heart's no room for you."

"The Lord refreshed my soul with many sweet passages of his word. O the New Jerusalem! my soul longed for it. O the song of Moses and the Lamb! And that blessed song, that no man can learn but they who are "redeemed from the earth!""

> "Lord, I'm a stranger here alone;
> "Earth no true comforts can afford;
> "Yet, absent from my dearest one,
> "My soul delights to cry 'My Lord!'
> " Jesus, my Lord. my only love,
> " Possess my soul, nor thence depart:
> " Grant me kind visits, heavenly Dove;
> "My God shall then have all my heart."

April 27. "I arose and retired early for secret devotions; and in prayer, God was pleased to pour such ineffable comforts into my soul, that I could do nothing for some time but say over and over, "O my sweet Savior! whom have I in Heaven but thee? and there is none upon earth that I desire beside thee." If I had a thousand lives, my soul would gladly have laid them all down at once, to have been with Christ. My soul never enjoyed so much of heaven before; it was the most refined and most spiritual season of communion with God I ever yet felt.

April 28.—"I withdrew to my usual place of retirement, in great peace and tranquility, spent about two hours in secret duties, and felt much as I did yesterday morning, only weaker, and more overcome. I seemed to depend wholly on my dear Lord; weaned from all other dependencies. I knew not what to say to my God, but only *lean on his bosom*, as it were, and breathe out my desires after a perfect conformity to him in all things. Thirsting desires after *perfect holiness*, and insatiable longings possessed my soul. God was so precious to me that the world, with all its enjoy ments, was infinitely vile. I had no more value for the favor of men, than for pebbles. The LORD was my ALL, and that he over-ruled all, greatly delighted me. I think that my faith and dependence on God scarce ever rose so high. I saw him such a fountain of good- ness that it seemed impossible I should distrust nim again, or be any way anxious about any thing that should happen to me. I now had great satisfaction in praying for absent friends, and for the enlargement of Christ's kingdom in the world. Much of the power of these divine enjoyments remained with me through the day. In the evening my heart seemed to melt, and I trust was really humbled for indwelling corruption, and I "mourned like a dove." I felt that all my un- happiness arose from my being a *sinner*. With resig- nation, I could bid welcome to all *other* trials; but sin hung heavy upon me; for God discovered to me the corruption of my heart. I went to bed with a heavy heart, *because I was a sinner;* though I did not in the least doubt of God's love. O that God would " purge away my dross, and take away my tin," and make me ten times refined!

May 1.—" I was enabled to cry to God with fer- vency for ministerial qualifications, that he would ap- pear for the advancement of his own kingdom, and that he would bring in the Heathen. Had much assis- tance in my studies. This has been a profitable week to me; I have enjoyed many communications of the blessed Spirit in my soul.

May 3.—" Had a sense of vile ingratitude. In the morning I withdrew to my usual place of retirement, and mourned for my abuse of my dear Lord; spent the day in fasting and prayer. God gave me much power of wrestling for his cause and kingdom; and it was a happy day to my soul. God was with me all the day; and I was more above the world than ever in my life.

May 13.—(At Wethersfield.) "Saw so much of the wickedness of my heart that I longed to get away from myself. I never before thought that there was so much spiritual *pride* in my soul. I felt almost pressed to death with my own vileness. O what a "body of death" is there in me! Lord deliver my soul! I could not find any convenient place for retirement, and was greatly exercised. Rode to Hartford in the afternoon; had some refreshment and comfort in religious exercises with christian friends; but longed for more retirement. O, the closest walk with God is the sweetest heaven that can be enjoyed on earth!

June 14.—" Felt somewhat of the sweetness of communion with God, and the constraining force of his love; how admirably it captivates the soul, and makes all the desires and affections centre in God!—I set apart this day for secret fasting and prayer, to entreat God to direct and bless me with regard to the great work which I have in view, of *preaching the gospel*—and that the Lord would return to me, and individually "show me the light of his countenance." Had little life and power in the forenoon: near the middle of the afternoon God enabled me to wrestle ardently in intercession for absent friends: but just at night the Lord visited me marvellously in prayer. I think my soul never was in such an agony before. I felt no restraint, for the treasures of divine grace were opened to me. I wrestled for absent friends, for the ingathering of souls, for *multitudes* of poor souls, and for many that I thought were the children of God, in many distant p^laces. I was in such an agony, from half an hour before sunset, till near dark, that I was all over wet with sweat: but yet it seemed to me that I had wasted away the day, and had done nothing. O, my dear Savior did *sweat blood* for poor souls! I longed for more compassion toward them. Felt still in a sweet frame, under a sense of divine love and grace; and went to bed in such a frame, with my heart set on God.

June 15.—" Had the most ardent longings after God. At noon, in my secret retirement, I could do nothing but tell my dear Lord, in a sweet calm, that he knew I desired nothing but *himself*, nothing but *holiness;* that he had given me these desires, and he only could give me the thing desired. I never seemed to be so unhinged from myself, and to be so wholly devoted to God. My heart was swallowed up in God most of the day. In the evening I had such a view of the soul being, as it were, enlarged, to contain more holiness, that it seemed ready to separate from my body. I then wrestled in an agony for divine blessings; had my heart drawn out in prayer for some christian friends, beyond what I ever had before. I feel differently now from what I ever did under any enjoyments before; more engaged to *live to God* for ever, and less pleased with my own frames. I am not satisfied with my frames, nor feel at all more easy after such strugglings than before; for it seems far too little, if I could always be so. O how short do I fall of my duty in my sweetest moments!

June 18.—" Considering my great unfitness for the work of the *ministry*, my present deadness, and total inability to do any thing for the glory of God that way, feeling myself very helpless, and at a great loss what the Lord would have me to do; I set apart this day for

prayer to God, and spent most of the day in that duty
but was amazingly deserted most of the day. Yet I
found God graciously near, once in particular; while I
was pleading for more compassion for immortal souls,
my heart seemed to be opened at once, and I was enabled to cry with great ardency for a few minutes. O,
I was distressed to think, that I should offer such dead
cold services to the living God! My soul seemed to
breathe after holiness, a life of constant devotedness to
God. But I am almost lost sometimes in the pursuit
of this blessedness, and ready to sink, because I continually fall short, and miss of my desire. O that the
Lord would help me to hold out, yet a little while, until
the happy hour of deliverance comes!

June 30.—" Spent this day alone in the woods, in
fasting and prayer; underwent the most dreadful conflicts in my soul. I saw myself so vile that I was
ready to say, " I shall now perish by the hand of
Saul." I thought that I had no power to stand for the
cause of God, but was almost afraid of the shaking of
a leaf. Spent almost the whole day in prayer, incessantly. I could not bear to think of Christians showing me any respect. I almost despaired of doing any
service in the world: I could not feel any hope or
comfort respecting the heathen, which used to afford
me some refreshment in the darkest hours of this nature. I spent the day in bitterness of soul. Near
night I felt a little better; and afterward enjoyed
some sweetness in secret prayer.

July 1.—" Had some enjoyment in prayer this morning; and far more than usual in secret prayer to-night,
and desired nothing so ardently as that *God should do
with me just as he pleased.*

July 2.—" Felt composed in secret prayer in the

morning. My desires ascended to God this day, as
I was traveling: was comfortable in the evening.
Blessed be God for all my consolations.

July 3.—" My heart seemed again to sink. The disgrace I was laid under at college seemed to damp my
spirits; as it opens the mouths of opposers. I had no
refuge but in God. Blessed be his name, that I may
go to him at all times, and find him a " present help."

Lord's day, July 4.—" Had considerable assistance.
In the evening I withdrew, and enjoyed a happy season in secret prayer. God was pleased to give me the
exercise of faith, and thereby brought the invisible
and eternal world near to my soul; which appeared
sweetly to me. I hoped that my weary pilgrimage in
the world would be *short ;* and that it would not be
long before I should be brought to my heavenly home
and Father's house. I was resigned to God's will, to
tarry his time, to do his work, and suffer his pleasure.
I felt *thankfulness* to God for all my pressing *desertions*
of late; for I am persuaded that they have been made
a means of making me more humble, and much more
resigned. I felt pleased to be little, to be nothing, and
to lie in the dust. I enjoyed life and consolation in
pleading for the dear children of God, and the kingdom of Christ in the world: and my soul earnestly
breathed after holiness, and the enjoyment of God.
" O come, Lord Jesus, come quickly."

July 29.—" I was examined by the Association met
at Danbury, as to my *learning,* and also my *experience*
in religion, and received a licence from them to preach
the Gospel of Christ. Afterward felt much devoted
to God; joined in prayer with one of the ministers,
my peculiar friend, in a convenient place; and went
to bed resolving to live devoted to God all my days."

CHAPTER III

From his being licensed to preach, till he was commissioned as a Missionary.

July 30.—Nov. 25, 1742

July 30, 1742.—" Rode from Danbury to South-bury; preached there, from 1 Pet. 4 : 8. Had much of the comfortable presence of God in the exercise. I seemed to have power with God in prayer, and power to get hold of the hearts of the people in preaching.

Aug. 12. (Near Kent.)—" This morning and last night I was exercised with sore inward trials : I had no power to pray; but seemed shut out from God. I had in a great measure lost my hopes of God's sending me among the Heathen afar off, and of seeing them flock home to Christ. I saw so much of my vileness, that I wondered that God would let me live. and that people did not stone me ; much more that they would ever hear me preach ! It seemed as though I never could preach any more; yet about nine or ten o'clock the people came over, and I was forced to preach ; and blessed be God, he gave me his presence and Spirit in prayer and preaching; so that I was much assisted, and spake with power, from Job, 14 : 14. Some Indians residing here, cried out in great distress, and all appeared greatly concerned. After we had prayed and exhorted them to seek the Lord with constancy, and hired an Englishwoman to keep a kind of *school* among them, we came away."

Lord's day, Aug. 15.—" Felt much comfort and devotedness to God this day. At night, it was refreshing to get alone with God, and *pour out my soul.* O,

who can conceive of the sweetness of communion
with the blessed God, but those who have experience
of it! Glory to God for ever, that I may taste heaven
below.

Aug. 17.—" Exceedingly depressed in spirit, it cuts
and wounds my heart to think how much self-exaltation, spiritual pride, and warmth of temper, I have
formerly had intermingled with my endeavors to promote God's work: and sometimes I long to lie down
at the feet of opposers, and confess what a poor imperfect creature I have been, and still am. The Lord
forgive me, and make me, for the future, " wise as a
serpent, and harmless as a dove !" Afterward enjoyed considerable comfort and delight of soul.

Aug. 19.—" This day, being about to go from Mr.
Bellamy's, at Bethlehem, where I had resided some
time, I prayed with him and two or three other Christian friends. We gave ourselves to God with all our
hearts, to be his for ever: eternity looked very near
to me while I was praying. If I never should see
these Christians again in this world, it seemed but a
few moments before I should meet them in another
world.

Aug. 23.—" Had a sweet season in secret prayer:
the Lord drew near to my soul, and filled me with
peace and divine consolation. O, my soul tasted the
sweetness of heaven; and was drawn out in prayer
for the world, that it might come home to Christ!
Had much comfort in the thoughts and hopes of the
ingathering of the Heathen; was greatly assisted in
intercession for Christian friends."

Sept. 1.—" Went to Judea to the ordination of Mr.
Judd. Mr. Bellamy preached from Matt. 24 · 46.
' Blessed is that servant whom his Lord, when he

cometh, shall find so doing.' I felt very solemn; had my thoughts much on that time when our Lord will come, which refreshed my soul much; only I was afraid I should not be found faithful, because I have so vile a heart. My thoughts were much in eternity where I love to dwell. Blessed be God for this solemn season. Rode home to night with Mr. Bellamy, conversed with some friends till it was very late, and then retired to rest in a comfortable frame.

Sept. 4.—"Much out of health, exceedingly depressed in my soul, and at awful distance from God. Toward night, spent some time in profitable thoughts on Rom. 8 : 2. Near night, had a very sweet season in prayer; God enabled me to wrestle ardently for the advancement of the Redeemer's kingdom; pleaded earnestly for my own dear brother John, (who at length became his successor as a Missionary to the Indians,) that God would make him more of a pilgrim and stranger on the earth, and fit him for singular serviceableness in the world; and my heart sweetly exulted in the Lord, in the thoughts of any distresses that might alight on him or on me, in the advancement of Christ's kingdom. It was a sweet and comfortable hour unto my soul, while I was indulged with freedom to plead, not only for myself, but also for many other souls.

Sept. 16.—" At night, enjoyed much of God, in secret prayer: felt an uncommon resignation to be and do what God pleased. Some days past I felt great perplexity on account of my past conduct: my bitterness, and want of Christian kindness and love, has been very distressing to my soul: the Lord forgive me my unchristian warmth, and want of a spirit of meekness!

Oct. 21.—" Had a very deep sense of the vanity of

the world, most of the day; had little more regard to
it, than if I had been to go into eternity the next hour.
Through divine goodness, I felt very serious and
solemn. *O I love to live on the brink of eternity*, in my
views and meditations! This gives me a sweet, awful
and reverential sense and apprehension of God and
divine things, when I see myself as it were, standing
before the judgment seat of Christ.

Oct. 22.—" Uncommonly weaned from the world to
day: my soul delighted to be a " stranger and pilgrim
on the earth ;" I felt a disposition in me never to have
any thing to do with this world. The character given
of some of the ancient people of God, in Heb. 11 : 13,
was very pleasing to me, " They confessed that they
were pilgrims and strangers on the earth," by their
daily practice; and O that I could always do so!
Spent some time in a pleasant grove, in prayer and
meditation. O it is sweet to be thus weaned from
friends, and from myself, and dead to the present
world, that so I may live wholly to and upon the
blessed God! Saw myself little, low and vile as I am
in myself. In the afternoon preached at Bethlehem
from Deut. 8 : 2. God helped me to speak to the
hearts of dear Christians. Blessed be the Lord for this
season: I trust they and I shall rejoice on this account
to all eternity. Dear Mr. Bellamy came in while I
was making the first prayer, (having returned home
from a journey,) and after meeting we walked away
together, and spent the evening in sweetly conversing
on divine things, and praying together, with tender
love to each other, and retired to rest with our hearts
in a serious spiritual frame.

Oct. 26.—" [At West Suffield.] Was in great distress, under a sense of my own unworthiness. It

seemed to me that I deserved rather to be driven out of the place, than to have any body treat me with kindness, or come to hear me preach. And verily my spirits were so depressed at this time (as at many others) that it was impossible I should treat immortal souls with faithfulness. I could not deal closely and faithfully with them, I felt so infinitely vile in myself. O what *dust and ashes* I am, to think of preaching the Gospel to others! Indeed, I never can be faithful for one moment, but shall certainly "daub with untempered mortar," if God do not grant me special help. In the evening I went to the meeting-house, and it looked to me near as easy for one to rise out of the grave and preach, as for me. However, God afforded me some life and power, both in prayer and sermon; and was pleased to lift me up, and show me that he could enable me to preach. O the wonderful goodness of God to so vile a sinner! Returned to my lodgings, and enjoyed some sweetness in prayer alone, and mourned that I could not live more to God.

November 4.—" [At Lebanon.] Saw much of my nothingness most of this day; but felt concerned that I had no more sense of my insufficiency and unworthiness. O it is sweet *lying in the dust!* But it is distressing to feel in my soul that hell of corruption which still remains in me. In the afternoon had a sense of the sweetness of a strict, close, and constant devotedness to God, and my soul was comforted with his consolations. My soul felt a pleasing, yet painful concern, lest I should spend some moments *without God*. O may I always *live to God!* In the evening I was visited by some friends, and spent the time in prayer, and such conversation as tended to our edification. It was a comfortable season to my soul: I felt an

intense desire to spend every moment for God. God
is unspeakably gracious to me continually. In times
past, he has given me inexpressible sweetness in the
performance of duty. Frequently my soul has enjoyed
much of God; but has been ready to say, "Lord, it is
good to be here," and so to indulge sloth, while I have
lived on my enjoyments. But of late, God has been
pleased to keep my soul *hungry*, almost continually;
so that I have been filled with a kind of pleasing pain.
When I really enjoy God I feel my desires of him the
more insatiable, and my thirstings after holiness the
more unquenchable; and the Lord will not allow me
to feel as though I were fully supplied and satisfied,
but keeps me still reaching forward. I feel barren and
empty, as though I could not live without more of
God; I feel ashamed and guilty *before him*. I see that
"the law is spiritual, but I am carnal." I do not, I
cannot live to God. O for holiness! O for more of
God in my soul! O this pleasing pain! It makes my
soul press after God; the language of it is, "Then
shall I be satisfied, when I awake in God's likeness,"
but never, never before: and consequently, I am engaged to "press toward the mark," day by day. O
that I may feel this continual hunger, and not be re-
tarded, but rather animated, by every cluster from Canaan, to reach forward in the narrow way for the full
enjoyment and possession of the heavenly inheritance!
O that I may never loiter in my heavenly journey!"

Lord's day, Nov. 7.—" [At Millington.] It seemed
as if such an unholy wretch as I never could arrive at
that blessedness, to be "holy, as God is holy." At
noon, I longed for sanctification, and conformity to
God. O that is THE ALL, THE ALL. The Lord help me
to *press after God* for ever.

Nov. 8.—" Toward night, enjoyed much sweetness in secret prayer. so that my soul longed for an arrival in the heavenly country, the blessed paradise of God. Through divine goodness I have scarce seen the day for two months, in which *death* has not looked so pleasant to me, at one time or other of the day, that I could have rejoiced that it should be my last, notwithstanding my present inward trials and conflicts. I trust the Lord will finally make me a conqueror, and more than a conqueror; and that I shall be able to use that triumphant language, " O death, where is thy sting ! O grave, where is thy victory !""

Nov. 19.—" [At New-Haven.] Received a letter from the Rev. Mr. Pemberton, of New-York, desiring me speedily to go down thither, and consult in reference to the evangelizing of the Indians in those parts; and to meet certain gentlemen there who were intrusted with those affairs. My mind was instantly seized with concern; so I retired, with two or three Christian friends, and prayed ; and indeed it was a sweet time with me. I was enabled to leave myself, and all my concerns with God ; and taking leave of friends, I rode to Ripton, and was comforted in an opportunity to see and converse with dear Mr. Mills."

Nov. 24.—" Came to New-York; felt still much concerned about the importance of my business; made many earnest requests to God for his help and direction; was confused with the noise and tumult of the city ; enjoyed but little time alone with God ; but my soul longed after him.

Nov. 25.—" Spent much time in prayer and supplication : was examined in reference to my Christian experience, my acquaintance with divinity, and some other studies and my qualifications for the important work of evangelizing the heathen ,* and was made sensible of my great ignorance and unfitness for public service. I had the most abasing thoughts of myself; I felt that I was the worst wretch that ever lived : it pained my very heart, that any body should show me any respect. Alas! methought how sadly they are deceived in me! how miserably would they be disappointed if they knew my inside! O my heart! And in this depressed condition I was forced to go and preach to a considerable assembly, before some grave and learned ministers; but felt such a pressure from a sense of my vileness, ignorance, and unfitness to appear in public, that I was almost overcome with it; my soul was grieved for the congregation, that they should sit there to hear such a *dead dog* as I preach. I thought myself infinitely indebted to the people, and longed that God would reward them with the rewards of his grace. I spent much of the evening alone."

CHAPTER IV

From his appointment as a Missionary, to his commencing his Mission among the Indians at Kavnaumeck, in New-York.

Nov. 26, 1742.—March 31, 1743

Nov. 26, 1742.—"Had still a sense of my great vileness, and endeavored as much as I could to keep alone. O what a nothing, what dust and ashes am I! Enjoyed

---

* Mr. Brainerd was examined by the correspondents in New York, New-Jersey, and Pennsylvania, of the Society in Scotland for propagating Christian knowledge; to whom was committed the management of their affairs in those parts, and who were now met at New-York.

some peace and comfort in spreading my complaints before the God of all grace.

Nov. 27.—"Committed my soul to God with some degree of comfort; left New-York about nine in the morning; came away with a distressing sense still of my unspeakable unworthiness. Surely I may well love all my brethren; for none of them all is so vile as I: whatever they do outwardly, yet it seems to me none is conscious of so much guilt before God. O my leanness, my barrenness, my carnality, and past bitterness, and want of a gospel temper! These things oppress my soul. Rode from New-York, thirty miles, to White Plains, and most of the way continued lifting up my heart to God for mercy and purifying grace; and spent the evening much dejected in spirit.

Dec. 1.—"My soul breathed after God, in sweet spiritual and longing desires of conformity to him, and was brought to rest itself on his rich grace, and felt strength and encouragement to do or suffer any thing, that divine providence should allot me. Rode about twenty miles, from Stratfield to Newtown."

Within the space of the next nine days he went a journey from Newtown to Haddam, his native town; and after staying there some days, returned again into the western part of Connecticut, and came to Southbury.

Dec. 11.—"Conversed with a dear friend, to whom I had thought of giving a liberal education, and being at the whole charge of it, that he might be fitted for the gospel ministry.* I acquainted him with my thoughts

---

* Brainerd, having now undertaken the business of a missionary to the Indians, and having some estate left him by his father, judged that there was no way in which he could spend it more for the glory of God, than by being at the charge of

on the subject, and so left him to consider of it, till I should see him again. Then I rode to Bethlehem, came to Mr. Bellamy's lodgings, and spent the evening with him in sweet conversation and prayer. We commended the concern of sending my friend to college to the God of all grace. Blessed be the Lord for this evening's opportunity together.

Lord's day, Dec. 12.—"I felt, in the morning, as if I had little or no power either to pray or preach; and felt a distressing need of divine help. I went to meeting trembling; but it pleased God to assist me in prayer and sermon. I think my soul scarce ever penetrated so far into the immaterial world, in any one prayer that I ever made, nor were my devotions ever so free from gross conceptions and imaginations framed from beholding material objects. I preached with some satisfaction, from Matt. 6 : 33. "But seek ye first the kingdom of God," &c.; and in the afternoon, from Rom. 15 : 30. "And now I beseech you brethren," &c. There was much affection in the assembly. This has been a sweet Sabbath to me; and blessed be God, I have reason to think that my religion has become more spiritual by means of my late inward conflicts. Amen. May I always be willing that God should use his own methods with me!

Dec. 14.—"Some perplexity hung on my mind; I was distressed last night and this morning for the interests of Zion, especially on account of the *false appearances of religion*, that do but rather breed confu-

educating some young man of talents and piety for the ministry. The young man here spoken of was selected for this purpose, and received his education at Brainerd's expense, so long as his benefactor lived, which was till he was carried through his third year in college.

sion, especially in some places.   I cried to God for
help, to enable me to bear testimony against those
things, which, instead of promoting, do but hinder the
progress of vital piety.   In the afternoon, rode down
to Southbury, and conversed again with my friend
on the important subject of his pursuing the work of
the ministry; and he appeared much inclined to devote himself to it, if God should succeed his attempts
to qualify himself for so great a work.   In the evening
I preached from 1 Thess. 4:8, and endeavored, though
with tenderness, to undermine false religion.   The
Lord gave me some assistance.

Dec. 15.—"Enjoyed something of God to-day, both
in secret and social prayer; but was sensible of much
barrenness and defect in duty, as well as my inability to
help myself for the time to come, or to perform the
work and business I have to do.   Afterward, felt much
of the sweetness of religion, and the tenderness of the
gospel-temper.   I found a dear love to all mankind,
and was much afraid lest some motion of anger or
resentment should, from time to time creep into my
heart.   Had some comforting, soul-refreshing discourse
with dear friends, just as we took our leave of each
other; and supposed it might be we should not meet
again till we came to the eternal world.*   I doubt not
but, through grace, some of us shall have a happy

* It had been determined by the Commissioners, who employed Brainerd as a missionary, that he should go, as soon as
might be conveniently, to the Indians living near the Forks of
Delaware river, and the Indians on Susquehanna river.   The
distance of those places, and his probable exposure to many
hardships and dangers, was the occasion of his taking leave
of his friends in this manner.

meeting there, and bless God for this season, as well as many others.   Amen.

Dec. 18.   " Spent much time in prayer in the woods; and seemed raised above the things of the world: my soul was strong in the Lord of Hosts; but was sensible of great barrenness.

Dec. 23.—" Enjoyed, I trust, the presence of God this morning in secret.   O, how divinely sweet is it to come into the secret of his presence, and abide in his pavilion !

Dec. 27.—" Enjoyed a precious season indeed; had a melting sense of divine things, of the pure spirituality of the religion of Christ Jesus.   In the evening I preached from Matt. 6 : 33. with much freedom, power and pungency: the presence of God attended our meeting.   O, the sweetness, the tenderness I felt in my soul! If ever I felt the temper of Christ, I had some sense of it now.   Blessed be my God, I have seldom enjoyed a more comfortable and profitable day than this.   O, that I could spend all my time for God!

Jan. 14, 1743.—" My spiritual conflicts to-day were unspeakably dreadful, heavier than the mountains and over-flowing floods.   I was deprived of all sense of God, even of the being of a God; and that was my misery.   The torments of the damned, I am sure, will consist much in a *privation of God*, and consequently of *all good*.   This taught me the absolute dependence of a creature upon God the Creator, for every crumb of happiness it enjoys.   O, I feel that, if there is no God, though I might live for ever here, and enjoy not only this, but all other worlds, I should be ten thousand times more miserable than a reptile.

Lord's day, Jan. 23.—" I scarce ever felt myself so unfit to exist as now: saw I was not worthy of a place among the Indians, where I am going, if God permit: thought I should be ashamed to look them in the face, and much more to have any respect shown me there. Indeed I felt myself banished from the earth, as if all places were too good for such a wretch. I thought I should be ashamed to go among the very savages of Africa; I appeared to myself a creature fit for nothing, neither heaven nor earth. None know but those who feel it, what the soul endures that is sensibly shut out from the presence of God: alas! it is more bitter than death.

Feb. 2.—" Preached my farewell sermon last night, at the house of an aged man, who had been unable to attend on public worship for some time. This morning spent the time in prayer, almost wherever I went; and having taken leave of friends, I set out on my journey toward the Indians; though I was first to spend some weeks at East-Hampton, on Long-Island, by leave of the commissioners; the winter season being judged unfavorable for the commencement of the mission.

Feb. 12.—[At East-Hampton.] "Enjoyed a little more comfort; was enabled to meditate with some composure of mind; and especially in the evening, found my soul more refreshed in prayer than at any time of late; my soul seemed to " take hold of God's strength," and was comforted with his consolations. O, how sweet are some glimpses of divine glory! how strengthening and quickening!

Feb. 15. "Early in the day I felt some comfort, afterward I walked into a neighboring grove, and felt more as a stranger on earth, I think, than ever before; dead to any of the enjoyments of the world. In the evening had divine sweetness in secret duty: God was then my portion, and my soul rose above those *deep waters*, into which I have sunk so low of late. My soul then cried for Zion, and had sweetness in so doing."

Feb. 17.—"Preached this day at a little village in East-Hampton; and God was pleased to give me his gracious presence and assistance, so that I spake with freedom, boldness, and some power. In the evening spent some time with a dear Christian friend ; and felt serious, as on the brink of eternity. Our interview was truly a little emblem of heaven itself. I find my soul is more refined and weaned from a dependence on my frames and spiritual feelings.

Feb. 18.—"Had some enjoyment most of the day, and found access to the throne of grace. Blessed be the Lord for any intervals of heavenly delight and composure, while I am engaged in the field of battle. O, that I might be serious, solemn, and always vigilant, while in an evil world! Had some opportunity alone to-day, and found some freedom in study. O, I long to *live to God!*"

During the next two weeks it appears that for the most part he enjoyed much spiritual peace and comfort. In his diary for this space of time, are expressed such things as these; mourning over indwelling sin, unprofitableness; deadness to the world; longing after God, and to live to his glory; heart melting desires after his eternal home; fixed reliance on God for his help; experience of much divine assistance, both in the private and public exercises of religion; inward strength and courage in the service of God; very frequent refreshment, consolation, and divine sweetness in meditation, prayer, preaching, and Christian conversation. And it appears by his account, that this space of time was filled up with great diligence and earnestness in serving God; in study, prayer, meditation, preaching, and privately instructing and counseling.

March 7.—"This morning when I arose I found my heart go forth after God in longing desires of conformity to him, and in secret prayer found myself sweetly quickened and drawn out in praises to God for all he had done to and for me, and for all my inward trials and distress of late. My heart ascribed glory, glory, glory to the blessed God! and bid welcome to all inward distress again, if God saw meet to exercise me with it. Time appeared but an inch long, and eternity at hand; and I thought I could with patience and cheerfulness bear any thing for the cause of God; for I saw that a moment would bring me to a world of peace and blessedness. My soul, by the strength of the Lord, rose far above this lower world, and all the vain amusements and frightful disappointments of it.

Lord's day, March 13. "At noon, I thought it impossible for me to preach, by reason of bodily weakness and inward deadness. In the first prayer, I was so weak that I could scarcely stand; but in the sermon, God strengthened me, so that I spake near an hour and a half with sweet freedom, clearness, and some tender power, from Gen. 5:24. "And Enoch walked with God." I was sweetly assisted to insist on a *close walk with God,* and to leave this as my parting advice to God's people here, that they should "walk with God." May the God of all grace succeed my poor labors in this place!

March 14. "In the morning was very busy in preration for my journey, and was almost continually engaged in ejaculatory prayer. About ten took leave of the dear people of East-Hampton; my heart grieved and mourned, and rejoiced at the same time; rode near fifty miles to a part of Brook-Haven, and lodged there, and had refreshing conversation with a Christian friend."

In two days more he reached New-York; but complains of much desertion and deadness on the road. He stayed one day in New-York, and on Friday went to Mr. Dickinson's at Elizabeth-Town.

March. 19. "Was bitterly distressed under a sense of my ignorance, darkness, and unworthiness; got alone, and poured out my complaint to God in the bitterness of my soul. In the afternoon rode to Newark, and had some sweetness in conversation and prayer with Mr. Burr. O blessed be God for ever and ever, for any enlivening and quickening seasons.

Lord's day, March 20. "Preached in the forenoon: God gave me some assistance, and enabled me to speak with real tenderness, love, and impartiality. In the evening preached again; and of a truth God was pleased to assist a poor worm. Blessed be God, I was enabled to speak with life, power, and desire of the edification of God's people; and with some power to sinners. In the evening I was watchful, lest my heart should by any means be drawn away from God. O when shall I come to that blessed world where every power of my soul will be incessantly and eternally wound up in heavenly employments and enjoyments, to the highest degree!"

On Monday he went to Woodbridge, New-Jersey, where he met the Correspondents; who, instead of sending him to the Indians at the Forks of the Delaware, as before intended, directed him to go to a number of Indians at Kaunaumeek; a place in New-York, in the woods between Stockbridge and Albany. This alteration was occasioned by two things. 1. Information which the correspondents had received of some contention between the white people and the Indians on the Delaware, concerning their lands; which they sup-

posed would be a hinderance to the success of a missionary among them at that time. 2. Some intimations
which they had received from Mr. Sergeant, Missionary to the Indians at Stockbridge, concerning the Indians at Kaunaumeek, and the hopeful prospect of success which a Missionary might have among them.

On the day following he set out on his journey for
Kaunaumeek, and arrived at Mr. Sergeant's house in
Stockbridge March 31.

CHAPTER V

*His labors for nearly a year among the Indians at Kaunaumeek
—temporal deprivations and sufferings—establishes a school—
confession offered to the faculty of Yale College—days of fasting—methods of instructing the Indians—visit to New-Jersey and Connecticut—commencement of labor among the Indians at the Forks of the Delaware—Ordination.*

April 1, 1743.—June 12, 1744

April 1, 1743. "I rode to Kaunaumeek, in the wilderness, near twenty miles from Stockbridge, and about
an equal distance from Albany, where the Indians live
with whom I am concerned;and lodged with a poor
Scotchman, about a mile and a half distant from them,
on a little heap of straw, in a log room without any
floor. I was greatly exercised with inward trials, and
seemed to have no God to go to. O that God would
help me:

April 7. "Appeared to myself exceedingly ignorant,
weak, helpless, unworthy, and altogether unequal to
my work. It seemed to me that I should never do
any service, or have any success among the Indians.

My soul was weary of my life; I longed for death, beyond measure. When I thought of any godly soul departed, my soul was ready to envy him his privilege,
thinking, "O when will my turn come! must it be
years first!" But I know these ardent desires, at this
and other times, rose partly from the want of resignation to God under all miseries; and so were but impatience. Toward night I had the exercise of faith in
prayer, and some assistance in writing. O that God
would keep me near him!

Lord's day, April 10. "Rose early in the morning
and walked out and spent a considerable time in the
woods, in prayer and meditation. Preached to the Indians, both forenoon and afternoon. They behaved
soberly in general: two or three in particular appeared
to be under some religious concern; with whom I discoursed privately; and one told me, "that her heart
had cried ever since she first heard me preach."

April 16.—" In the afternoon preached to my people;
but was more discouraged with them than before;
feared that nothing would ever be done for them to
any happy effect. I retired and poured out my soul
to God for mercy; but without any sensible relief.
Soon after, two ungodly men came, with a design, as
they said, to hear me preach the next day; but none
can tell how I felt to hear their *profane* talk. O, I
longed that some dear Christian should know my distress. I got into a kind of hovel, and there groaned
out my complaint to God; and withal felt more sensible gratitude and thankfulness to God, that he had
made me to differ from these men, as I knew, through
grace, he had.

Lord's day, April 17.—" In the morning was again
distressed as soon as I awaked, hearing much talk

about the world, and the things of it. I perceived that the men were in some measure afraid of me; and I discoursed about sanctifying the Sabbath, if possible to solemnize their minds; but when they were at a little distance, they again talked freely about secular affairs. O I thought what a *hell* it would be to live with such men to eternity! The Lord gave me some assistance in preaching, all day, and some resignation, and a small degree of comfort in prayer, at night.

April 19.—" In the morning I enjoyed some sweet repose and rest in God; felt some strength and confidence in him; and my soul was in some measure refreshed and comforted. Spent most of the day in writing, and had some exercise of grace, sensible and comfortable. My soul seemed lifted above the *deep waters*, wherein it has long been almost drowned; felt some spiritual longings and breathings after God; and found myself engaged for the advancement of Christ's kingdom in my own soul.

April 20.—" Set apart this day for fasting and prayer, to bow my soul before God for the bestowment of divine grace; especially that all my spiritual afflictions, and inward distresses, might be sanctified to my soul. And endeavored also to remember the goodness of God to me the year past, this day being my birth day. Having obtained help of God, I have hitherto lived, and am now arrived at the age of twenty-five years. My soul was pained to think of my barrenness and deadness; that I have lived so little to the glory of the eternal God. I spent the day in the woods alone, and there poured out my complaint to God. O that God would enable me to live to his glory for the future!

May 10.—" Was in the same state as to my mind,

that I have been in for some time; extremely oppressed with a sense of guilt, pollution, and blindness, "The iniquity of my heels hath compassed me about: the sins of my youth have been set in order before me; they have gone over my head, as an heavy burden, too heavy for me to bear." Almost all the actions of my life past seem to be covered over with sin and guilt; and those of them that I performed in the most conscientious manner, now fill me with shame and confusion, that I cannot hold up my face. O, the pride, selfishness, hypocrisy, ignorance, bitterness, party zeal, and the want of love, candor, meekness, and gentleness, that have attended my attempts to promote the interests of religion; and this, when I have reason to hope I had real assistance from above, and some sweet intercourse with heaven! But alas, what corrupt mixtures attended my best duties!"

May 18.—" My circumstances are such that I have no comfort of any kind, but what I have in God. I live in the most lonesome wilderness; have but one single person to converse with that can speak English.* Most of the talk I hear, is either Highland Scotch, or Indian. I have no fellow-christian to whom I may unbosom myself, or lay open my spiritual sorrows; with whom I may take sweet counsel in conversation about heavenly things, and join in social prayer. I live poorly with regard to the comforts of

---

* This person was BRAINERD's interpreter, an ingenious young Indian, belonging to Stockbridge, whose name was *John Wauwaumpequunnaunt.* He had been instructed in the Christian religion by Mr. Sergeant; had lived with the Rev. Mr. Williams, of Long-Meadow; had been further instructed by him, at the charge of Mr. Hollis, of London; and understood both English and Indian very well, and wrote a good hand.

life : most of my diet consists of boiled corn, hasty-
pudding, &c. I lodge on a bundle of straw, my labor
is hard and extremely difficult, and I have little appearance of success to comfort me. The Indians have
no land to live on but what the Dutch people lay claim
to ; and these threaten to drive them off. They have
no regard to the *souls* of the poor Indians ; and by
what I can learn, they hate me because I come to
preach to them. But that which makes all my difficulties grievous to be borne, is, that *God hides his face
from me.*

May 20.—" Was much perplexed some part of the
day ; but toward night had some comfortable meditations on Isa. 40 : 1. " Comfort ye, comfort ye my
people, saith your God," and enjoyed some sweetness
in prayer. Afterward my soul rose so far above the
deep waters, that I dared to rejoice in God. I saw that
there was sufficient matter of consolation in the blessed
God."

On Monday, May 30, he set out on a journey to
New-Jersey to consult the commissioners, and obtain
orders from them to set up a school among the Indians
at Kaunaumeek, and that his interpreter might be
appointed the schoolmaster ; which was accordingly done. He proceeded from New-Jersey to New-
Haven, where he arrived on Monday, June 6 ; attempted a reconciliation with the faculty of the college ; and spent this week in visiting his friends in
those parts, and in his journey homeward, till Saturday, in a pretty comfortable frame of mind. On Saturday, in his way from Stockbridge to Kaunaumeek, he
was lost in the woods, and lay all night in the open air ;
but happily found his way in the morning, and came
to his Indians on Lord's day, June 12, and had greater

assistance in preaching among them than ever before, since his first coming among them.

From this time forward he was the subject of various frames and exercises of mind, in the general much after the same manner as hitherto from his first coming to Kaunaumeek, till he got into his own house, (a little hut, which he made chiefly with his own hands, by long and hard labor.) He found that the distance of the family with whom he at first lodged, debarred him from many favorable opportunities of access to the Indians, especially morning and evening; and after about three months, removed and lived with the Indians in one of their wigwams. Here he continued for about one month, when he completed the small house of which he now speaks.

Although he was much dejected during most of this period, yet he had many intermissions of his melancholy, and some seasons of comfort, sweet tranquillity and resignation of mind, and frequently special assistance in public services, as appears in his diary. The manner of his relief from his sorrow, once in particular, is worthy to be mentioned in his own words.

July 25.—" Had little or no resolution for a life of holiness; was ready almost to renounce my hope of living to God. And O now dark it looked, to think of being unholy for ever! This I could not endure. The cry of my soul was, Psalm 65 : 3. " Iniquities prevail against me." But I was in some measure relieved by a comfortable meditation on God's eternity, that he never had a beginning. Whence I was led to admire his greatness and power, in such a manner, that I stood still, and praised the Lord for his own glories and perfections : though I was (and if I should for ever be) an unholy creature, my soul was comforted to apprehend an eternal, infinite, powerful, holy God."

July 30.—"Just at night, moved into *my own house*, and lodged there that night; found it much better spending the time alone than in the *wigwam* where I was before.

Lord's day, July 31.—"Felt more comfortably than some days past. Blessed be the Lord, who has now given me a place of retirement. O that I may *find God* in it, and that he would dwell with me for ever!

Aug. 1.—"Was still busy in further labors on my house. Felt a little sweetness of religion, and thought hat it was worth while to follow after God through a housand snares, deserts, and death itself. O that I might always *follow after holiness*, that I may be fully conformed to God! Had some degree of sweetness in secret prayer, though I had much sorrow.

Aug. 3.—"Spent most of the day in writing. Enjoyed some sense of religion. Through divine goodness I am now uninterruptedly alone, and find my retirement comfortable. I have enjoyed more sense of divine things within a few days last past than for some time before. I longed after holiness, humility, and meekness: O that God would enable me to 'pass the time of my sojourning here in his fear,' and always *live to him!*

Aug. 4.—"Was enabled to pray much through the whole day; and through divine goodness found some intenseness of soul in the duty, as I used to do, and some ability to persevere in my supplications. I had some apprehensions of divine things, which afforded me courage and resolution. It is good, I find, to *persevere in attempts* to pray, if I cannot *pray with perseverance,* i. e. continue long in my addresses to the Divine Being I have generally found that *the more I do* in secret prayer, the more I have *delighted to do,*

and the more I have enjoyed a spirit of prayer; and
frequently I have found the contrary, when by journeying or otherwise I have been much deprived of retirement. A seasonable, steady performance of SECRET
DUTIES IN THEIR PROPER HOURS, and a CAREFUL IMPROVE-
MENT OF ALL TIME, filling up every hour with some
profitable labor, either of heart, head, or hands, are excellent means of spiritual peace and boldness before
God. Filling up our time *with* and *for* God, is the way
to rise up and lie down in peace.

Aug. 13.—"Was enabled in secret prayer to raise
my soul to God, with desire and delight. It was indeed
a blessed season. I found the comfort of being a
Christian; and " counted the sufferings of the present
life not worthy to be compared with the glory " of divine
enjoyments even in this world. All my past sorrows
seemed kindly to disappear, and I "remembered no
more the sorrow, for joy." O, how kindly, and with
what a filial tenderness, the soul confides in " the Rock
of Ages," at such a season, that he will " never leave it
nor forsake it," that he will cause " all things to work
together for its good!" I longed that others should
know how good a God the Lord is. My soul was full
of tenderness and love, even to the most inveterate of
my enemies. I longed that they should share in the
same mercy; and loved that God should so do just as
he pleased with me and every thing else. I felt peculiarly serious, calm, and peaceful, and encouragement
to press after holiness as long as I live, whatever difficulties and trials may be in my way. May the Lord
always help me so to do! Amen, and Amen.

Aug. 15.—"Spent most of the day in labor, to procure something to keep my horse on in the winter.
Had not much spiritual enjoyment in the morning;

was very weak in body through the day; and thought that this frail body·would soon drop into the dust; and had some very realizing apprehensions of a speedy entrance into another world. In this weak state of body, I was not a little distressed for want of suitable food. I had no bread, nor could I get any. I am forced to go or send ten or fifteen miles for all the bread I eat; and sometimes it is mouldy and sour before I eat it, if I get any considerable quantity. And then again I have none for some days together, for want of an opportunity to send for it, and cannot find my horse in the woods to go myself; and this was my case now; but through divine goodness I had some Indian *meal*, of which I made cakes, and fried them. Yet I felt contented with my circumstances, and sweetly resigned to God. In prayer I enjoyed great freedom; and blessed God as much for my present circumstances as if I had been a king; and thought that I found a disposition to be contented in *any* circumstances. Blessed be God."

In his diary for Saturday, he says he was somewhat melancholy and sorrowful in mind; and adds, " I never feel comfortably, but when I find my soul going forth after God. If I cannot be holy, I must necessarily be miserable for ever.

Lord's day, Aug. 21.—"Was much straitened in the forenoon exercise; my thoughts seemed to be all scattered to the ends of the earth. At noon, I fell down before the Lord, groaned under my vileness, barrenness, and deadness; and felt as if I was guilty of soul murder, in speaking to immortal souls in such a manner as I had then done. In the afternoon God was pleased to give me some assistance, and I was enabled to set before my hearers the nature and necessity of true repentance. Afterward had some small degree of thankfulness. Was very ill and full of pain in the evening and my soul mourned that I had spent so much time to so little profit.

Aug. 23.—"Studied in the forenoon, and enjoyed some freedom. In the afternoon labored abroad: endeavored to pray, but found not much enjoyment or intenseness of mind. Toward night was very weary, and tired of this world of sorrow: the thoughts of death and immortality appeared very desirable, and even refreshed my soul. Those lines turned in my mind with pleasure,

> " Come death, shake hands; I'll kiss thy bands;
> " 'Tis happiness for me to die.—
> " What!—dost thou think that I will shrink?
> " I'll go to immortality."

" In evening prayer, God was pleased to draw near my soul, though very sinful and unworthy; so that I was enabled to wrestle with God, and to persevere in my requests for grace. I poured out my soul for all the world, friends and enemies. My soul was concerned, not so much for souls as such, but rather for Christ's kingdom, that it might appear in the world, that God might be known to be God, in the whole earth. And O my soul abhorred the very thought of a *party* in re ligion! Let the truth of God appear, wherever it is; and God have glory for ever. Amen. This was indeed a comfortable season. I thought I had some foretaste of the enjoyments and employments of the upper world. O that my soul was more attempered to it!

Aug. 31.—[On a journey to New-York.] "Was in a sweet, serious, and I hope, Christian frame. Eternal things engrossed all my thoughts; and I longed to be in the world of spirits. O how happy is it to have

all our thoughts swallowed up in that world: to feel
one's self a stranger in this world, diligently seeking
a road through it, the best, the sure road to the heavenly Jerusalem!"

He went forward on his journey, and after tarrying
two or three days at New-York, set out from that city
toward New-Haven, intending to be there at the commencement.

Lord's day, Sept. 11.—" [At Horse-Neck.]   In the
afternoon I preached from Titus, 3 : 8. I think God
never helped me more in painting true religion, and
in detecting clearly, and tenderly discountenancing
false appearances of religion, wild fire, party zeal, spiritual pride, &c. as well as a confident dogmatical spirit,
and its spring, viz. *ignorance of the heart.* In the evening took much pains in private conversation to suppress some confusions which I perceived were among
that people.

Sept. 13.—" Rode to New-Haven. Was sometimes
dejected; not in the sweetest frame. Lodged at ****.
Had some profitable Christian conversation. I find,
though my inward trials were great, and a life of solitude gives them greater advantage to settle, and pene-
trate to the very inmost recesses of the soul; yet it is
better to be alone than incumbered with noise and tumult. I find it very difficult maintaining any sense of
divine things while removing from place to place. diverted with new objects, and filled with care and business. A settled steady business is best adapted to a life
of strict religion.

Sept. 14.—" This day I ought to have taken my *degree;* but God sees fit to deny it me. And though I
was greatly afraid of being overwhelmed with perplexity and confusion, when I should see my *class-*

mates take theirs; yet, at the very time, God enabled
me with calmness and resignation to say, " the will of
the Lord be done." Indeed, through divine goodness,
I have scarcely felt my mind so calm, sedate, and comfortable for some time. I have long feared this season,
and expected my humility, meekness, patience and resignation would be much tried; but found much more
pleasure and divine comfort than I expected. Felt
spiritually serious, tender and affectionate in private
prayer with a dear Christian friend to-day.

Sept. 15.—" Had some satisfaction in hearing the
ministers discourse. It is always a comfort to me to
hear religious and spiritual conversation. O that ministers and people were more spiritual and devoted to
God! Toward night, with the advice of Christian
friends, I offered the following reflections in writing,
to the rector and trustees of the college—which are for
substance the same that I had freely offered to the
rector before, and intreated him to accept—that if possible I might cut off all occasion of offence from those
who seek occasion. What I offered, is as follows:

" ' Whereas I have said before several persons, concerning Mr. Whittelsey, one of the tutors of Yale College, that I
did not believe he had any more grace than the chair I then
leaned upon; I humbly confess, that herein I have sinned
against God, and acted contrary to the rules of his word, and
have injured Mr. Whittelsey. I had no right to make thus
free with his character; and had no just reason to say as I did
concerning him. My fault herein was the more aggravated,
in that I said this concerning one who was so much my superior, and one whom I was obliged to treat with special respect
and honor, by reason of the relation I stood in to him in the
college. Such a manner of behavior I confess did not become a Christian; it was taking too much upon me, and did
not savor of that humble respect which I ought to have ex-

pressed toward Mr. Whittelsey. I have long since been convinced of the falseness of those apprehensions, by which I
then justified such a conduct. I have often reflected on this
act with grief; I hope, on account of the sin of it: and am
willing to lie low, and be abased before God and man for it.
I humbly ask the forgiveness of the governors of the college
and of the whole society; but of Mr. Whittelsey in particular.
And whereas I have been accused by one person of saying
concerning the reverend rector of Yale College, that I wondered he did not expect to drop down dead for fining the
scholars that followed Mr. Tennent to Milford; I seriously
profess that I do not remember my saying any thing to this
purpose: but if I did, which I am not certain I did not, I
utterly condemn it, and detest all such kind of behavior; and
especially in an under-graduate toward the rector. And I
now appear to judge and condemn myself for going once to
the separate meeting in New-Haven, a little before I was expelled, though the rector had refused to give me leave. For
this I humbly ask the rector's forgiveness. And whether the
governors of the college shall ever see cause to remove the
academical censure I lie under, or no, or to admit me to the
privileges I desire; yet I am willing to appear, if they think
fit, openly to own, and to humble myself for those things I
have herein confessed.' "

" God has made me willing to do any thing that I
can do consistently with truth, for the sake of peace,
and that I might not be a stumbling block to others.
For this reason I can cheerfully forego and give up
what I verily believe, after the most mature and im-
partial search, is my right, in some instances. God
has given me the disposition, that, if a man has done
me a hundred injuries, and I (though ever so much
provoked to it) have done him only one, I feel disposed
and heartily willing humbly to confess my fault to him,
and on my knees to ask forgiveness of him; though at
the same time he should justify himself in all the in-

juries he has done me, and should only make use of
my humble confession to blacken my character the
more, and represent me as the only person guilty; yea,
though he should as it were insult me, and say, "he
knew all this before, and that I was making work for
repentance." Though what I said concerning Mr.
Whittelsey was only spoken in private, to a friend or
two; and being partly overheard, was related to the
rector, and by him extorted from my friends; yet, seeing it was divulged and made public, I was willing to
confess my fault therein publicly. But I trust God
will plead my cause."

I was witness to the very Christian spirit which
Brainerd showed at that time; being then at New
Haven, and one whom he thought fit to consult on
that occasion. This was my first opportunity of a personal acquaintance with him. There truly appeared
in him a great degree of calmness and humility, without the least appearance of rising of spirit for any ill
treatment which he supposed he had suffered, or the
least backwardness to abase himself before them who,
as he thought, had wronged him. What he did was
without any objection or appearance of reluctance,
even in private to his friends, to whom he freely opened himself. Earnest application was made on his behalf to the authority of the college, that he might have
his degree then given him; and particularly by the
Rev. Mr. Burr of Newark, one of the correspondents
of the society in Scotland; he being sent from New-
Jersey to New-Haven, by the rest of the commissioners,
for that end; and many arguments were used, but without success. Indeed, the governors of the college were
so far satisfied with the reflections which Brainerd
had made on himself, that they appeared willing to

admit him again into college; but not to give him his degree, till he should have remained there at least twelve months, which being contrary to what the correspondents, to whom he was now engaged, had declared to be their mind, he did not consent to it. He desired his degree, as he thought it would tend to his being more extensively useful; but still when he was denied it, he manifested no disappointment or resentment.

Sept. 20.—"[At Bethlehem.] Had thoughts of going forward on my journey to my Indians; but toward night was taken with a hard pain in my teeth, and shivering cold; and could not possibly recover a comfortable degree of warmth the whole night following. I continued very full of pain all night; and in the morning had a very hard fever, and pains almost over my whole body. I had a sense of the divine goodness in appointing this to be the place of my sickness, among my friends, who were very kind to me. I should probably have perished if I had first got home to my own house in the wilderness, where I have none to converse with but the poor, rude, ignorant Indians. Here, I saw, was mercy in the midst of affliction. I continued thus, mostly confined to my bed, till Friday night; very full of pain most of the time; but, through divine goodness, not afraid of death. Then I saw the extreme folly of those who put off their turning to God till a sick bed. Surely this is not a time proper to prepare for eternity. On Friday evening my pains went off somewhat suddenly. I was exceedingly weak, and almost fainted; but was very comfortable the night following. I thought we were to prize the continuation of life, only on this account, that we may "show forth God's goodness and works of grace."

Oct. 4.—" This day rode home to my own house and people. The poor Indians appeared very glad of my return. Found my house and all things in safety. I presently fell on my knees, and blessed God for my safe return. I have taken many considerable journies since this time last year, and yet God has never suffered one of my bones to be broken, or any distressing calamity to befal me, excepting the ill turn I had in my last journey. I have been often exposed to cold and hunger in the wilderness, where the comforts of life were not to be had; have frequently been lost in the woods; and sometimes obliged to ride much of the night; and once lay out in the woods all night; yet blessed be God, he has preserved me!

Nov. 3.—" Spent this day in secret fasting and prayer, from morning till night. Early in the morning I had some small degree of assistance in prayer. Afterward read the story of Elijah the prophet, 1 Kings, 17th, 18th, and 19th chapters; and also 2 Kings, 2d, and 4th chapters. My soul was much moved, observing the faith, zeal, and power of that holy man; how he wrestled with God in prayer, &c. My soul then cried with Elisha, "Where is the Lord God of Elijah!" O I longed for more faith! My soul breathed after God, and pleaded with him, that a "double portion of that spirit" which was given to Elijah, might "rest on me." And that which was divinely refreshing and strengthening to my soul, was, I saw that God is the *same* that he was in the days of Elijah. Was enabled to wrestle with God by prayer, in a more affectionate, fervent, humble, intense, and importunate manner, than I have for many months past. Nothing seemed too hard for God to perform; nothing too great for me to hope for from him. I had for many

months entirely lost all hope of being made instrumental of doing any special service for God in the
world ; it has appeared entirely impossible, that one so
vile should be thus employed for God. But at this
time God was pleased to revive this hope. Afterward
read from the 3d chapter of Exodus to the 20th,
and saw more of the *glory* and *majesty of God*
discovered in those chapters than ever I had seen before ; frequently in the mean time falling on my knees
and crying to God for the faith of Moses, and for a
manifestation of the *divine glory.* Especially the
3d, 4th, and part of the 14th and 15th chapters were unspeakably sweet to my soul: my soul blessed God that
he had shown himself so gracious to his servants of
old. The 15th chapter seemed to be the very language
which my soul uttered to God in the season of my first
spiritual comfort, when I had just got through the *Red
Sea*, by a *way* that I had no expectation of. O how
my soul then *rejoiced in God!* And now those things
came fresh and lively to my mind ; now my soul
blessed God afresh that he had opened that unthought
of way to deliver me from the fear of the Egyp-
tians, when I almost despaired of life. Afterward
read the story of Abraham's pilgrimage in the land of
Canaan. My soul was melted, in observing his *faith*,
how he leaned on God ; how he *communed* with God ;
and what a *stranger* he was here in the world. After
that, read the story of Joseph's sufferings, and God's
goodness to him : blessed God for these examples of
faith and patience. My soul was ardent in prayer,
was enabled to wrestle ardently for myself, for Christian friends, and for the church of God ; and felt more
desire to see the power of God in the conversion of
souls, than I have done for a long season. Blessed be

God for this season of fasting and prayer!—May his goodness always abide with me, and draw my soul to him!

Nov. 10.—" Spent this day in fasting and prayer alone. In the morning was very dull and lifeless, melancholy and discouraged. But after some time, while reading 2 Kings, 19, my soul was moved and affected; especially reading verse 14, and onward. I saw there was no other way for the afflicted children of God to take, but to go to God with all their sorrows. Hezekiah, in his great distress, went and spread his complaint before the Lord. I was then enabled to see the mighty power of God, and my extreme need of that power; and to cry to him affectionately and ardently for his power and grace to be exercised toward me. Afterward, read the story of David's trials, and observed the course he took under them, how he strengthened his hands in God; whereby my soul was carried out after God, enabled to cry to him, and rely upon him, and felt strong in the Lord. Was afterward refreshed, observing the blessed temper that was wrought in David by his trials: all bitterness, and desire of revenge, seemed wholly taken away; so that he mourned for the death of his enemies. 2 Sam. 1 : 17, and 4 : 9–12. Was enabled to bless God that he had given me something of this divine temper, that my soul freely *forgives*, and heartily *loves my enemies*.

Nov. 29.—" Began to study the Indian tongue, with Mr. Sergeant, at Stockbridge.* Was perplexed for want

* The commissioners who employed him, had directed him to spend much time this winter with Mr. Sergeant, to learn the language of the Indians; which necessitated him very often to ride backward and forward, twenty miles through the unin-

of more retirement. I love to live alone in my own little cottage, where I can spend much time in prayer, &c.

Dec. 22.—"Spent this day alone in fasting and prayer, and reading in God's word the exercises and deliverances of his children. Had, I trust, some exercise of faith, and realizing apprehension of divine power, grace, and holiness; and also of the unchangeableness of God, that he is the same as when he delivered his saints of old out of great tribulation. My soul was sundry times in prayer enlarged for God's church and people. O that Zion might become the "joy of the whole earth !" It is better to wait upon God with patience, than to put confidence in any thing in this lower world. "My soul, wait thou on the Lord ;" for "from him comes thy salvation."

Lord's day, Jan. 1, 1744.—"In the morning had some small degree of assistance in prayer. Saw myself so vile and unworthy that I could not look my people in the face when I came to preach. O my meanness, folly, ignorance, and inward pollution !—In the evening had a little assistance in prayer, so that the duty was delightful, rather than burdensome. Reflected on the goodness of God to me in the past year, &c. Of a truth God has been kind and gracious to me, though he has caused me to pass through many sorrows; he has provided for me bountifully, so that I have been enabled, in about fifteen months past, to bestow to charitable uses about an *hundred pounds* New-England money, that I can now remember. Blessed be the Lord

habited woods between Stockbridge and Kaunaumeek; which many times exposed him to extreme hardship in the severe seasons of the winter.

that has so far used me as *his steward*, to distribute a
portion of his goods. May I always remember, that
all I have comes from God. Blessed be the Lord, that
has carried me through all the toils, fatigues and hardships of the year past, as well as the spiritual sorrows
and conflicts that have attended it. O that I could
begin this year *with God*, and spend the whole of it to
his glory, either in life or death!

Jan. 3.—"Was employed much of the day in writing ; and spent some time in other necessary employment. But my time passes away so swiftly, that I am
astonished when I reflect on it, and see how little I do.
My state of solitude does not make the hours hang
heavy upon my hands. O what reason of thankfulness have I on account of this retirement! I find that
I do not, and it seems I cannot, lead a *Christian life*
when I am abroad, and cannot spend time in devotion,
Christian conversation, and serious meditation, as I
should do. Those weeks that I am obliged now to be
from home, in order to learn the Indian tongue, are
mostly spent in perplexity and barrenness, without
much sweet relish of divine things; and I feel myself
a stranger at the throne of grace for want of more frequent and continued retirement. When I return home
and give myself to meditation, prayer, and fasting, a
new scene opens to my mind, and my soul longs for
mortification, self-denial, humility, and divorcement
from all things of the world. This evening my heart was
somewhat warm and fervent in prayer and meditation,
so that I was loth to indulge sleep. Continued in
those duties till about midnight.

Jan. 6.—"Feeling my extreme weakness, and want of
grace, the pollution of my soul, and danger of temptations on every side, I set apart this day for fasting and

prayer, neither eating nor drinking from evening to evening, beseeching God to have mercy on me. My soul intensely longed that the dreadful spots and stains of sin might be washed away from it. Saw something of the power and all-sufficiency of God. My soul seemed to rest on his power and grace; longed for resignation to his will, and mortification to all things here below. My mind was greatly fixed on divine things: my resolutions for a life of mortification, continual watchfulness, self-denial, seriousness and devotion, were strong and fixed; my desires ardent and intense; my conscience tender, and afraid of every appearance of evil. My soul grieved with reflection on past levity, and want of resolution for God. I solemnly renewed my dedication of myself to God, and longed for grace to enable me always to keep covenant with him. Time appeared very short, eternity near, and a great name, either in or after life, together with all earthly pleasures and profits, but an empty bubble, a deluding dream.

Jan. 7. "Spent this day in seriousness, with steadfast resolutions for God, and a life of mortification. Studied closely, till I felt my bodily strength fail. Felt some degree of resignation to God, with an acquiescence in his dispensations. Was grieved that I could do so little for God before my bodily strength failed. In the evening, though tired, was enabled to continue instant in prayer for some time. Spent the time in reading, meditation, and prayer, till the evening was far spent: was grieved to think that I could not *watch unto prayer* the whole night. But blessed be God, heaven is a place of continual and incessant devotion though the earth is dull.

Jan. 14. "This morning, enjoyed a most solemn

season in prayer: my soul seemed enlarged and assisted to pour out itself to God for grace, and for every
blessing I wanted for myself, for dear christian friends,
and for the church of God; and was so enabled to
"see Him who is invisible," that my soul *rested upon
him* for the performance of every thing I asked agreeable to his will. It was then my happiness to 'continue
instant in prayer,' and I was enabled to continue in it
for near an hour. My soul was then "strong in the
Lord, and in the power of his might." Longed exceedingly for an angelic holiness and purity, and to have
all my thoughts, at all times, employed in divine and
heavenly things. Felt the same divine assistance in
prayer sundry times in the day. My soul confided in
God for myself, and for his Zion: trusted in divine
power and grace, that he would do glorious things in
his church on earth, for his own glory.

Feb. 3. "Enjoyed more freedom and comfort than
of late; was engaged in meditation upon the different
whispers of the various powers and affections of a
pious mind, exercised with a great variety of dispensations; and could not but write, as well as meditate,
on so entertaining a subject. I hope the Lord gave me
some true sense of divine things this day; but alas,
how great and pressing are the remains of indwelling
corruption! I am now more sensible than ever, that
God alone is "the author and finisher of our faith," *i. e.*
that the whole and every part of sanctification, and
every good word, work, or thought, found in me, is the
effect of his power and grace; that "without him I can
do nothing," in the strictest sense, and that, "he works
in us to will and to do of his own good pleasure," and
from no other motive. O how amazing it is that people can talk so much about men's power and goodness;

when if God did not hold us back every moment, we should be devils incarnate! This my bitter experience, for several days last past, has abundantly taught me concerning myself.

Feb. 7. "My soul felt and tasted that the Lord is gracious; that he is the supreme good, the only soul-satisfying happiness; that he is a complete, sufficient, and almighty portion. The language of my heart was, "Whom have I in heaven but thee? and there is none upon earth that I desire beside thee." O, I feel that it is heaven to please him, and to be just what he would have me to be! O that my soul were "holy, as he is holy!" O that it were "pure, even as Christ is pure;" and "perfect, as my Father in heaven is perfect!" These I feel are the sweetest commands in God's book, comprising all others. And shall I break them! must I break them! am I under the necessity of it as long as I live in the world! O my soul, wo, wo is me, that I am a sinner, who continually grieve and offend this blessed God, infinite in goodness and grace! O methinks if he would punish me for my sins, it would not wound my heart so deep to offend him; but though I sin continually, yet he continually repeats his kindness to me! O methinks I could bear any sufferings; but how can I bear to grieve and dishonor this blessed God! How shall I yield ten thousand times more honor to him? What shall I do to glorify and worship this best of beings? O that I could consecrate myself, soul and body, to his service for ever! O that I could give up myself to him, so as never more to attempt to be my own, or to have any will or affections that are not perfectly conformed to him! But, alas! I find I cannot be thus entirely devoted to God; I cannot live, and not sin. O ye angels, do ye glorify him incessantly; and if possi-

ble, prostrate yourselves lower before the blessed King
of heaven! I long to bear a part with you; and, if it
were possible, to help you.   O when we have done all
that we can, to all eternity, we shall not be able to offer
the ten thousandth part of the homage which the glorious God deserves!

March 3. "In the morning, spent (I believe) an
hour in prayer, with great intenseness and freedom,
and with the most soft and tender affection toward all
mankind.   I longed that those who, I have reason to
think, owe me ill will, might be eternally happy.   It
seemed refreshing to think of meeting them in heaven,
how much soever they had injured me on earth: had
no disposition to insist upon any confession f. om them,
in order to reconciliation, and the exercise of love and
kindness to them.   O it is an emblem of heaven itself,
to love all the world with a love of kindness, forgiveness, and benevolence; to feel our souls sedate, mild,
and meek; to be void of all evil surmisings and sus-
picions, and scarce able to think evil of any man upon
any occasion; to find our hearts simple, open, and free,
to those that look upon us with a different eye!—
Prayer was so sweet an exercise to me, that I knew
not how to cease, lest I should lose the spirit of prayer.
Felt no disposition to eat or drink, for the sake of the
pleasure of it, but only to support my nature, and fit
me for divine service.   Could not be content without
a very particular mention of a great number of dear
friends at the throne of grace; as also the particular
circumstances of many, as far as they were known.

March 10. "In the morning, felt exceeding dead to
the world, and all its enjoyments.   I thought I was
ready and willing to give up life and all its comforts,
as soon as called to it; and yet then had as much com-

fort of life as almost ever I had. I longed to be per-
petually and entirely *crucified* to all things here below,
by the *cross of Christ.* My soul was sweetly resigned
to God's disposal of me, in every regard; and I saw
that nothing had happened but what was best for me.
I confided in God, that he would never leave me,
though I should "walk through the valley of the shadow of death." It was then my meat and drink to be
holy, to live to the Lord, and die to the Lord. And I
thought that I then enjoyed such a heaven as far exceeded the most sublime conceptions of an unregenerate soul; and even unspeakably beyond what I myself could conceive of at another time. I did not wonder that Peter said, "Lord, it is good to be here," when
thus refreshed with divine glories. My soul was full
of love and tenderness in the duty of intercession;
especially felt a most sweet affection to some precious
godly ministers, of my acquaintance. Prayed earnestly for dear Christians, and for those I have reason to
fear are my enemies; and could not have spoken a
word of bitterness, or entertained a bitter thought,
against the vilest man living. Had a sense of my own
great unworthiness. ' My soul seemed to breathe forth
love and praise to God afresh, when I thought he would
let his children love and receive me as one of their
brethren and fellow citizens. When I thought of their
treating me in that manner, I longed to lie at their feet;
and could think of no way to express the sincerity and
simplicity of my love and esteem of them, as being
much better than myself.

Lord's day, March 11. "My soul was in some measure *strengthened in God,* in morning devotion; so that
I was released from trembling fear and distress. Preached to my people from the parable of the *sower*, Matt.

13, and enjoyed some assistance both parts of the day;
had some freedom, affection, and fervency in addressing my poor people; longed that God should take hold
of their hearts, and make them spiritually alive. And
indeed I had so much to say to them, that I knew not
how to leave off speaking."

This was the last Sabbath in which he ever performed public service at Kaunaumeek, and these the
last sermons which he ever preached to the Indians
there. The methods he adopted for their salvation, he
thus describes in a letter to Rev. Mr. Pemberton of
New-York.

"In my labors with them, in order to "turn them
from darkness to light," I studied what was most *plain*
and *easy*, and best suited to their capacities; and endeavored to set before them from time to time, as they
were able to receive them, the most *important* and *necessary* truths of Christianity; such as most immediately concerned their speedy conversion to God, and
such as I judged had the greatest tendency, as means,
to effect that glorious change in them. But especially
I made it the scope and drift of all my labors, to lead
them into a thorough acquaintance with these two
things: (1.) The *sinfulness* and *misery* of the estate
they were naturally in; the evil of their hearts, the
pollution of their natures; the heavy guilt they were
under, and their exposedness to everlasting punishment; as also their utter inability to save themselves,
either from their sins, or from those miseries which
are the just punishment of them; and their unworthiness of any mercy at the hand of God, on account of
any thing they themselves could do to procure his
favor, and consequently their extreme need of Christ
to save them. And, (2.) I frequently endeavored to

open to them the *fullness*, *all-sufficiency*, and *freeness* of that *redemption* which the Son of God has wrought out by his obedience and sufferings, for perishing sinners: how this provision he had made was suited to all their wants; and how he called and invited them to accept of everlasting life freely, notwithstanding all their sinfulness.

"After I had been with the Indians several months, I composed sundry *forms of prayer*, adapted to their circumstances and capacities; which, with the help of my interpreter, I translated into the Indian language; and soon learned to pronounce their words, so as to pray with them in their own tongue. I also translated sundry *psalms* into their language, and soon after we were able to sing in the worship of God.

"When my people had gained some acquaintance with many of the simplest truths of Christianity, so that they were capable of receiving and understanding others, I gave them an *historical* account of God's dealings with his ancient professing people, the Jews; some of the rites and ceremonies they were obliged to observe, as their sacrifices, &c.; and what these were designed to represent to them; as also some of the surprising *miracles* God wrought for their salvation, while they trusted in him; and sore *punishments* he sometimes brought upon them, when they forsook and sinned against him. Afterward I proceeded to give them a relation of the birth, life, miracles, sufferings, death, and resurrection of Christ; as well as his ascension, and the wonderful effusion of the Holy Spirit consequent thereupon.

"And having thus endeavored to prepare the way by such a general account of things, I next proceeded to read and *expound* to them the Gospel of St. Matthew

(at least the substance of it) in course, wherein they
had a more distinct and particular view of what they
had had before some general notion. These exposi-
tions I attended almost every *evening*, when there was
any considerable number of them at home; except
when I was obliged to be absent myself, in order to
learn the Indian language with the Rev. Mr. Sargeant.
Besides these means of instruction, there was likewise
an English *school* constantly kept by my interpreter
among the Indians; which I used frequently to visit,
in order to give the children and young people some
proper instructions, and serious exhortations suited to
their age.

" The degree of knowledge to which some of them
attained was considerable. Many of the truths of Christianity seemed fixed in their minds, especially in some
instances, so that they would speak to me of them,
and ask such questions about them as were necessary
to render them more plain and clear to their understandings. The children, also, and young people, who
attended the school, made considerable proficiency (at
least some of them) in their learning; so that had they
understood the English language well, they would
have been able to read somewhat readily in a psalter.

" But that which was most of all desirable, and gave
me the greatest encouragement amidst many difficulties and disconsolate hours, was, that the truths of
God's word seemed, at times, to be attended with some
power upon the hearts and consciences of the Indians.
And especially this appeared evident in a few individuals, who were awakened to some sense of their miserable estate by nature, and appeared solicitous for
deliverance from it. Several of them came, of their
own accord to discourse with me about their soul's

concerns; and some, with tears, inquired what they should do to be saved?"

The Indians at Kaunaumeek being but few in number, and Brainerd having been laboring among them about a year, and having prevailed upon them to be willing to leave Kaunaumeek, and remove to Stockbridge, to live constantly under Mr. Sergeant's ministry; he thought he might now do more service for Christ among the Indians elsewhere: and therefore went to New-Jersey, and laid the matter before the Commissioners; who met at Elizabeth-Town, on the occasion, and determined that he should forthwith leave Kaunaumeek, and go to the Delaware Indians.

By the invitations which Brainerd had lately received, it appears, that it was not from necessity, or for want of opportunities to settle in the ministry, that he determined to forsake all the outward comforts, he might thus have enjoyed, to spend his life among *savages*, and endure the difficulties and self-denials of an Indian *mission*. He had, just as he was leaving Kaunaumeek, had an earnest invitation to a settlement at East-Hampton, one of the pleasantest towns on Long-Island. The people there were unanimous in their desires to have him for their pastor, and for a long time continued in earnest pursuit of him, and were hardly brought to relinquish their endeavors, and give up their hopes of obtaining him. Besides this, he had an invitation to preach with reference to a settlement in Millington, near his native town, and in the midst of his friends. Nor did Brainerd choose the business of a missionary to the Indians, rather than accept of those invitations, because he was unacquainted with the difficulties and sufferings which attended such a service; for he had had experience of these difficul-

ties in summer and winter; having spent about a year
in a lonely desert among these savages, where he had
gone through extreme hardships, and been the subject
of a train of outward and inward sorrows, which were
now fresh in his mind.

After this he continued two or three days in New-
Jersey, very ill; and then returned to New-York; and
from thence into New-England; and went to his native
town of Haddam, where he arrived on Saturday, April
14. And he continues still his bitter complaints of want
of retirement. While he was in New-York, he says
thus, "O it is not the pleasures of the world which can
comfort me! If *God* deny his presence, what are the
pleasures of the *city* to me? One hour of sweet retirement where *God is*, is better than the whole world."

April 17.—"In the evening, at my brother's, singing
hymns with friends, my soul seemed to melt; and in
prayer afterward, enjoyed the exercise of *faith*, and
was enabled to be fervent in spirit: found more of
God's presence than I have done any time in my late
wearisome journey. Eternity appeared very near;
my nature was very weak, and seemed ready to be dis-
solved; the sun declining, and the shadows of the
evening drawing on apace. O I longed to fill up the
remaining moments all for God! Though my body
was so feeble, and wearied with preaching and much
private conversation, yet I wanted to sit up all night to
do something for God. To God, the giver of these
refreshments, be glory for ever and ever. Amen.

April 18.—"Was very weak, and enjoyed but little
spiritual comfort. Was exercised with one who ca-
villed against original sin. May the Lord open his
eyes to see the fountain of sin in himself!"

After this he visited several ministers in Connecti-

cut; and then travelled towards Kaunaumeek, and
came to Mr. Sergeant's, at Stockbridge, Thursday,
April 26, having performed the journey in a very weak
state of body.

April 27 and 28.—" Spent some time in visiting
friends, and discoursing with my people, (who were
now moved down from their own place to Mr. Sergeant's) and found them very glad to see me returned.
Was exercised in my mind with a sense of my own
unworthiness.

Lord's day, April 29.—" Preached for Mr. Sergeant both parts of the day, from Rev. 14 : 4. Enjoyed
some freedom in preaching, though not much spirituality. In the evening, my heart was in some measure lifted up in thankfulness to God for any assistance.

April 30.—" Rode to Kaunaumeek, but was extremely ill; did not enjoy the comfort I hoped for in
my own house.

May 1.—" Having received new orders to go to a
number of Indians on Delaware river, in Pennsylvania, and my people here being mostly removed to Mr.
Sergeant's, I this day took all my clothes, books, &c.
and disposed of them, and set out for Delaware river ;
but made it my way to return to Mr. Sergeant's, which
I did this day, just at night. Rode several hours in
the rain through the howling wilderness, although I
was so disordered in body, that little or nothing but
blood came from me.

May 8.—" Travelled about forty-five miles to a place
called *Fishkill ;* and lodged there. Spent much of my
time, while riding, in prayer that God would go with
me to the Delaware. My heart sometimes was ready
to sink with the thoughts of my work, and going alone

in the wilderness, I knew not where; but still it was comfortable to think that others of God's children had ' wandered about in dens and caves of the earth ;' and Abraham, when he was called to go forth, 'went out not knowing whither he went.' O that I might follow after God !"

The next day he went forward on his journey; crossed the Hudson, and went to Goshen in the Highlands; and so traveled across the woods, from the Hudson to the Delaware, about a hundred miles, through a desolate and hideous country, above New-Jersey, where were very few settlements ; in which journey he suffered much fatigue and hardship. He visited some Indians in the way, at a place called *Miunissinks*, and discoursed with them concerning Christianity. Was considerably melancholy and disconsolate, being alone in a strange wilderness. On Saturday, May 12, he came to a settlement of Irish and Dutch people, and proceeding about twelve miles further arrived at *Sakhauwotung*, an Indian settlement within the Forks of the Delaware.

Lord's day, May 13.—" Rose early ; felt very poorly after my long journey, and after being wet and fatigued. Was very melancholy; have scarcely ever seen such a gloomy morning in my life ; there appeared to be no *Sabbath ;* the children were all at play; I, a stranger in the wilderness, and knew not where to go ; and all circumstances seemed to conspire to render my affairs dark and discouraging. Was disappointed respecting an *Interpreter*, and heard that the Indians were much scattered. O, I mourned after the presence of God, and seemed like a creature banished from his sight! yet he was pleased to support my sinking soul amidst all my sorrows; so that I never enter-

tained any thought of quitting my business among the
poor Indians; but was comforted to think that death
would ere long set me free from these distresses.
Rode about three or four miles to the Irish people,
where I found some that appeared sober and concerned about religion. My heart then began to be a
little encouraged : went and preached first to the Irish
and then to the Indians; and in the evening was a
little comforted : my soul seemed to rest on God, and
take courage.

Lord's day, May 20.—" Preached twice to the poor
Indians; and enjoyed some freedom in speaking, while
I attempted to remove their prejudices against Christianity. My soul longed continually for assistance
from above; for I saw I had no strength sufficient for
that work. Afterward preached to the Irish people;
was much assisted in the first prayer, and somewhat
in the sermon. Several persons seemed much concerned for their souls, with whom I discoursed afterward with much freedom and some power. Blessed
be God for any assistance afforded to an unworthy
worm. O that I could live to him !

Lord's day, May 27.—" Visited my Indians in the
morning, and attended upon a funeral among them;
was affected to see their heathenish practices. O that
they might be ' turned from darkness to light !' Afterward got a considerable number of them together, and
preached to them; and observed them very attentive.
After this preached to the white people from Heb.
2 : 3. ' How shall we escape if we neglect so great
salvation?' Was enabled to speak with some freedom
and power : several people seemed much concerned
for their souls; especially one who had been educated
a Roman Catholic. Blessed be the Lord for any help.

May 28.—"Set out from the Indians above the Forks
of the Delaware, on a journey toward Newark, in
New-Jersey, according to my orders. Rode through
the wilderness; was much fatigued with the heat;
lodged at a place called Black River; was exceedingly tired and worn out.

Lord's day, June 10.—"[At Newark.] In the morning was much concerned how I should perform the
work of the day: and trembled at the thoughts of being left to myself. Enjoyed very considerable assistance in all parts of the public service. Had an opportunity again to attend on the ordinance of the Lord's
Supper, and through divine goodness was refreshed in
it: my soul was full of love and tenderness toward the
children of God, and toward all men. At night I
enjoyed more spirituality and sweet desire of holiness,
than I have felt for some time: was afraid of every
thought and every motion, lest thereby my heart
should be drawn away from God. O that I might
never leave the blessed God! 'Lord, in thy presence
is fulness of joy.' O the blessedness of living to God!

June 11.—"This day the Presbytery met at Newark, in order to my *ordination*. Was very weak and
disordered in body; yet endeavored to repose my confidence in God. Spent most of the day alone; especially the forenoon. At three in the afternoon preached
my probation sermon from Acts, 26 : 17, 18, being a
text given me for that purpose. Felt not well either
in body or mind: however, God carried me through
comfortably. Afterward passed an examination before
the Presbytery. Was much tired, and my mind burdened with the greatness of that charge I was in the
most solemn manner about to take upon me: my mind
was so pressed with the weight of the work incum-

bent upon me, that I could not sleep this night, though very weary and in great need of rest.

June 12.—" Was this morning further examined respecting my *experimental acquaintance with Christianity.* At 10 o'clock my *ordination* was attended ; the sermon preached by the Rev. Mr. Pemberton. At this time I was affected with a sense of the important trust committed to me; yet was composed and solemn without distraction ; and I hope that then, as many times before, I gave myself up to God, to be for *him*, and not for *another*. O that I might always be engaged in the service of God, and duly remember the solemn charge I have received in the presence of God, angels, and men. Amen."

CHAPTER VI

Labors for the Indians at and near the Forks of Delaware—idolatrous feast and dance—journey through the wilderness to Opeholhaupung or the Susquehanna—erects a cottage at Forks of the Delaware—some evidences of a work of the Spirit among the Indians—journey to New-England to obtain money to support a colleague—visit to the Indians on the Susquehanna—journey to Crossweeksung in New-Jersey.

June 13, 1744.—June 18, 1745

June 13, 1744. [At Elizabeth Town.]—" Spent considerable time in writing an account of the Indian affairs, to be sent to Scotland ; some, in conversation with friends; but had not much spiritual enjoyment."

On *Tuesday, June* 19, he set out on his journey, and in three days reached his residence near the Forks of Delaware. Performed the journey under much weakness of body, but had comfort in his soul, from day to day.

Lord's day, June 24.—"Extremely feeble; scarcely able to walk: however visited my Indians, and took much pains to instruct them; labored with some that were much disaffected toward Christianity. My mind was much burdened with the weight and difficulty of my work. My whole dependence and hope of success seemed to be on God; who alone I saw could make them willing to receive instruction. My heart was much engaged in prayer, sending up silent requests to God, even while I was speaking to them. O that I could always go in the strength of the Lord!

June 25.—"Was somewhat better in health than of late; and was able to spend a considerable part of the day in prayer and close study. Had more freedom and fervency in prayer than usual of late; especially longed for the presence of God in my work, and that the poor Heathen might be converted. And in evening prayer my faith and hope in God were much raised. *To an eye of reason every thing that respects the conversion of the Heathen is as dark as midnight;* and yet I cannot but hope in God for the accomplishment of something glorious among them. My soul longed much for the advancement of the Redeemer's kingdom on earth. Was very fearful lest I should admit some vain thought, and so lose the sense I then had of divine things. O for an abiding heavenly temper!

June 26.—"In the morning, my desires seemed to rise, and ascend up freely to God. Was busy most of the day in *translating prayers* into the language of the Delaware Indians; met with great difficulty, because my interpreter was altogether unacquainted with the business. But though I was much discouraged with

the extreme difficulty of that work, yet God supported
me; and especially in the evening, gave me sweet refreshment.   In prayer my soul was enlarged, and my
faith drawn into sensible exercise; was enabled to cry
to God for my poor Indians; and though the work of
their conversion appeared *impossible with man*, yet *with
God* I saw *all things were possible*. My faith was much
strengthened, by observing the wonderful assistance
God afforded his servants Nehemiah and Ezra, in reforming his people and re-establishing his ancient
church. I was much assisted in prayer for my dear
Christian friends, and for others whom I apprehended
to be Christless; but was more especially concerned
for the poor heathen, and those of my own charge;
was enabled to be instant in prayer for them; and
hoped that God would bow the heavens and come down
for their salvation. It seemed to me that there could
be no impediment sufficient to obstruct that glorious
work, seeing the living God, as I strongly hoped, was
engaged for it. I continued in a solemn frame, lifting
up my heart to God for assistance and grace, that I
might be more mortified to this present world, that my
whole soul might be taken up continually in concern
for the advancement of Christ's kingdom. Earnestly
desired that God would purge me more, that I might
be as a chosen vessel to bear his name among the
Heathen.

June 28.—"Spent the morning in reading several
parts of the holy scripture, and in fervent prayer for
my Indians, that God would set up his kingdom among
them, and bring them into his church. About nine I
withdrew to my usual place of retirement in the woods,
and there again enjoyed some assistance in prayer.
My great concern was for the conversion of the hea-

then to God; and the Lord helped me to plead with
him for it. Toward noon rode up to the Indians in
order to preach to them; and while going my heart
went up to God in prayer for them; could freely tell
God he knew that the cause in which I was engaged
was not mine; but that it was his own cause, and that
it would be for his own glory to convert the poor Indians: and blessed be God I felt no desire of their
conversion that I might receive honor from the world
as being the instrument of it. Had some freedom in
speaking to the Indians.

June 30.—" My soul was very solemn in reading
God's word,'especially the ninth chapter of Daniel. I
saw how God had called out his servants to prayer,
and made them wrestle with him, when he designed
to bestow any great mercy on his church. And, alas!
I was ashamed of myself to think of my dullness and
inactivity when there seemed to be so much to do for
the upbuilding of Zion. O how does Zion lie waste!
I longed that the church of God might be enlarged;
was enabled to pray, I think, in faith; my soul seemed
sensibly to confide in God, and was enabled to wrestle
with him. Afterward walked abroad to a place of
sweet retirement; enjoyed some assistance in prayer,
had a sense of my great need of divine help, and felt
my soul sensibly depend on God. Blessed be God,
this has been a comfortable week to me.

Lord's day, July 1.—" After I came to them my
mind was confused, and I felt nothing sensibly of that
sweet reliance on God with which my soul has been
comforted in days past. Spent the forenoon in this
posture of mind, and preached to the Indians without
any heart. In the afternoon I felt still barren when I
began to preach, and for about half an hour: I seemed

to myself to know nothing, and to have nothing to say to the Indians; but soon after I found in myself a spirit of love, and warmth, and power, to address the poor Indians, and God helped me to plead with them, to ' turn from all the vanities of the heathen to the living God;' I am persuaded that the Lord touched their consciences; for I never saw such attention raised in them. When I came away from them, I spent the whole time I was riding to my lodgings, three miles distant, in prayer and praise to God. After I had rode more than two miles it came into my mind to dedicate myself to God again, which I did with great solemnity and unspeakable satisfaction; especially gave up myself to him renewedly in the work of the ministry. This I did by divine grace, I hope, without any exception or reserve; not in the least shrinking back from any difficulties that might attend this great and blessed work. I seemed to be most free, cheerful, and full in this dedication of myself. My whole soul cried, ' Lord, to thee I dedicate myself! O accept of me, and let me be thine for ever. Lord, I desire nothing else; I desire nothing more. O come, come, Lord, accept a poor worm. My heart rejoiced in my particular work as a *missionary;* rejoiced in my necessity of self-denial in many respects, and I still continued to give up myself to God, and to implore mercy of him, praying incessantly every moment with sweet fervency. My nature being very weak of late, and much spent, was now considerably overcome: my fingers grew very feeble, and somewhat numb, so that I could scarcely stretch them out straight, and when I lighted from my horse could hardly walk; my joints seemed all to be loosed. But I felt abundant *strength in the inner man.* Preached to the white people; God

helped me much, especially in prayer. Sundry of my
poor Indians were so moved as to come to meeting
also, and one appeared much concerned.

July 3.—" Was still very weak. This morning was
enabled to pray under a feeling sense of my need of
help from God, and I trust had some faith in exercise;
and, blessed be God, was enabled to plead with him a
considerable time. Truly God is good to me. But
my soul mourned, and was grieved at my sinfulness
and barrenness, and longed to be more engaged for
God. Near nine, withdrew again for prayer, and
through divine goodness had the blessed spirit of
prayer; my soul loved the duty, and longed for God
in it. O it is sweet to be *the Lord's*, to be sensibly devoted to him! What a blessed portion is God! How
glorious, how lovely in himself! O my soul longed to
improve time wholly for God! Spent most of the day
in translating prayers into Indian. In the evening
was enabled again to wrestle with God in prayer with
fervency. Was enabled to maintain a self-diffident
and watchful frame of spirit, and was jealous, and
afraid lest I should admit carelessness and self-confidence.

July 6.—" Awoke this morning in the fear of God,
and spent my first waking minutes in prayer for sanctification, that my soul may be washed from its exceeding pollution and defilement. After I arose I spent
some time in reading God's word, and in prayer. I
cried to God under a sense of my great indigence. I
am of late most of all concerned for ministerial qualifications, and the conversion of the heathen. Last
year I longed to be prepared for a world of glory, and
speedily to depart out of this world; but of late all my
concern almost is for the conversion of the heathen,

and for that end I long to live. But blessed be God I
have less desire to live for any of the pleasures of the
world than I ever had. I long and love to be a pilgrim, and want grace to imitate the life, labors and
sufferings of St. Paul among the heathen. And when
I long for holiness now, it is not so much for myself
as formerly, but rather thereby I may become an 'able
minister of the New Testament,' especially to the
heathen.

July 7.—" Was very much disordered this morning,
and my vigor all spent and exhausted; but was affected and refreshed in reading the sweet story of Elijah's
translation, and enjoyed some affection and fervency in
prayer; longed much for ministerial gifts and graces,
that I might do something in the cause of God. Afterward was refreshed and invigorated while reading
ALLEINE's first *Case of Conscience,* &c.—was enabled
then to pray with some ardor of soul—was afraid of
carelessness and self-confidence, and longed for holiness.

Lord's day, July 8.—" Was ill last night—not able
to rest quietly. Had some small degree of assistance
in preaching to the Indians, and afterward was enabled
to preach to the white people with some power, especially in the close of my discourse, from Jer. 3 : 23.
' Truly in vain is salvation hoped for from the hills,'
&c. The Lord also assisted me in some measure in
the first prayer; blessed be his name. Near night,
though very weary, was enabled to read God's word
with some sweet relish of it, and to pray with affection, fervency, and I trust with faith; my soul was
more sensibly dependant on God than usual. Was
watchful, tender, and jealous of my own heart, lest I
should admit carelessness and vain thoughts, and

grieve the blessed Spirit, so that he should withdraw his sweet, kind, and tender influences. Longed to 'depart, and be with Christ,' more than at any time of late. My soul was exceedingly united to the saints of ancient times, as well as those now living; especially my soul melted for the society of Elijah and Elisha. Was enabled to cry to God with a child-like spirit, and to continue instant in prayer for some time. Was much enlarged in the sweet duty of intercession; was enabled to remember great numbers of dear friends, and precious souls, as well as Christ's ministers. Continued in this frame, afraid of every idle thought, till I dropped asleep.

July 21.—" This morning I was greatly oppressed with guilt and shame from a sense of inward vileness and pollution. About nine withdrew to the woods for prayer, but had not much comfort; I appeared to myself the vilest, meanest creature upon earth, and could scarcely live with myself; so mean and vile I appeared, that I thought I should never be able to hold up my face in heaven, if God, of his infinite grace, should bring me thither. Toward night my burden respecting my work among the Indians began to increase much, and was aggravated by hearing sundry things which looked very discouraging, in particular that they intended to meet together the next day for an idolatrous feast and dance. Then I began to be in anguish; I thought that I must in conscience go and endeavor to break them up, yet knew not how to attempt such a thing. However, I withdrew for prayer hoping for strength from above. In prayer I was exceedingly enlarged, and my soul was as much drawn out as I ever remember it to have been in my life. I was in such anguish, and pleaded with such earnest ness and importunity, that when I rose from my knees I felt extremely weak and overcome; I could scarcely walk straight; my joints were loosed; the sweat ran down my face and body, and nature seemed as if it would dissolve. So far as I could judge, I was wholly free from selfish ends in my fervent supplications for the poor Indians. I knew that they were met together to worship devils, and not God; and this made me cry earnestly that God would now appear and help me in my attempts to break up this idolatrous meeting. My soul pleaded long, and I thought that God would hear, and would go with me to vindicate his own cause: I seemed to confide in God for his presence and assistance. And thus I spent the evening, praying incessantly for divine assistance, and that I might not be self-dependent, but still have my whole dependance upon God. What I passed through was remarkable, and indeed inexpressible. All things here below vanished, and there appeared to be nothing of any considerable importance to me, but holiness of heart and life, and the conversion of the heathen to God. All my cares, fears and desires, which might be said to be of a worldly nature, disappeared, and were, in my esteem, of little more importance than a puff of wind. I exceedingly longed that God would get to himself a name among the heathen; and I appealed to him with the greatest freedom, that he knew I ' preferred him above my chief joy.' Indeed, I had no notion of joy from this world; I cared not where or how I lived, or what hardships I went through, so that I could but gain souls to Christ. I continued in this frame all the evening and night. While I was asleep I dreamed of these things; and when I waked, (as I frequently did,) the first thing I thought of was this great work of pleading for God against Satan.

Lord's day, July 22.—" When I waked my soul was
burdened with what seemed to be before me. I cried
to God, before I could get out of my bed; and as soon
as I was dressed I withdrew into the woods, to pour
out my burdened soul to God, especially for assistance
in my great work; for I could scarcely think of any
thing else. I enjoyed the same freedom and fervency
as the last evening; and did with unspeakable freedom
give up myself afresh to God, for life or death, for all
hardships to which he should call me, among the
heathen; and felt as if nothing could discourage me
from this blessed work. I had a strong hope that God
would ' bow the heavens and come down,' and do
some marvellous work among the heathen. While I
was riding to the Indians, three miles, my heart was
continually going up to God for his presence and assistance; and hoping, and almost expecting, that God
would make this the day of his power and grace
amongst the poor Indians. When I came to them, I
found them engaged in their frolic; but through divine
goodness I persuaded them to desist and attend to my
preaching: yet still there appeared nothing of the
special power of God among them. Preached again
to them in the afternoon, and observed the Indians
were more sober than before; but still saw nothing
special among them. Hence satan took occasion to
tempt and buffet me with these cursed suggestions,
There is no God, or if there be, he is not able to convert the Indians, before they have more knowledge,
&c. I was very weak and weary, and my soul borne
down with perplexity; but was mortified to all the
world, and was determined still to wait upon God for
the conversion of the heathen, though the devil tempted me to the contrary.

July 24.—" Rode about seventeen miles westward, over a hideous mountain, to a number of Indians. Got together near thirty of them : preached to them in the evening, and lodged among them. Was weak, and felt in some degree disconsolate ; yet could have no freedom in the thought of any other circumstances or business in life. All my desire was the conversion of the heathen ; and all my hope was in God. God does not suffer me to please or comfort myself with hopes of seeing friends, returning to my dear acquaintance, and enjoying worldly comforts.

Lord's day, August 5.—" Though very weak, I visited and preached to the poor Indians twice, and was strengthened vastly beyond my expectations. Indeed the Lord gave me some freedom and fervency in addressing them ; though I had not strength enough to stand, but was obliged to sit down the whole time. Toward night was extremely weak, faint, sick, and full of pain. I seem to myself like a man that has all his estate embarked in one small boat, unhappily going adrift down a swift torrent. The poor owner stands on the shore, and looks, and laments his loss. But, alas ! though my all seems to be adrift, and I stand and see it, I dare not lament ; for this sinks my spirits more, and aggravates my bodily disorders ! I am forced, therefore, to divert myself with trifles ; although at the same time I am afraid, and often feel as if I was guilty of the misimprovement of time. And oftentimes my conscience is so exercised with this miserable way of spending time, that I have no peace ; though I have no strength of mind or body to improve it to better purpose. O that God would pity my distressed state !"

The next three weeks his illness was less severe

and he was in some degree capable of business, both
public and private, though he had some turns wherein
his indisposition prevailed to a great degree. He had
generally also much more inward assistance and
strength of mind. He often expresses great longings
for the enlargement of Christ's kingdom, especially
by the conversion of the heathen to God ; and speaks
of this hope as all his delight and joy. He continues
still to express his usual desires after holiness, living
to God, and a sense of his own unworthiness. He
several times speaks of his appearing to himself the
vilest creature on earth ; and once says, that he verily
thought there were none of God's children who fell
so far short of that holiness, and perfection in their
obedience, which God requires, as he. He speaks of
his feeling more dead than ever to the enjoyments of
the world. He sometimes mentions the special assistance which he had at this time, in preaching to the
Indians, and the appearances of religious concern
among them. He speaks also of assistance in prayer
for absent friends, and especially ministers and candidates for the ministry ; and of much comfort which
he enjoyed in the company of some ministers who
came to visit him.

Sept. 1.—" Was so far strengthened, after a season
of great weakness, that I was able to spend two or
three hours in writing on a divine subject. Enjoyed
some comfort and sweetness in things divine and sacred ; and as my bodily strength was in some measure
restored, so my soul seemed to be somewhat vigorous,
and engaged in the things of God.

Lord's day, Sept. 2.—" Was enabled to speak to my
poor Indians with much concern and fervency ; and I
am persuaded that God enabled me to exercise faith in

him, while I was speaking to them. I perceived that
some of them were afraid to hearken to and embrace
Christianity, lest they should be enchanted and poi-
soned by some of the *powaws :* but I was enabled to
plead with them not to fear these; and, confiding in
God for safety and deliverance, I bid a challenge to all
these *powers of darkness*, to do their worst on *me* first.
I told my people that I was a Christian, and asked
them why the powaws did not bewitch and poison me.
I scarcely ever felt more sensible of my own unworthiness, than in this action. I saw that the honor of
God was concerned; and desired to be preserved—not
from selfish views—but for a testimony of the divine
power and goodness, and of the truth of Christianity,
and that God might be glorified. Afterward, I found
my soul rejoice in God for his assisting grace."

After this, he went a journey into New-England, and
was absent from the place of his abode, at the Forks
of Delaware, about three weeks. He was in a feeble
state the greater part of the time. But in the latter
of the journey he found that he gained much in health
and strength.

Sept. 26.—" Rode home to the Forks of Delaware.
What reason have I to bless God, who has preserved
me in riding more than four hundred and twenty
miles, and has ' kept all my bones, that not one of
them has been broken !' My health likewise is greatly recovered. O that I could dedicate my all to God !
This is all the return I can make to him."

When he began to preach here, he had not more
than from twenty to twenty-five hearers; their numbers at length increased to forty, or more; and often
most belonging to those parts came together to hear
him preach. In a letter to Rev. Mr. Pemberton, he says

" The *effects* which the truths of God's word have had upon some of the Indians in this place, are somewhat encouraging. A number of them are brought to renounce *idolatry*, and to decline partaking of those feasts which they used to offer in sacrifice to certain supposed unknown powers. And some few among them have, for a considerable time, manifested a serious concern for their soul's eternal welfare, and still continue to ' inquire the way to Zion,' with such diligence, affection, and becoming solicitude, as gives me reason to hope that ' God who, I trust, has begun this work in them,' will carry it on, until it shall issue in their saving conversion to himself. These not only detest their old idolatrous notions, but strive also to bring their friends off from them. And as they are seeking salvation for their own souls, so they seem desirous, and some of them take pains, that others might be excited to do the same.

" There are also many *difficulties*, that attend the christianizing of these poor pagans.

" In the first place, their minds are filled with *prejudices* against Christianity, on account of the *vicious* lives and *unchristian* behavior of some that are called Christians. These not only set before them the worst examples, but some of them take pains, expressly in words, to dissuade them from becoming Christians, foreseeing that if these should be converted to God, ' the hope of their unlawful gain' would thereby be lost.

" Again : these poor heathens are extremely attached to the *customs, traditions, and fabulous notions of their fathers.* And this one seems to be the foundation of all their other notions, viz. that ' it was not the same God made them, who made the white people,' but another, who commanded them to live by hunting.

&c., and not to conform to the customs of the white people. Hence, when they are desired to become Christians, they frequently reply, that ' they will live as their fathers lived, and go to their fathers when they die.' And if the miracles of Christ and his apostles be mentioned to prove the truth of Christianity, they also mention sundry miracles which their fathers have told them were anciently wrought among the Indians, and which satan makes them believe were so. They are much attached to idolatry, frequently making feasts, which they eat in honor to some *unknown* beings, who, they suppose, speak to them in *dreams;* promising them success in hunting, and other affairs, in case they will sacrifice to them. They oftentimes also offer their sacrifices to the spirits of the dead, who, they suppose, stand in need of favors from the living, and yet are in such a state as that they can well reward all the offices of kindness that are shown them. And they impute all their calamities to the neglect of these sacrifices.

" Furthermore, they are much awed by those among themselves who are called *powaws,* who are supposed to have a power of enchanting, or poisoning them to death, or at least in a very distressing manner. And they apprehended it would be their sad fate to be thus enchanted in case they should become Christians.

" The *manner of their living* is likewise a great disadvantage to the design of their being christianized. They are almost continually roving from place to place, and it is but rare that an opportunity can be had with some of them for their instruction."

Oct. 1.—" Was engaged in making preparations for my intended journey to the Susquehanna. Withdrew several times to the woods for secret duties, and endeavored to plead for the divine presence to go with me to the poor Pagans, to whom I was going to preach the Gospel. Toward night rode about four miles, and met brother Byram, who was come at my desire to be my companion in travel to the Indians. I rejoiced to see him, and I trust God made his conversation profitable to me. I saw him, as I thought, more dead to the world, its anxious cares and alluring objects, than I was; and this made me look within myself, and gave me a greater sense of my guilt, ingratitude, and misery.

Oct. 2.—" Set out on my journey in company with dear brother Byram and my interpreter, and two chief Indians from the Forks of Delaware. Traveled about twenty-five miles, and lodged in one of the last houses on our road; after which there was nothing but a hideous and howling *wilderness.*

Oct. 3.—" We went on our way into the wilderness, and found the most difficult and dangerous traveling by far, that ever any of us had seen. We had scarce any thing else but lofty mountains, deep valleys, and hideous rocks, to make our way through. However, I had some spiritual enjoyment part of the day, and my mind intensely engaged in meditation on a divine subject. Near night my horse hung one of her legs in the rocks and fell down under me, but through divine goodness I was not hurt. However, she broke her leg ; and being in such a hideous place, and near thirty miles from any house, I saw nothing that could be done to preserve her life, and so was obliged to kill her, and to prosecute my journey on foot. This accident made me admire the divine goodness to me that my bones were not broken, and the multitude of them filled with strong pain. Just at dark we kindled a fire, cut up a few bushes, and made a shelter over our heads to save us from the frost, which was very hard that night, and committing ourselves to God by prayer, we lay down on the ground and slept quietly."

The next·day they went forward on their journey. and at night took up their lodgings in the woods in like manner.

Oct. 5.—" We reached the Susquehanna river at a place called *Opeholhaupung*, and found there twelve Indian houses. After I had saluted the king in a friendly manner I told him my business, and that my desire was to teach them *Christianity*. After some consultation the Indians gathered, and I preached to them. And when I had done I asked if they would hear me again. They replied that they would consider of it, and soon after sent me word that they would immediately attend if I would preach, which I did with freedom, both times. When I asked them again, whether they would hear me further, they replied, they would the next day. I was exceeding sensible of the impossibility of doing any thing for the poor Heathen without special assistance from above; and my soul seemed to rest on God, and leave it to him to do as he pleased in that which I saw was his own cause. Indeed, through divine goodness, I had felt somewhat of this frame most of the time while I was traveling thither; and in some measure before I set out.

Oct. 6.—" Rose early and besought the Lord for help in my great work. Near noon, preached again to the Indians; and in the afternoon visited them from house to house, and invited them to come and hear me again the next day, and put off their hunting design. which they were just entering upon, till Monday 'This night' I trust, 'the Lord stood by me,' to encourage and strengthen my soul: I spent more than an hour in secret retirement; was enabled to 'pour out my heart before God,' for the increase of grace in my soul, for ministerial endowments, for success among the poor Indians, for God's ministers and people, for distant dear friends, &c. Blessed be God!

Oct. 8.—"Visited the Indians with a design to take my leave of them, supposing they would this morning go out to hunting early; but beyond my expectation and hope, they desired to hear me preach again. I gladly complied with their request, and afterward endeavored to answer their *objections* against Christianity.

Oct. 9.—"We rose about four in the morning, and commending ourselves to God by prayer, and asking his special protection, set out on our journey homeward about five, and traveled with great steadiness till past six at night; and then made us a fire and a shelter of bark, and so rested. I had some clear and comfortable thoughts on a divine subject, by the way, toward night. In the night, the wolves howled around us; but God preserved us."

The next day they rose early, and at night came to an Irish settlement, with which Brainerd was acquainted, and lodged there. On the following day both he and Mr. Byram preached to the people.

Oct. 12.—"Rode home to my lodgings; where I poured out my soul to God in secret prayer, and endeavored to bless him for his abundant goodness to me in my late journey. I scarcely ever enjoyed more health, at least of later years; and God marvellously and almost miraculously, supported me under the fatigues of the way, and traveling on foot. Blessed be the Lord, who continually preserves me.

Lord's day, Oct. 14.—"I went to the place of public

worship, lifting up my heart to God for assistance and grace, in my great work; and God was gracious to me, helping me to plead with him for holiness, and to use the strongest arguments with him, drawn from the incarnation and sufferings of Christ, for this very end, that men might be made holy. Afterward, I was much assisted in preaching. I know not that ever God helped me to preach in a more close and distinguishing manner for the trial of men's state. Through the infinite goodness of God, I felt what I spoke; and he enabled me to treat on divine truth with uncommon clearness.

Oct. 24—"Near noon, rode to my people; spent some time, and prayed with them; felt the frame of a *pilgrim* on earth; longed much to leave this gloomy mansion; but yet found the exercise of patience and resignation. And as I returned home from the Indians, spent the whole time in lifting up my heart to God. In the evening enjoyed a blessed season alone in prayer; was enabled to cry to God with a child-like spirit, for the space of near an hour; enjoyed a sweet freedom in supplicating for myself, for dear friends, ministers, and some who are preparing for that work, and for the church of God; and longed to be as lively myself in God's service as the angels.

Oct. 26.—" In the morning my soul was melted with a sense of divine goodness and mercy to such a vile unworthy worm. I delighted to lean upon God, and place my whole trust in him. My soul was exceedingly grieved for sin, and prized and longed after holiness; it wounded my heart deeply, yet sweetly, to think how I had abused a kind God. I longed to be perfectly holy that I might not grieve a gracious God; who will continue to love notwithstanding his love is

abused! I longed for holiness more for this end than
I did for my own happiness' sake; and yet this was
my greatest happiness, never more to dishonor, but
always to glorify the blessed God.

Oct. 31.—"Was sensible of my barrenness and de-
cays in the things of God: my soul failed when I
remembered the fervency which I had enjoyed at the
throne of grace. O, I thought, if I could but be spiritual, warm, heavenly minded, and affectionately breathing after God, this would be better than life to me!
My soul longed exceedingly for death, to be loosed
from this dullness and barrenness, and made for ever
active in the service of God. I seemed to live for nothing, and to do no good: and O the burden of such
a life! O death, death, my kind friend, hasten and
deliver me from dull mortality, and make me spiritual
and vigorous to eternity!"

Nov. 5.—He set out on a journey to New-York, and
was from home more than a fortnight. He was exposed to cold and storms, became greatly fatigued,
and when he returned from New-York to New-Jersey
was taken ill, and detained some time.

Nov. 21.—" Rode from Newark to Rockciticus in the
cold, and was almost overcome with it. Enjoyed some
sweetness in conversation with dear Mr. Jones, while
I dined with him. My soul loves the people of God,
and especially the ministers of Jesus Christ who feel
the same trials that I do.

Nov. 22.—" Came on my way from Rockciticus to
the Delaware. Was very much disordered with a
cold and pain in my head. About six at night I lost
my way in the wilderness, and wandered over rocks
and mountains, down hideous steeps, through swamps
and most dreadful and dangerous places; and the night

being dark, so that few stars could be seen, I was greatly exposed. I was much pinched with cold, and distressed with pain in my head, attended with sickness at my stomach; so that every step I took was distressing to me. I had little hope, for several hours together, but that I must lie out in the woods all night in this distressed case. But about nine o'clock I found a house, through the abundant goodness of God, and was kindly entertained. Thus I have frequently been exposed, and sometimes lain out the whole night : but God has hitherto preserved me; and blessed be his name. Such fatigues and hardships as these serve to wean me from the earth; and I trust will make heaven the sweeter. Formerly, when I was thus exposed to cold, rain, &c. I was ready to please myself with the thoughts of enjoying a comfortable house, a warm fire, and other outward comforts; but now these have less place in my heart, (through the grace of God,) and my eye is more to God for comfort. In this world I expect tribulation; and it does not now, as formerly, appear strange to me. I do not in such seasons of difficulty flatter myself that it will be better hereafter; but rather think *how much worse it might be ;* how much greater trials *others* of God's children have endured; and how much greater are yet *perhaps reserved for me.* Blessed be God, that he makes the thoughts of my journey's end, and of my dissolution a great comfort to me under my sharpest trials; and scarce ever lets these thoughts be attended with terror or melancholy; but they are attended frequently with great joy.

Nov. 23.—" Visited a sick man; discoursed and prayed with him. Then visited another house, where was one dead and laid out : looked on the corpse, and longed that my time might come to *depart* and be *with Christ.* Then went home to my lodgings about one o'clock. Felt poorly; but was able to read most of the afternoon."

Within the space of the next twelve days he spent much time in hard labor, with others, to make for himself a little cottage or hut, to live in by himself through the winter. Yet he frequently preached to the Indians, and speaks of special assistance which he had from time to time, in addressing himself to them; and of his sometimes having considerable encouragement from the attention which they gave. But on Tuesday, December 4, he was sunk into great discouragement, to see most of them going in company to an idolatrous *feast* and *dance,* after he had taken abundant pains to dissuade them from these things.

Dec. 6.—" Having now a happy opportunity of being retired in a house of my own, which I have lately procured and moved into; considering that it is now a long time since I have been able, either on account of bodily weakness or for want of retirement, or some other difficulty, to spend any time in secret fasting and prayer; considering also the greatness of my work, the extreme difficulties that attend it, and that my poor Indians are now *worshipping devils,* notwithstanding all the pains I have taken with them, which almost overwhelms my spirit; moreover, considering my extreme barrenness, spiritual deadness and dejection, of late; as also the power of some particular corruptions; I set apart this day for secret prayer and fasting, to implore the blessing of God on myself, on my poor people, on my friends, and on the church of God. At first I felt a great backwardness to the duties of the day on account of the seeming impossibility of performing them; but the Lord helped me to break through this difficulty. God was pleased, by the use of means, to give me some clear conviction of my sinfulness, and a discovery of *the plague of my own heart*, more affecting than what I have of late had. And especially I saw my sinfulness in this, that when God had withdrawn himself, then, instead of living and dying in pursuit of him, I have been disposed to one of these two things: either to yield an unbecoming respect to some *earthly* objects, as if happiness were to be derived from them; or to be secretly froward and impatient, and unsuitably *desirous of death*, so that I have sometimes thought I could not bear to think that my life must be lengthened out. That which often drove me to this impatient desire of death, was a despair of doing any good in life: and I chose death rather than a life spent for nothing. But now God made me sensible of my sin in these things, and enabled me to cry to him for forgiveness. Yet this was not all I wanted, for my soul appeared exceedingly polluted, my heart seemed like a nest of vipers, or a cage of unclean and hateful birds; and therefore I wanted to be purified 'by the blood of sprinkling, that cleanseth from all sin.' This, I hope, I was enabled to pray for in faith. I enjoyed much more intenseness, fervency, and spirituality, than I expected; God was better to me than my fears. Toward night, I felt my soul rejoice, that God is unchangeably happy and glorious; and that he will be glorified, whatever becomes of his creatures. I was enabled to persevere in prayer until sometime in the evening; at which time I saw so much need of divine help, in every respect, that I knew not how to leave off, and had forgot that I needed food. Blessed be the Lord for any help in the past day.

Dec. 7. "Spent some time in prayer, in the morning; enjoyed some freedom and affection in the duty, and had longing desires of being made ' faithful to the death.' Spent a little time in writing on a divine subject; then visited the Indians, and preached to them; but I had no heart to speak to them, and could not do it, but as I forced myself: I knew they must hate to hear me, as having but just got home from their idolatrous feast and devil-worship. In the evening, had some freedom in prayer and meditation.

Dec. 12.—" Was very weak; but somewhat assisted in secret prayer, and enabled with pleasure and sweetness to cry, 'Come, Lord Jesus! come, Lord Jesus! come quickly.' My soul 'longed for God, for the living God.' O how delightful it is to pray under such sweet influences! O how much better is this than one's necessary food! I had at this time no disposition to eat, (though late in the morning;) for earthly food appeared wholly tasteless. O how much ' better is thy love than wine,' than the sweetest wine!—I visited and preached to the Indians in the afternoon; but under much dejection. Found my *Interpreter* under some concern for his soul; which was some comfort to me; and yet filled me with new care. I longed greatly for his conversion; lifted up my heart to God for it, while I was talking to him; came home, and poured out my soul to God for him; enjoyed some freedom in prayer, and was enabled, I think, to leave all with God.

Dec. 18.—"Went to the Indians, and discoursed to them near an hour, without any power to come close to their hearts. But at last I felt some fervency, and God helped me to speak with warmth. My *Interpreter* also was amazingly assisted; and presently most of the grown persons were much affected, and the tears ran down their cheeks. One old man, I suppose an hundred years old, was so much affected that he wept, and seemed convinced of the importance of what I taught them. I staid with them a considerable time, exhorting and directing them; and came away, lifting up my heart to God in prayer and praise, and encouraged and exhorted my *Interpreter* to 'strive to enter in at the strait gate.' Came home, and spent most of the evening in prayer and thanksgiving; and found myself much enlarged and quickened. Was greatly concerned that the Lord's work, which seemed to be begun, might be carried on with power, to the conversion of poor souls, and the glory of divine grace.

Dec. 19.—"Spent a great part of the day in prayer to God for the outpouring of his Spirit on my poor people; as also to bless his name for awakening my *Interpreter* and some others, and giving us some tokens of his presence yesterday. And blessed be God, I had much freedom, five or six times in the day, in prayer and praise, and felt a weighty concern upon my spirit for the salvation of those precious souls, and the enlargement of the Redeemer's kingdom among them. My soul hoped in God for some success in my ministry: blessed be his name for so much hope.

Dec. 21.—"Was enabled again to pray with freedom, cheerfulness, and hope. God was pleased to make the duty comfortable and pleasant to me; so that I delighted to persevere, and repeatedly to engage in it. Toward noon visited my people, and spent the whole time in the way to them in prayer, longing to see *the power of God* among them, as there appeared something of it the last Tuesday; and I found it sweet to rest and hope in God. Preached to them twice, an [1] at two distinct places: had considerable freedom each time, and so had my *Interpreter*. Several of them followed me from one place to the other; and I thought there was some divine influence discernible among them. In the evening was assisted in prayer again. Blessed be the Lord.

Dec. 25.—"Enjoyed very little quiet sleep last night, by reason of bodily weakness, and the closeness of my studies yesterday; yet my heart was somewhat lively in prayer and praise. I was delighted with the divine glory and happiness, and rejoiced that God was God, and that he was unchangeably possessed of glory and blessedness. Though God *held my eyes waking*, yet he helped me to improve my time profitably amidst my pains and weakness, in continued meditations on Luke, 13:7. 'Behold, these three years I come seeking fruit.' &c. My meditations were sweet; and I wanted to set before sinners their sin and danger."

He continued in a very low state, as to his bodily health, for some days, which seems to have been a great hindrance to him in his religious exercises and pursuits. But yet he expresses some degree of divine assistance, from day to day, through the remainder of this week. He preached several times this week to his Indians; and there appeared still some concern among them for their souls.

Jan. 9, 1745.—"In the morning God was pleased to remove that gloom which has of late oppressed my mind, and gave me freedom and sweetness in prayer; I was encouraged, strengthened, and enabled to plead for grace myself, and mercy for my poor Indians; and was sweetly assisted in my intercessions with God for others. Blessed be his holy name for ever and ever. Amen, and Amen. Those things that of late have appeared most difficult and almost impossible, now appeared not only possible, but easy. My soul so much delighted to continue instant in prayer, at this blessed season, that I had no desire for my necessary food: I even dreaded leaving off praying at all, lest I should lose this spirituality, and this blessed thankfulness to God which I then felt. I felt now quite willing to live, and undergo all trials that might remain for me in a world of sorrow; but still longed for heaven, that I might glorify God in a perfect manner. 'O come, Lord Jesus, come quickly.'

Lord's day, Feb. 3.—" In the morning I was somewhat relieved of that gloom and confusion with which my mind has of late been greatly exercised ; and was enabled to pray with some composure and comfort. Still I went to my Indians trembling; but God was pleased to hear my cries, and to afford me great assistance; so that I felt peace in my own soul; and was satisfied, that if not one of the Indians should be profited by my preaching, but they should all be damned, yet I should be accepted and rewarded as faithful ; for I am persuaded, God enabled me to be so. Had some good degree of help afterward at another place ; and much longed for the conversion of the poor Indians."

On the next Sabbath he preached at Greenwich, in New-Jersey. In the evening he rode eight miles to visit a sick man at the point of death, and found him speechless and senseless.

Feb. 11.—" About the break of day the sick man died. I was affected at the sight; spent the morning with the mourners; and after prayer and some discourse with them, returned to Greenwich, and preached again from Psalm 89 : 15. The Lord gave me some assistance; I felt a sweet love to souls. and to the

kingdom of Christ; and longed that poor sinners might
'know the joyful sound.' Several persons were much
affected. After meeting, I was enabled to discourse,
with freedom and concern, to some persons who applied to me under spiritual trouble. Left the place,
sweetly composed, and rode home to my house about
eight miles distant. Discoursed to friends, and inculcated divine truths upon some. In the evening was in
the most solemn frame which I almost ever remember
to have experienced. I know not that ever death appeared more real to me, or that ever I saw myself in
the condition of a dead corpse, laid out, and dressed for
a lodging in the silent grave, so evidently as at this
time. And yet I felt exceedingly tranquil; my mind
was composed and calm, and *death* appeared *without
a sting*. I think I never felt such an universal
mortification to all created objects as now. O, how
great and solemn a thing it appeared to die! O, how
it lays the greatest honor in the dust! And O, how
vain and trifling did the riches, honors, and pleasures
of the world appear! I could not, I dare not so much
as think of any of them; for *death, death* appeared at
the door. O, I could see myself dead, and laid out,
and inclosed in my coffin, and put down into the cold
grave, with the greatest solemnity, but without terror!
I spent most of the evening in conversing with a dear
Christian friend. Blessed be God for the comforts of
the past day.

Feb. 15.—" Was engaged in writing almost the
whole day. In the evening was much assisted in
meditating on that precious text, John, 7 : 37. 'Jesus
stood and cried,' &c. I had then a sweet sense of the
free grace of the gospel; my soul was encouraged,
warmed, and quickened. My desires were drawn out

after God in prayer; and my soul was watchful, afraid
of losing such a guest as I then entertained. I continued long in prayer and meditation, intermixing one
with the other; and was unwilling to be diverted by
any thing at all from so sweet an exercise. I longed
to proclaim the grace I then meditated upon, to the
world of sinners. O how *quick* and *powerful* is the
word of the blessed God.

Lord's day, Feb. 17.—" Preached to the *white* people
[my *interpreter* being absent,] in the wilderness, upon
the sunny side of a hill; had a considerable assembly,
consisting of people who lived, at least many of them,
not less than thirty miles asunder; some of them came
near twenty miles. I discoursed to them all day, from
John, 7 : 37. 'Jesus stood and cried, saying, that if any
man thirst,' &c. In the afternoon, it pleased God to
grant me great freedom and fervency in my discourse;
and I was enabled to imitate the example of Christ in
the text, who *stood and cried.* I think I was scarce
ever enabled to exhibit the free grace of God to perishing sinners with more freedom and plainness in my
life. Afterward, I was enabled earnestly to invite the
children of God to come renewedly, and drink of this
fountain of the water of life, from whence they have
heretofore derived unspeakable satisfaction. It was a
very comfortable time to me. There were many tears
in the assembly ; and I doubt not but that the Spirit of
God was there, convincing poor sinners of their need
of Christ. In the evening I felt composed and comfortable, though much tired. I had some sweet sense
of the excellency and glory of God; my soul rejoiced
that he was 'God over all, blessed for ever;' but was
too much crowded with company and conversation,
and longed to be more alone with God. O that I could

for ever bless God for the mercy of this day, who 'answered me in the joy of my heart.'

Lord's day, Feb. 24.—" In the morning was much perplexed. My *interpreter* being absent, I knew not how to perform my work among the Indians. However, I rode to them, got a Dutchman to interpret for me, though he was but poorly qualified for the business. Afterward I came and preached to a few white people, from John, 6 : 67. Here the Lord seemed to unburden me in some measure, especially toward the close of my discourse : I felt freedom to open the *love of Christ* to his own dear *disciples.* When the rest of the world forsake him, and are forsaken by him, he then turns to his own, and says, *Will ye also go away?* I had a sense of the free grace of Christ to his own people, in such seasons of general apostacy, and when they themselves in some measure backslide with the world. O the free grace of Christ, that he seasonably reminds his people of their danger of *backsliding,* and invites them to persevere in their adherence to himself! I saw that backsliding souls, who seemed to be about to go away with the world, might return, and be welcome, to him immediately ; without any thing to recommend them ; notwithstanding all their former backslidings. Thus my discourse was suited to my own soul's case ; for of late, I have found a great want of this sense and apprehension of divine grace ; and have often been greatly distressed in my own soul, because I did not suitably apprehend this fountain opened to purge away sin ; and have been too much laboring for spiritual ife, peace of conscience, and progressive holiness, in my own strength. Now God showed me, in some measure, *the arm* of all strength, and *the fountain* of all grace. In the evening, I felt solemn, resting on free grace for assistance, acceptance, and peace of conscience.

March 6.—" Spent most of the day in preparing for a journey to New-England; and sometime in prayer with a special reference to it. Was afraid I should forsake the Fountain of living waters, and attempt to derive satisfaction from *broken cisterns,* my dear friends and acquaintance, whom I might meet in my journey. I looked to God to keep me from this *vanity* as well as others. Toward night, and in the evening, was visited by some friends, some of whom I trust were real Christians; who discovered an affectionate regard to me, and seemed grieved that I was about to leave them; especially as I did not expect to make any considerable stay among them, if I should live to return.* O how kind has God been to me! how he has raised up friends in every place where his providence has called me! Friends are a great comfort; and it is God who gives them; it is He who makes them friendly to me. 'Bless the Lord, my soul, and forget not all his benefits.'"

The next day he set out on his journey; and it was about five weeks before he returned. The special design of this journey, he himself declares afterward, in his diary for March 21, where, speaking of his conversing with a certain minister in New-England, he says, "Contrived with him how to raise some money among Christian friends, in order to support a colleague with me in the wilderness, (I having now spent two years in a very solitary manner,) that we might be together: as Christ sent out his disciples two and two:

---

* It seems by what afterward appears, that he had a design to remove and live among the Indians on the Susquehanna river.

and as this was the principal concern I had in view, in taking this journey, so I took pains in it, and hope God will succeed it, if for his glory." He first went into various parts of New-Jersey, and visited several ministers there; then went to New-York; and from thence into New-England, going to various parts of Connecticut. He then returned to New-Jersey, and met a number of ministers at Woodbridge, "who," he says "met there to consult about the affairs of Christ's kingdom." He seems, for the most part, to have been free from melancholy in this journey; and many times to have had extraordinary assistance in public ministrations, and his preaching was sometimes attended with very hopeful appearances of a good effect on the auditory. He also had many seasons of special comfort and spiritual refreshment, in conversation with ministers and other Christian friends, and also in meditation and prayer when alone.

April 13.—"Rode home to my own house at the Forks of Delaware; was enabled to remember the goodness of the Lord, who has now preserved me while riding full six hundred miles in this journey; and kept me that none of my bones have been broken. Blessed be the Lord, who has preserved me in this tedious journey, and returned me in safety to my own house. Verily it is God who has upheld me, and guarded my goings.

Lord's day, April 14.—"Was disordered in body with the fatigues of the late journey; but was enabled however to preach to a considerable assembly of white people, gathered from all parts round about, with some freedom, from Ezek. 33:11. 'As I live saith the Lord,' &c. Had much more assistance than I expected."

This week he went a journey to Philadelphia, in or-

der to engage the Governor to use his interest with
the chief of the Six Nations, with whom he maintained a strict friendship, that he would give him leave to
live at Susquehanna, and instruct the Indians who are
within their territories.

April 26.—"Conversed with a Christian friend with
some warmth; and felt a spirit of mortification to the
world, in a very great degree. Afterward, was enabled to pray fervently, and to rely on God sweetly,
for 'all things pertaining to life and godliness.' Just
in the evening, was visited by a dear Christian friend,
with whom I spent an hour or two in conversation, on
the very soul of religion. There are many with whom
I can talk *about religion;* but alas! I find few with
whom I can talk *religion itself;* but, blessed be the
Lord there are some that love to feed on the kernel,
rather than the shell.

April 30.—"Was scarce able to walk about, and was
obliged to betake myself to bed much of the day; and
passed away the time in a very solitary manner; being
neither able to read, meditate, nor pray, and had none
to converse with in this wilderness. O how heavily
does time pass away when I can do nothing to any
good purpose; but seem obliged to trifle away precious
time! But of late I have seen it my duty to *divert*
myself by all lawful means, that I may be fit, at least
some small part of my time, to labor for God. And
here is the difference between my present diversions,
and those I once pursued, when in a natural state.
Then I made a God of my diversions, delighted in
them with a neglect of God, and drew my highest satisfaction from them. Now I use them as means to
help me in living to God; fixedly delighting in *him*,
and not in them, drawing my highest satisfaction from

him. Then they were my *all;* now they are only *means* leading to my all. And those things that are the greatest diversion, when pursued with this view, do not tend to hinder, but promote my spirituality; and I see now, more than ever, that they are absolutely necessary.

May 2.—"In the evening, being a little better in health, I walked into the woods, and enjoyed a sweet season of meditation and prayer. My thoughts ran upon Psalm 17: 15. 'I shall be satisfied, when I awake, with thy likeness.' And it was indeed a precious text to me. I longed to preach to the whole world; and it seemed to me they must needs all be melted in hearing such precious divine truths as I then had a view of. My thoughts were exceeding clear, and my soul was refreshed. Blessed be the Lord, that in my late and present weakness, now for many days together, my mind is not gloomy, as at some other times.

May 7.—"Spent the day mainly in making preparation for a journey into the wilderness. Was still weak, and concerned how I should perform so difficult a journey; but wanted bodily strength to spend the day in fasting and prayer."

The next day he set out on his journey to the Susquehanna, with his interpreter. He endured great hardships and fatigues in his way thither through the wilderness; where, after having lodged one night in the open woods, he was overtaken with a north-easterly storm, in which he was ready to perish. Having no manner of shelter, and not being able to make a fire in so great a rain, he could have no comfort if he stopped; he therefore determined to go forward in hope of meeting with some shelter, without which he thought it impossible to live the night through; but their horses happening to eat poison, for the want of other food, at a place where they lodged the night before, were so sick that they could neither ride nor lead them, but were obliged to drive them and travel on foot; until, through the mercy of God, just at dusk they came to a bark hut, where they lodged that night. After he came to the Susquehanna he traveled about a hundred miles on the river, and visited many towns and settlements of the Indians; saw some of seven or eight tribes, and preached to different nations, by different interpreters. He was sometimes much discouraged, and sunk in his spirits, through the opposition which appeared in the Indians to Christianity. At other times he was encouraged by the disposition which some of these people manifested to hear, and their willingness to be instructed. He here met with some who had formerly been his hearers at Kaunaumeek, and had removed hither; who saw and heard him again with great joy. He spent a fortnight among the Indians on this river, and passed through many labors and hardships, lodging on the ground for several weeks, and sometimes in the open air. At length he became extremely ill, as he was riding in the wilderness, being seized with an ague, followed with a burning fever and extreme pains in his head and bowels, attended with a great evacuation of blood; so that he thought he must have perished in the wilderness. But at last coming to an Indian trader's hut, he got leave to stay there; and though without physic or food proper for him, it pleased God, after about a week's distress, to relieve him so far that he was able to ride. He returned homeward from *Juncauta*, an island far down the river, where were a considerable number of Indians, who appeared more free from prejudices against Chris-

tianity than most of the other Indians; and arrived at
the Forks of Delaware on Thursday, May 30, after
having rode in this journey about three hundred and
forty miles. He came home in a very week state, and
under dejection of mind; which was a great hindrance
to him in religious exercises. However, on the Sabbath, after having preached to the Indians, he preached
to the white people with some success, from Isaiah,
53 : 10. " Yet it pleased the Lord to bruise him," &c.
some being awakened by his preaching. The next
day he was much exercised for want of spiritual life
and fervency.

June 5.—" Felt thirsting desires after God, in the
morning. In the evening, enjoyed a precious season
of retirement : was favored with some clear and sweet
meditations upon a sacred text; divine things opened
with clearness and certainty, and had a divine stamp
upon them. My soul was also enlarged and refreshed
in prayer; I delighted to continue in the duty; and was
sweetly assisted in praying for my fellow Christians,
and dear brethren in the ministry. Blessed be the dear
Lord for such enjoyments. O how sweet and precious
it is to have a clear apprehension and tender sense of
the *mystery of godliness,* of true holiness, and of likeness to the best of beings ! O what a blessedness it is
to be as much like God as it is possible for a creature
to be like his great Creator ! Lord give me more of *thy
likeness ;* ' I shall be satisfied, when I awake, with it.' "

On Friday, June 7, he went a journey of near fifty
miles, to Neshaminy, to assist at a sacramental occasion,
to be attended at Mr. Beatty's meeting-house; being invited thither by him and his people.

June 8.—" Was exceedingly weak and fatigued with
riding in the heat yesterday; but being desired, I

preached in the afternoon, to a crowded audience, from Isaiah, 40 : 1. 'Comfort ye, comfort ye my people, saith your God.' God was pleased to give me great freedom, in opening the sorrows of his people, and in setting before them comforting considerations. And, blessed be the Lord, it was a sweet melting season in the assembly.

Lord's day, June 9.—" Felt some longing desires of the presence of God to be with his people on the solemn occasion of the day. In the forenoon Mr. Beatty preached; and there appeared some warmth in the assembly. Afterward, I assisted in the administration of the Lord's supper: and toward the close of it, I discoursed to the multitude extempore, with some reference to that sacred passage, Isaiah, 53 : 10. 'Yet it pleased the Lord to bruise him.' Here God gave me great assistance in addressing sinners: and the word was attended with amazing power: many scores, if not hundreds, in that great assembly, consisting of three or four thousand, were much affected; so that there was a 'very great mourning, like the mourning of Hadadrimmon.'

June 10.—"Preached with a good degree of clearness and some sweet warmth from Psalm 17 : 15. 'I shall be satisfied, when I awake, with thy likeness.' And blessed be God, there was a great solemnity, and attention in the assembly, and sweet refreshment among God's people; as was evident then and afterward.

June 11.—"Spent the day mainly in conversation with dear Christian friends; and enjoyed some sweet sense of divine things. O how desirable it is to keep company with God's dear children! 'These are the excellent ones of the earth,' in whom, I can truly say 'is all my delight.' O what delight will it afford, to meet them all in a state of perfection! Lord prepare me for that state.

June 18.—" Set out from New-Brunswick with a design to visit some Indians at a place called *Crossweek-sung*, in New-Jersey, toward the sea. In the afternoon, came to a place called *Cranberry*, and meeting with a serious minister, Mr. Macknight, I lodged there with him. Had some enlargement and freedom in prayer with a number of people."

CHAPTER VII

Being part 1st of his public journal of "the Rise and Progress of a remarkable work of grace among the Indians in New-Jersey and Pennsylvania, kept by order of the Society in Scotland for propagating Christian knowledge."—Commencement of his labors at Crossweeksung.—Renewal of labor at the Forks of Delaware.—Conversion of his Interpreter.—Return to Crossweeksung.—Outpouring of the spirit.—Visit to the Forks of Delaware and the Susquehanna.—A Powaw.—A Conjurer.—Renewal of labor at Crossweeksung.—Remarks on the works of Divine Grace.

June 19.—Nov. 5, 1745

[We are now come to that part of Brainerd's Life, when he had the greatest success in his labors for the good of souls, and in his particular business as a missionary to the Indians. After all his agonizing in prayer, and travailing in birth for their conversion—his raised hopes and expectations, disappointments and encouragements; after panting in a way of persevering prayer, labor, and suffering, as it were through a long night; at length the day dawns: "Weeping continues·for a

night, but joy comes in the morning." He went forth
weeping, " bearing precious seed," but now he comes
" with rejoicing, bringing his sheaves with him." The
desired event is brought to pass at last ; but at a time,
in a place, and upon subjects, that scarce ever entered
his heart.]

" Crossweeksung, in New-Jersey, June 17, 1745

June 19.—" I had spent most of my time for more than
a year past among the Indians at the Forks of Delaware, in Pennsylvania. During that time I made two
journies to the Susquehanna, to treat with the Indians on
that river respecting Christianity ; and not having had
any considerable appearance of special success in either
of those places, my spirits were depressed, and I was
not a little discouraged. Hearing that there were a
number of Indians at a place called *Crossweeksung,* in
New-Jersey, nearly eighty miles south east from the
Forks of Delaware, I determined to make them a visit,
and see what might be done toward christianizing
them ; and accordingly arrived among them this day.

" I found very few persons at the place I visited, and
perceived that the Indians in these parts were very
much scattered. There were not more than two or
three families in a place ; and these small settlements
were six, ten, fifteen, twenty, or thirty miles, and some
more from that place. However, I preached to those
few I found ; who appeared well disposed, serious and
attentive, and not inclined to cavil and object, as the
Indians had done elsewhere. When I had concluded
my discourse, I informed them (there being none but
a few women and children) that I would willingly
visit them again the next day. Whereupon they
readily set out and traveled ten or fifteen miles, in

order to give notice to some of their friends at that distance. These women, like the woman of Samaria, seemed desirous that others should see the man who had told them what they had done in their past lives, and the misery that attended their idolatrous ways.

June 20.—" Visited and preached to the Indians again as I proposed. Numbers were gathered at the invitations of their friends, who had heard me the day before. These also appeared as attentive, orderly and well disposed, as the others: and none made any objections, as Indians in other places have usually done.

June 22.—" Preached to the Indians again. Their number, which at first consisted of seven or eight persons, was now increased to nearly thirty. There was not only a solemn attention among them, but some considerable impression, it was apparent, was made upon their minds by divine truth. Some began to feel their misery, and perishing state, and appeared concerned for a deliverance from it.

Lord's day, June 23.—Preached to the Indians, and spent the day with them. Their number still increased; and all with one consent, seemed to rejoice in my coming among them. Not a word of opposition was heard from any of them against Christianity, although in times past they had been as much opposed to any thing of that nature as any Indians whatsoever. Some of them, not many months before, were enraged with my Interpreter because he attempted to teach them something of Christianity.

June 24.—" Preached to the Indians at their desire. and upon their own motion. To see poor Pagans desirous of hearing the gospel of Christ, animated me to discourse to them; although I was now very weak, and my spirits much exhausted. They attended with the greatest seriousness and diligence; and some concern for their soul's salvation was apparent among them.

June 27.—" Visited and preached to the Indians again. Their number now amounted to about forty persons. Their solemnity and attention still continued, and a considerable concern for their souls became very apparent among numbers of them.

June 28.—" The Indians being now gathered, a considerable number of them, from their several and distant habitations, requested me to preach twice a day to them ; being desirous to hear as much as they possibly could while I was with them. I cheerfully complied with their request, and could not but admire the goodness of God, who I was persuaded had inclined them thus to inquire after the way of salvation.

June 29.—" Preached twice to the Indians. Saw, as I thought, the hand of God very evidently, and in a manner somewhat remarkable, making provision for their subsistence together, in order to their being instructed in divine things; for this day, and the day before, with only walking a little way from the place of our daily meeting, they killed three deer, which were a seasonable supply for their wants, and without which, they could not have subsisted together in order to attend the means of grace.

Lord's day, June 30.—" Preached twice this day also. Observed yet more concern and affection among the poor heathen than ever; so that they even constrained me to tarry yet longer with them, although my constitution was exceedingly worn out, and my health much impaired by my late fatigues and labors; and especially by my late journey to the Susquehanna in May last, in which I lodged on the ground for several weeks together.

July 1.—" Preached again twice to a very serious
and attentive assembly of Indians; they having now
learned to attend on the worship of God with Christian decency in all respects.   There were now between
forty and fifty persons of them present, old and young.
I spent a considerable time in discoursing with them
in a more private way; inquiring of them what they
remembered of the great truths which had been taught
them from day to day; and may justly say, it was
amazing to see how they had received and retained
the instructions given them, and what a measure of
knowledge some of them had acquired in a few days.

July 2.—" Was obliged to leave these Indians at
Crossweeksung, thinking it my duty, as soon as health
would admit, again to visit those at the Forks of Delaware.   When I came to take leave of them, and to
speak particularly to each of them, they all earnestly
inquired when I would come again, and expressed a
great desire of being further instructed. Of their own
accord they agreed, that, when I should come again,
they would all meet and live together during my continuance with them ; and that they would use their utmost endeavors to gather all the other Indians in
these parts who were yet more remote.   When I
parted from them, one told me, with many tears, ' She
wished God would change her heart;' another, that
' she wanted to find Christ ;' and an old man who had
been one of their chiefs, wept bitterly with concern for
his soul.   I then promised them to return as speedily
as my health and business elsewhere would permit,
and felt not a little concern at parting, lest the good
impressions, then apparent upon numbers of them,
might decline and wear off, when the means came to
cease. Yet I could not but hope, that He, who I

trusted had begun a good work among them, and who I knew did not stand in need of means to carry it on, would mantain and promote it. At the same time, I must confess, that I had often seen encouraging appearances among the Indians elsewhere, prove wholly abortive, and it appeared that the favor would be too great, if God should now, after I had passed through so considerable a series of almost fruitless labors and fatigues, and after my rising hopes had been so often frustrated among these poor pagans, give me any special success in my labors with them, I could not believe, and scarcely dared to hope, that the event would be so happy; and scarcely ever found myself more suspended between hope and fear in any affair, or at any time, than in this.

" This encouraging disposition, and readiness to receive instruction, now apparent among the Indians, seems to have been the happy effect of the conviction which one or two of them met with, some time since, at the Forks of the Delaware; who have since endeavored to show their friends the evil of idolatry. Though the other Indians seemed but little to regard, and rather to deride them; yet this, perhaps, has put them into a thinking posture of mind, or at least given them some thoughts about Christianity, and excited in some of them a curiosity to hear; and so made way for the present encouraging attention. An apprehension that this might be the case here, has given me encouragement that God may, in such a manner, bless the means which I have used with the Indians in other places; where, as yet there is no appearance of it. If so, may his name have the glory of it; for I have learnt, by experience, that he only can open the ear, engage the attention, and incline the hearts of poor benighted, prejudiced pagans, to receive instruction."

Forks of Delaware, in Pennsylvania, July, 1745

Lord's day, July 14.—" Discoursed to the Indians twice. Several of them appeared concerned, and were, I have reason to think, in some measure convinced, by the Divine Spirit, of their sin and misery ; so that they wept much the whole time of divine service. Afterward discoursed to a number of white people then present.

July 18.—" Preached to my people, who attended diligently beyond what had been common among these Indians ; and some of them appeared concerned for their souls.

Lord's day, July 21.—" Preached to the Indians first, then to a number of white people present; and in the afternoon to the Indians again. Divine truth seemed to make very considerable impressions upon several of them, and caused the tears to flow freely.

" On this day *my interpreter and his wife* publicly professed their faith in Christ, being the first hopeful converts among the Indians. They have both been awakened to a solemn concern for their souls ; have, to appearance, been brought to a sense of their misery and *undoneness* in themselves ; have both appeared to be comforted with divine consolations ; and it is apparent that both have passed a *great*, and I cannot but hope, a saving change.

" It may perhaps be satisfactory and agreeable, that I should give some BRIEF RELATION OF THIS MAN'S EXERCISES AND EXPERIENCE since he has been with me ; especially since he is employed as my *interpreter* to others. When I first employed him in this business,

in the beginning of the summer of 1744, he was well
fitted for his work, in regard to his acquaintance with
the Indian and English languages, as well as with the
manners of both nations; and in respect to his desire
that the Indians should conform to the manners and
customs of the English, and especially to their manner
of living. But he seemed to have little or no impression of religion upon his mind, and in that respect was
very *unfit* for his work; being incapable of understand ·
ing and communicating to others many things of importance, so that I labored under great disadvantages'
in addressing the Indians, for want of his having an
experimental, as well as more doctrinal acquaintance
with divine truths; and, at times, my spirits sunk, and
I was much discouraged under this difficulty; especially when I observed that divine truth made little or
no impression upon his mind for many weeks together. He indeed behaved soberly after I employed
him; although before he had been a hard drinker, and
seemed honestly engaged, as far as he was capable, in
the performance of his work. Especially he appeared
very desirous that the Indians should renounce their
heathenish notions and practices, and conform to the
customs of the Christian world. But still he seemed
to have no concern about his own soul, until he had
been with me a considerable time.

"Near the latter end of July, 1744, I preached to an
assembly of white people, with more freedom and fervency than I could possibly address the Indians with,
without their having first obtained a greater measure
of doctrinal knowledge. At this time he was present,
and was somewhat awakened to a concern for his soul;
so that the next day he discoursed freely with me
about his spiritual concerns, and gave me an opportu-

nity to use further endeavors to fasten the impressions of his perishing state upon his mind. I could plainly perceive, for some time after this, that he addressed the Indians with more concern and fervency than he had formerly done.

"But these impressions seemed quickly to decline, and he remained in a great measure careless and secure, until some time late in the autumn of the year following; when he fell into a weak and languishing state of body, and continued much disordered for several weeks together. At this season divine truth took hold of him, and made deep impressions upon his mind. He was brought under great concern for his soul; and his exercises were not now transient and unsteady, but constant and abiding, so that his mind was burdened from day to day; and it was now his great inquiry, ' What he should do to be saved?' This spiritual trouble prevailed, until his sleep in a great measure departed from him, and he had little rest day or night; but walked about under great pressure of mind, for he was still able to walk, and appeared like another man to his neighbors, who could not but observe his behavior with wonder. After he had been some time under this exercise, while he was striving to obtain mercy, he says there seemed to be *an impassable mountain* before him. He was pressing toward heaven, as he thought; but ' his way was hedged up with thorns, so that he could not stir an inch further.' He looked this way, and that way, but could find no way at all. He thought if he could but make his way through these thorns and briers, and climb up the first steep pitch of the mountain, that then there might be hope for him; but no way or means could he find to accomplish this. Here he labored for a time, but all in

vain. He saw it was impossible, he says, for him ever
to help himself through this insupportable difficulty—
' It signified just nothing at all for him to struggle and
strive any more.' Here, he says, he gave over striving,
and felt that it was a gone case with him as to his own
power, and that all his attempts were, and for ever
would be, vain and fruitless. Yet he was more calm
and composed under this view of things, than he had
been while striving to help himself.

"While he was giving me this account of his exercises, I was not without fears that what he related was
but the working of his own *imagination*, and not the
effect of any divine *illumination* of mind. But before
I had time to discover my fears, he added, that at this
time he felt himself in a miserable and perishing condition; that he saw plainly what he had been doing all
his days; and that he had ' never done one good thing,'
as he expressed it. He knew he was not guilty of some
wicked actions of which he knew some others guilty.
He had not been accustomed to steal, quarrel, and
murder; the latter of which vices are common among
the Indians. He likewise knew that he had done many
things that were right; he had been kind to his neighbors, &c. But still his cry was, that ' *he had never done
one good thing ;*' meaning that he had never done any
thing from a right principle, and with a right *view*.
' And now I thought,' said he, ' that I must sink down
to hell; that there was no hope for me, because I
never could do any thing that was good : and if God
let me alone ever so long, and I should try ever so
much, still I should do nothing but what is bad.'

"This further account of his exercises satisfied me
that it was not the mere working of his imagination,
since he appeared so evidently to die to himself, and

to be divorced from a dependence upon his own righteousness and good deeds, to which mankind in a fallen
state are so much attached, and upon which they are
so ready to hope for salvation.

"There was one thing more in his view of things
at this time, which was very remarkable.   He not only
saw, he says, what a miserable state he *himself* was in;
but he likewise saw that the *world around him,* in general, were in the same perishing circumstances, notwithstanding the profession which many of them made
of christianity, and the hope which they entertained of
obtaining everlasting happiness.   This he saw clearly,
'as if he was now waked out of sleep, or had a cloud
taken from his eyes.'   He saw that the life which he
had lived was the way to eternal death, that he was
now on the brink of endless misery; and when he
looked around he saw multitudes of others, who had
lived the same life with himself, persons who had no
more goodness than he, and yet dreamed that they
were safe enough, as he had formerly done.   He was
fully persuaded, by their conversation and behavior,
that they had never felt their sin and misery, as he
now felt his.

"After he had been for some time in this condition,
sensible of the impossibility of helping himself by any
thing he could do, or of being delivered by any *created*
arm; so that he had 'given up all for lost,' as to his
own attempts, and was become more calm and composed; then, he says, it was borne in upon his mind, as
if it had been audibly spoken to him,   'There is hope,
there is hope.'   Whereupon his soul seemed to rest,
and be in some measure satisfied, though he had no
considerable joy.

"He cannot here remember distinctly any views he

had of Christ, or give any clear account of his soul's
acceptance of him, which makes his experience appear
the more doubtful, and renders it less satisfactory to
himself and others than it might be if he could remember distinctly the apprehensions and actings of his
mind at this season.   But these exercises of soul were
attended and followed with a very great change in the
man; so that it might justly be said he was become
another man, if not *a new man.*   His conversation and
deportment were much altered; and even the careless
world could not but wonder what had befallen him, to
make so great a change in his temper, discourse, and
behavior.   Especially there was a surprising alteration
in his public performances.   He now addressed the Indians with admirable fervency, and scarcely knew
when to leave off.   Sometimes, when I had concluded
my discourse and was returning homeward, he would
tarry behind to repeat and inculcate what had been
spoken.

"His change is *abiding,* and his life, so far as I know,
unblemished to this day; though it is now more than
six months since he experienced this change; in which
space of time he has been as much exposed to *strong
drink* as possible, in divers places where it has been
moving as free as water; and yet has never, that I
know of, discovered any hankering desire after it.   He
seems to have a very considerable experience of *spiritual exercise,* and discourses feelingly of the conflicts
and consolations of a real Christian.   His heart echoes
to the soul-humbling doctrines of grace, and he never
appears better pleased than when he hears of the ab
solute sovereignty of God, and the salvation of sinners
in a way of mere free grace.   He has lately had also
more satisfaction respecting his own state and has

been much enlightened and assisted in his work; so that he has been a great comfort to me.

"After a strict observation of his serious and savory conversation, his christian temper, and unblemished behavior for such a length of time, as well as his experience, of which I have given an account; I think that I have reason to hope that he is 'created anew in Christ Jesus to good works.' His name is MOSES FINDA FAUTAURY. He is about *fifty* years of age, and is pretty well acquainted with the pagan notions and customs of his countrymen; and so is the better able now to expose them. He has, I am persuaded, already been, and I trust will yet be, a blessing to the other Indians.

July 23.—"Preached to the Indians, but had few hearers: Those who are constantly at home, seem, of late, to be under some impressions of a religious nature.

July 30.—"Discoursed to a number of my people, and gave them some particular advice and direction; being now about to leave them for the present, in order to renew my visit to the Indians in New-Jersey. They were very attentive to my discourse, and earnestly desirous to know when I designed to return to them again."

Crossweeksung, (*New-Jersey*,) *August*, 1745

Aug. 3.—"I visited the Indians in these parts in June last, and tarried with them a considerable time, preaching almost daily; at which season God was pleased to pour upon them a spirit of awakening and concern for their souls, and surprisingly to engage their attention to divine truths. I now found them serious, and a number of them under deep concern for an interest in Christ. Their convictions of their sinful and perish-

ing state were, in my absence from them, much promoted by the labors and endeavors of Rev. WILLIAM TEN-
NENT; to whom I had advised them to apply for direction; and whose house they frequented much while I
was gone. I preached to them this day with some
view to Rev. 22:17. 'And whosoever will, let him
take of the water of life freely;' though I could not
pretend to handle the subject methodically among
them. The Lord, I am persuaded, enabled me, in a
manner somewhat uncommon, to set before them the
Lord Jesus Christ as a kind and compassionate Savior,
inviting distressed and perishing sinners to accept everlasting mercy. A surprising concern soon became apparent among them. There were about twenty adult
persons together; many of the Indians at remote places not having as yet had time to come since my return hither; and not above two that I could see with
dry eyes.

"Some were much concerned, and discovered vehement longings of soul after Christ, to save them from
the misery they felt and feared.

Lord's day, Aug. 4.—"Being invited by a neighboring minister to assist in the administration of the Lord's
supper, I complied with his request, and took the Indians along with me; not only those who were together the day before, but many more who were coming to
hear me; so that there were nearly fifty in all, old and
young. They attended the several discourses of the
day; and some of them, who could understand English,
were much affected; and all seemed to have their concern in some measure raised.

"Now a change in their manners began to appear
very visible. In the evening, when they came to sup
together they would not taste a morsel until they had

sent to me to come and supplicate a blessing on their food; at which time sundry of them wept; especially when I reminded them how they had in times past eat their feasts in honor to *devils*, and neglected to thank God for them.

August 5.—"After a sermon had been preached by another minister, I preached, and concluded the public work of the solemnity from John, 7 : 37; and in my discourse addressed the Indians in particular, who sat in a part of the house by themselves; at which time one or two of them were struck with deep concern, as they afterward told me, who had been little affected before; and others had their concern increased to a considerable degree. In the evening, the greater part of them being at the house where I lodged, I discoursed to them, and found them universally engaged about their soul's concerns; inquiring 'what they should do to be saved.' All their conversation among themselves turned upon religious matters, in which they were assisted by my Interpreter, who was with them day and night.

" This day there was one woman, who had been much concerned for her soul ever since she first heard me preach in June last, who obtained comfort, I trust, solid and well grounded. She seemed to be filled with love to Christ. At the same time she behaved humbly and tenderly, and appeared afraid of nothing so much as of offending and grieving him whom her soul loved.

Aug. 6.—" In the morning I discoursed to the Indians at the house where we lodged. Many of them were much affected, and appeared surprisingly tender: so that a few words about the concerns of their souls would cause the tears to flow freely, and produce many sobs and groans. In the afternoon they being returned to the place where I had usually preached among them, I again discoursed to them there. There were about *fifty-five* persons in all; about *forty* that were capable of attending Divine service with understanding. I insisted on 1 John, 4 : 10. 'Herein is love.' &c. They seemed eager of hearing; but there appeared nothing very remarkable, except their attention, till near the close of my discourse; and then Divine truth was attended with a surprising influence, and produced a great concern among them. There were scarcely *three* in *forty* who could refrain from tears and bitter cries. They all as one seemed in an agony of soul to obtain an interest in Christ; and the more I discoursed of the love and compassion of God in sending his Son to suffer for the sins of men; and the more I invited them to come and partake of his love; the more their distress was aggravated, because they felt themselves unable to come. It was surprising to see how their hearts seemed to be pierced with the tender and melting invitations of the Gospel, when there was not a word of terror spoken to them.

"There were this day two persons who obtained relief and comfort; which, when I came to discourse with them particularly, appeared solid, rational, and scriptural. After I had inquired into the grounds of their comfort, and said many things which I thought proper to them; I asked them what they wanted that God should do farther for them? They replied, 'they wanted Christ should wipe their hearts quite clean,' &c. So surprising were now the doings of the Lord, that I can say no less of this day, and I need say no more of it, than that *the arm of the Lord* was powerfully and marvellously *revealed* in it.

Aug. 7.—"Preached to the Indians from Isaiah, 53 :

3-10. There was a remarkable influence attending
the word, and great concern in the assembly; but
scarcely equal to what appeared the day before; that
is, not quite so universal. However, most were much
affected, and many in great distress for their souls;
and some few could neither go nor stand, but lay flat
on the ground, as if pierced at heart, crying incessantly
for mercy. Several were newly awakened; and it
was remarkable that as fast as they came from remote
places round about, the Spirit of God seemed to seize
them with concern for their souls. After public service was concluded I found two persons more who
had newly met with comfort, of whom I had good
hopes; and a third of whom I could not but entertain
some hopes, whose case did not appear so clear as the
others; so that there were now six in all, who had got
some relief from their spiritual distresses; and five
whose experience appeared very clear and satisfactory.
It is worthy of remark, that those who obtained comfort first were in general deeply affected with concern
for their souls when I preached to them in June last.

Aug. 8.—" In the afternoon I preached to the Indians, their number was now about *sixty-five* persons;
men, women, and children. I discoursed upon Luke,
14 : 16-23, and was favored with uncommon freedom.
There was much visible concern among them while I
was discoursing publicly; but afterward, when I spoke
to one and another more particularly, whom I perceived under much concern, the power of God seemed
to descend upon the assembly ' *like a mighty rushing
wind*,' and with an astonishing energy bore down all
before it. I stood amazed at the influence which seized
the audience almost universally; and could compare
it to nothing more aptly than the irresistible force of a

mighty torrent, or swelling deluge, that with its insupportable weight and pressure bears down and sweeps before it whatever is in its way. Almost all persons of all ages were bowed down with concern together, and scarcely one was able to withstand the shock of this surprising operation. Old men and women who had been drunken wretches for many years, and some little children not more than six or seven years of age, appeared in distress for their souls, as well as persons of middle age. It was apparent that these children, some of them at least, were not merely frightened with seeing the general concern, but were made sensible of their danger, the badness of their hearts, and their misery without Christ, as some of them expressed it. The most stubborn hearts were now obliged to bow. A principal man among the Indians, who before was most secure and self-righteous, and thought his state good, because he knew more than the generality of the Indians had formerly done ; and who with a great degree of confidence the day before told me ' he had been a Christian more than ten years;' was now brought under solemn concern for his soul, and wept bitterly. Another man advanced in years, who had been a murderer, a *powaw* or conjurer, and a notorious drunkard, was likewise brought now to cry for mercy with many tears, and to complain much that he could be no more concerned, when he saw his danger so very great.

" They were almost universally praying and crying for mercy in every part of the house, and many out of doors ; and numbers could neither go nor stand. Their concern was so great, each one for himself, that none seemed to take any notice of those about them, but each prayed freely for himself. I am led to think they were, to their own apprehensions, as much retired

as if they had been individually by themselves, in the
thickest desert; or I believe rather that they thought
about nothing but themselves, and their own state,
and so were every one praying apart, although all together. It seemed to me that there was now an exact
fulfilment of that prophecy, Zech. 12 : 10, 11, 12; for
there was now 'a great mourning, like the mourning
of Hadadrimmon ;'—and each seemed to ' mourn
apart.' Methought this had a near resemblance to the
day of God's power, mentioned in Josh. 10 : 14; for I
must say I never saw *any day like it*, in all respects:
it was a day wherein I am persuaded the Lord did
much to destroy the kingdom of darkness among this
people.

" This concern, in general, was most rational and
just. Those who had been awakened any considerable
time, complained more especially of the badness of
their *hearts ;* and those who were newly awakened, of
the badness of their *lives* and *actions ;* and all were
afraid of the anger of God, and of everlasting misery
as the desert of their sins. Some of the white people
who came out of curiosity to hear what ' this babbler
would say' to the poor ignorant Indians, were much
awakened; and some appeared to be wounded with a
view of their perishing state. Those who had lately
obtained relief, were filled with comfort at this season.
They appeared calm and composed, and seemed to
rejoice in Christ Jesus. Some of them took their distressed friends by the hand, telling them of the goodness of Christ, and the comfort that is to be enjoyed in
him; and thence invited them to come and give up
their hearts to him. I could observe some of them, in
the most honest and unaffected manner, without any
design of being taken notice of, lifting up their eyes

to heaven, as if crying for mercy, while they saw the distress of the poor souls around them. There was one remarkable instance of awakening this day which I cannot fail to notice here. A young Indian woman, who, I believe, never knew before that she had a soul, nor ever thought of any such thing, hearing that there was something strange among the Indians, came, it seems, to see what was the matter. In her way to the Indians she called at my lodgings; and when I told her that I designed presently to preach to the Indians, laughed, and seemed to mock; but went however to them. I had not proceeded far in my public discourse before she felt effectually that she had a soul; and before I had concluded my discourse was so convinced of her sin and misery, and so distressed with concern for her soul's salvation, that she seemed like one pierced through with a dart, and cried out incessantly. She could neither go nor stand, nor sit on her seat without being held up. After public service was over she lay flat on the ground, praying earnestly, and would take no notice of, nor give any answer to any who spoke to her. I hearkened to what she said, and perceived the burden of her prayer to be, ' *Guttummaukalummeh wechaumeh kmeleh Nolah,*' i. e. ' *Have mercy on me, and help me to give you my heart.*' Thus she continued praying incessantly for many hours together. This was indeed a surprising day of God's power, and seemed enough to convince an Atheist of the truth, importance, and power of God's word.

Aug. 9.—"Spent almost the whole day with the Indians; the former part of it in discoursing to many of them privately, and especially to some who had lately received comfort, and endeavoring to inquire into the grounds of it, as well as to give them some proper instructions, cautions and directions.

"In the afternoon discoursed to them publicly. There were now present about *seventy* persons, old and young. I opened and applied the parable of the sower, Matt. 13. Was enabled to discourse with much plainness, and found afterward that this discourse was very instructive to them. There were many tears among them while I was discoursing publicly, but no considerable cry ; yet some were much affected with a few words spoken from Matt. 11 : 28, 'Come unto me all ye that labor,' &c. with which I concluded my discourse. But, while I was discoursing near night to two or three of the awakened persons, a Divine influence seemed to attend what was spoken to them in a powerful manner, which caused the persons to cry out in anguish of soul, although I spoke not a word of terror, but on the contrary, set before them the fullness and all-sufficiency of Christ's merits, and his willingness to save all that come to him, and thereupon pressed them to come without delay. The cry of these was soon heard by others, who, though scattered before, immediately gathered round. I then proceeded in the same strain of gospel invitation, till they were all melted into tears and cries except two or three; and seemed in the greatest distress to find and secure an interest in the great Redeemer. Some who had little more than a ruffle made in their passions the day before, seemed now to be deeply affected and wounded at heart; and the concern in general appeared nearly as prevalent as the day before. There was indeed a very *great mourning* among them, and yet every one seemed to *mourn apart*. For so great was their concern, that almost every one was praying and crying for himself, as if none had been near. ' *Guttummauhalummeh ; Guttummauhalummeh*,' i. e. ' *Have mercy upon me   have mercy upon me,*' was the common cry. It was very affecting to see the poor Indians, who the other day were hallooing and yelling in their *idolatrous* feasts and *drunken* frolics, now crying to God with such importunity for an interest in his dear Son! Found two or three persons who, I had reason to hope, had taken comfort upon good grounds since the evening before; and these, with others who had obtained comfort, were together, and seemed to rejoice much that God was carrying on his work with such power upon others.

August 10.—" Rode to the Indians, and began to discourse more privately to those who had obtained comfort and satisfaction; endeavoring to instruct, direct, caution, and comfort them. But others, being eager of hearing every word which related to spiritual concerns, soon came together one after another; and, when I had discoursed to the young converts more than half an hour, they seemed much melted with divine things, and earnestly desirous to be with Christ. I told them of the godly soul's perfect purity and full enjoyment of Christ, immediately upon its separation from the body; and that it would be for ever inconceivably more happy than *they* had ever been for any short space of time, when Christ seemed near to them in prayer or other duties. That I might make way for speaking of the resurrection of the body, and thence of the complete blessedness of the man; I said, ' But perhaps some of you will say, I love my body as well as my soul, and I cannot bear to think that my body shall lie dead, if my soul is happy.' To which they all cheerfully replied, ' *Muttoh, Muttoh;*' before I had opportunity to prosecute what I designed respecting the resurrection; i. e. ' *No, No,*' They did not regard their *bodies*, if their *souls* might be with Christ. Then they appeared willing to-be absent from the body, that they might be present with the Lord.

"When I had spent some time with them I turned to the other Indians, and spoke to them from Luke, 19 : 10. 'For the Son of man is come to seek and to save that which was lost.' I had not discoursed long before their concern rose to a great degree, and the house was filled with cries and groans. When I insisted on the compassion and care of the Lord Jesus Christ for those that were lost, who thought themselves undone, and could find no way of escape; this melted them down the more, and aggravated their distress, that they could not find and come to so kind a Savior.

"Sundry persons, who before had been slightly awakened, were now deeply wounded with a sense of their sin and misery. One man in particular, who was never before awakened, was now made to feel that ' the word of the Lord was quick and powerful, sharper than any two-edged sword.' He seemed to be pierced at heart with distress, and his concern appeared rational and scriptural, for he said that ' all the wickedness of his past life was brought fresh to his remembrance, and that he saw all the vile actions he had done formerly, as if done but yesterday.'

"Found one who had newly received comfort, after pressing distress from day to day. Could not but rejoice and admire the divine goodness in what appeared this day. There seems to be some good done by every discourse; some newly awakened every day, and some comforted. It was refreshing to observe the conduct of those who obtained comfort: while others were distressed with fear and concern, they were lifting up their hearts to God for them.

Lord's day, Aug. 11.—" Discoursed in the forenoon

from the parable of the *Prodigal Son.* Luke, 15. Observed no such remarkable effect of the word upon the assembly as in days past. There were numbers of careless spectators from the white people, of various characters. In the afternoon I discoursed upon a part of Peter's sermon. Acts, 2. And at the close of my discourse to the Indians, made an address to the white people; and divine truth seemed then to be attended with power, both to English and Indians. Several of the white heathen were awakened, and could not longer be idle spectators; but found they had souls to save or lose as well as the Indians; and a great concern spread through the whole assembly; so that this also appeared to be a day of God's power, especially toward the conclusion of it, although the influence attending the word seemed scarcely so powerful now as in some days past.

" The number of Indians, old and young, was now upward of *seventy;* and one or two were newly awakened this day who never had appeared to be moved with concern for their souls before. Those who had obtained relief and comfort, and had given hopeful evidences of having passed a saving change, appeared humble and devout, and behaved in an agreeable and Christian-like manner. I was refreshed to see the tenderness of conscience manifest in some of them; one instance of which I cannot but notice. Perceiving one of them very sorrowful in the morning, I inquired into the cause of her sorrow, and found the difficulty was that she had been angry with her child the evening before, and was now exercised with fears lest her anger had been inordinate and sinful; which so grieved her that she awoke and began to sob before day light, and continued weeping for several hours together.

August 14.—" Spent the day with the Indians. There
was one of them who had some time since put away
his wife, as is common among them, and taken another
woman; and being now brought under some serious
impressions, was much concerned about that affair in
particular, and seemed fully convinced of the wickedness of the practice, and earnestly desirous to know
what God would have him to do in his present circumstances. When the law of God respecting *marriage*
had been opened to them, and the cause of his leaving
his wife inquired into, and when it appeared that she
had given him no just occasion, by unchastity, to desert her, and that she was willing to forgive his past
misconduct and to live peaceably with him for the future, and that she, moreover, insisted on it as her right
to live with him; he was then told that it was his indispensable duty to renounce the woman whom he
had last taken, and receive the other, who was his
proper wife, and live peaceably with her during life.
With this he readily and cheerfully complied; and
thereupon *publicly* renounced the woman he had last
taken, and promised to live with and be kind to his
wife during life; she also promising the same to him.
Here appeared a clear demonstration of the power of
God's word upon their hearts. I suppose a few weeks
before the whole world could not have persuaded this
man to a compliance with Christian rules in this affair.

" I was not without fears that this proceeding might
be like putting ' new wine into old bottles;' and that
some might be prejudiced against Christianity, when
they saw the demands made by it. But the man being
much concerned about the matter, the determination
of it could be deferred no longer; and it seemed to have
a good, rather than an ill effect among the Indians, who

generally owned that the laws of Christ were good and right respecting the affairs of marriage. In the afternoon I preached to them from the apostle's discourse to Cornelius. Acts, 10 : 34. There appeared some affectionate concern among them, though not equal to what appeared in several of the former days. They still attended and heard as for their lives, and the Lord's work seemed still to be promoted and propagated among them.

August 15.—" Preached from Luke, 4 : 16–21. The word was attended with power upon the hearts of the hearers. There was much concern, many tears, and affecting cries among them ; and some were deeply wounded and distressed for their souls. There were some newly awakened who came but this week, and convictions seemed to be promoted in others. Those who had received comfort, were likewise refreshed and strengthened ; and the work of grace appeared to advance in all respects. The *passions* of the congregation in general were not so much moved as in some days past; but their *hearts* seemed as solemnly and deeply affected with divine truth as ever, at least in many instances, although the concern did not seem so universal, and to reach every individual in such a manner as it appeared to do some days before.

August. 16.—" Spent considerable time in conversing with the Indians. Found one who had got relief and comfort after pressing concern ; and could not but hope, when I came to discourse particularly with her, that her comfort was of the right kind. In the afternoon I preached to them from John, 6 : 26–34. Toward the close of my discourse divine truth was attended with considerable power upon the audience

and more especially after public service was over, when
I particularly addressed several distressed persons.

"There was a great concern for their souls spread
pretty generally among them; but especially there
were two persons newly awakened to a sense of their
sin and misery; one of whom was lately come, and
the other had all along been very attentive and desirous
of being awakened, but could never before have any
lively view of her perishing state. Now her concern
and spiritual distress was such, that I thought I had
never seen *any* more pressing. A number of *old* men
were also in distress for their souls; so that they could
not refrain from weeping and crying aloud; and their
bitter groans were the most convincing as well as affecting evidences of the reality and depth of their inward anguish. God is powerfully at work among
them. True and genuine convictions of sin are daily
promoted in many instances; and some are newly
awakened from time to time; although some few, who
felt a commotion in their passions in days past, seem
now to discover that their *hearts* were never duly affected. I never saw the work of God appear so inde-
pendent of means as at this time. I discoursed to the
people, and spake what I suppose had a proper tendency to promote convictions; but God's manner of
working upon them seemed so entirely supernatural,
and above means, that I could scarcely believe he used
me as an instrument, or what I spake as means of carrying on his work. For it appeared, as I thought, to
have no connection with or dependence on means in
any respect. Though I could not but continue to use
the means, which I thought proper for the promotion
of the work, yet God seemed, as I apprehended, to
work entirely without them. I seemed to do nothing,

and indeed to have nothing to do, but to ' stand still, and see the salvation of God ;' and found myself obliged and delighted to say, ' Not unto us,' not unto instruments and means, ' but to thy name be glory.' God appeared to work entirely alone, and I saw no room to attribute any part of this work to any created arm.

Aug. 17.—" Spent much time in private conferences with the Indians. Found one who had newly obtained relief and comfort, after a long season of spiritual trouble and distress; he having been one of my hearers at the Forks of Delaware for more than a year, and now having followed me here under deep concern for his soul; and had abundant reason to hope that his comfort was well grounded, and truly divine.

Lord's day, Aug. 18.—" Preached in the forenoon to a mixed assembly of white people, of divers denominations. Afterward preached to the Indians, from John 6 : 35–40. There was considerable concern visible among them, though not equal to what has frequently appeared of late.

Aug. 19.—" Preached from Isaiah, 55 : 1. ' Ho every one that thirsteth.' Divine truth was attended with power upon those who had received comfort, and others also. The former sweetly melted and refreshed with divine invitations ; the latter much concerned for their souls, that they might obtain an interest in these glorious gospel provisions which were set before them. There were numbers of poor impotent souls that waited at the pool for healing; and the angel seemed, as at other times of late, to trouble the waters, so that there was yet a most desirable and comfortable prospect of the spiritual recovery of diseased perishing sinners.

Aug 23.—" Spent some time with the Indians in private discourse; and afterward preached to them from John, 6 : 44-50. There was, as has been usual, a great attention, and some affection among them. Several appeared deeply concerned for their souls, and could not but express their inward anguish by tears and cries. But the amazing divine influence, which has been so powerfully among them in general, seems at present in some degree abated: at least in regard to its universality; though many who have obtained no special comfort still retain deep impressions of divine things.

Aug. 24.—"Spent the forenoon in discoursing to some of the Indians in reference to their publicly professing Christ. Numbers of them seemed to be filled with love to God, delighted with the thoughts of giving themselves up to him, and melted and refreshed with the hopes of enjoying the blessed Redeemer. Afterward I discoursed publicly from 1 Thess. 4 : 13-17. There was a solemn attention, and some visible concern and affection in the time of public service; which was afterward increased by some further exhortations given to them to come to Christ, and give up their hearts to him, that they might be fitted to 'ascend up and meet him in the air,' when he shall 'descend with a shout, and the voice of the archangel.'

"There were several Indians newly come, who thought their state good, and themselves happy, because they had sometimes lived with the white people under gospel light, had learned to read, were civil, &c., although they appeared utter strangers to their own hearts, and altogether unacquainted with the power of religion, as well as with the doctrines of grace. With these I discoursed particularly, after public worship; and was surprised to see their self-righteous disposition, their strong attachment to the covenant of works for salvation, and the high value they put upon their supposed attainments. Yet after much discourse, one appeared in a measure convinced that 'by the deeds of the law no flesh living can be justified;' and wept bitterly, inquiring ' what he must do to be saved.'

" This was very comfortable to others, who had gained some experimental knowledge of their own hearts; for before they were grieved with the conversation and conduct of these new comers, who boasted of their knowledge, and thought well of themselves but evidently discovered to those who had any experience of divine truth, that they knew nothing of their own hearts.

Lord's day, Aug. 25.—"Preached in the forenoon from Luke, 15: 3–7. A number of white people being present, I made an address to them at the close of my discourse to the Indians; but could not so much as keep them orderly; for scores of them kept walking and gazing about, and behaved more indecently than any Indians I have ever addressed. A view of their abusive conduct so sunk my spirits, that I could scarcely go on with my work.

" In the afternoon I discoursed from Rev. 3 : 20; at which time *fifteen* Indians made a public profession of their faith. After the crowd of spectators was gone I called them together, and discoursed to them in particular; at the same time inviting others to attend. I reminded them of the solemn obligations they were now under to live to God; warned them of the evil and dreadful consequences of careless living, especially after their public profession of Christianity; gave them directions for future conduct; and encouraged them to watchfulness and devotion, by setting

before them the comfort and happy conclusion of a
religious life.

"This was a desirable and sweet season indeed!
Their hearts were engaged and cheerful in duty; and
they rejoiced that they had, in a public and solemn
manner, dedicated themselves to God.   Love seemed
to reign among them! They took each other by the hand
with tenderness and affection, as if their hearts were
knit together, while I was discoursing to them; and
all their deportment toward each other was such, that
a serious spectator might justly be excited to cry out
with admiration, 'Behold how they love one another.'
Numbers of the other Indians, on seeing and hearing
these things, were much affected, and wept bitterly;
longing to be partakers of the same joy and comfort
which these discovered by their very countenances as
well as conduct.

Aug. 26.—"Preached to my people from John, 6:
51–55. After I had discoursed some time, I addressed
them in particular who entertained hopes that they
were passed from death unto life. Opened to them the
persevering nature of those consolations which Christ
gives his people, and which I trusted he had bestowed
upon some in that assembly; showed them that such
have already the beginnings of eternal life, and that
their heaven shall speedily be completed.

"I no sooner began to discourse in this strain than
the dear Christians in the congregation began to be
melted with affection to, and desire of the enjoyment
of Christ, and of a state of perfect purity. They wept
affectionately, yet joyfully; and their tears and sobs
discovered brokenness of heart, and yet were attended
with real comfort and sweetness   It was a tender, affectionate, humble and delightful meeting, and ap-

peared to be the genuine effect of a spirit of adoption, and very far from that spirit of bondage under which they not long since labored. The influence seemed to spread from these through the whole assembly; and there quickly appeared a wonderful concern among them. Many, who had not yet found Christ as an all-sufficient Savior, were surprisingly engaged in seeking after him. It was indeed a lovely and very interesting assembly. Their number was now about *ninety-five* persons, old and young, and almost all affected with joy in Christ Jesus, or with the utmost concern to obtain an interest in him.

"Being now convinced that it was my duty to take a journey far back to the Indians on the Susquehanna, it being now a proper season of the year to find them generally at home; after having spent some hours in public and private discourse with my people, I told them that I must now leave them for the present, and go to their brethren far remote, and preach to them; that I wanted the Spirit of God should go with me, without whom nothing could be done to any good purpose among the Indians—as they themselves had opportunity to see and observe by the barrenness of our meetings at some times, when there was much pains taken to affect and awaken sinners, and yet to little or no purpose; and asked them if they could not be willing to spend the remainder of the day in prayer for me, that God would go with me, and succeed my endeavors for the conversion of these poor souls. They cheerfully complied with the motion, and soon after I left them, the sun being about an hour and a half high, they began and continued praying till break of day, or very near; never mistrusting, as they tell me, till they went out and viewed the stars, and saw the morning

star a considerable height, that it was later than bed
time. Thus eager and unwearied were they in their
devotions! A remarkable night it was; attended, as my
Interpreter tells me, with a powerful influence upon
those who were yet under concern, as well as those
who had received comfort. There were, I trust, this
day, two distressed souls brought to the enjoyment of
solid comfort in Him in whom the weary find rest. It
was likewise remarkable, that this day an old Indian,
who had all his days been an idolater, was brought to
give up his rattles, which they use for music in their
idolatrous feasts and dances, to the other Indians, who
quickly destroyed them. This was done without any
interference of mine, I having not spoken to him about
it, so that it seemed to be nothing but the power of
God's word, without any particular application to this
sin, that produced this effect. Thus God has begun,
thus he has hitherto surprisingly carried on a work of
grace among these Indians. May the glory be ascribed
to Him who is the sole author of it."

Forks of Delaware, in Pennsylvania, Sept. 1745.

Lord's day, Sept. 1—"Preached to the Indians from
Luke, 11: 16–23. The word appeared to be attended
with some power, and caused some tears in the assembly. Afterward preached to a number of white people present, and observed many of them in tears; and
some who had formerly been as careless and uncon
cerned about religion, perhaps, as the Indians. To
ward night discoursed to the Indians again, and per
ceived a greater attention, and more visible concern
among them than has been usual in these parts.

Sept. 3.—"Preached to the Indians from Isaiah, 52
3–6. The Divine presence seemed to be in the mids

of the assembly, and a considerable concern spread among them. Sundry persons seemed to be awakened; among whom were two stupid creatures, whom I could scarce ever before keep awake while I was discoursing to them. I could not but rejoice at this appearance of things; although at the same time I could not but fear, lest the concern which they at present manifested might prove like a morning cloud, as something of that nature had formerly done in these parts.

Sept. 5.—" Discoursed to the Indians from the parable of the sower. Afterward I conversed particularly with a number of persons ; which occasioned them to weep, and even to cry out in an affecting manner, and seized others with surprise and concern. I doubt not but that a divine power accompanied what was then spoken. Several of these persons had been with me to Crossweeksung, and there had seen, and some of them, I trust *felt*, the power of God's word in an affecting and saving manner. I asked one of them, who had obtained comfort, and given hopeful evidence of being truly religious, ' Why he now cried ?' He replied, ' When he thought how Christ was slain like a lamb, and spilt his blood for sinners, he could not help crying when he was alone;' and thereupon burst into tears and cried again. I then asked his wife, who had likewise been abundantly comforted, why she cried? She answered, ' that she was grieved that the Indians *here* would not come to Christ, as well as those at Crossweeksung.' I asked her if she found a heart to pray for them, and whether Christ had seemed *to be near her of late in prayer*, as in times past, which is my usual method of expressing a sense of the divine presence. She replied, ' Yes, he had been near to her, and at times when she had been praying alone, her heart loved to pray so that she could not bear to leave the place, but wanted to stay and pray longer.'

Lord's day, Sept. 8.—" Discoursed to the Indians in the afternoon from Acts, 2 : 36–39. The word of God at this time seemed to fall with weight and influence upon them. There were but few present; but most that were, were in tears, and several cried out in distressing concern for their souls. There was one man considerably awakened, who never before discovered any concern for his soul. There appeared a remarkable work of the Divine Spirit among them generally, not unlike what has been of late at Crossweeksung. It seemed as if the divine influence had spread thence to this place, although something of it appeared here before in the awakening of my interpreter, his wife, and some few others. Several of the careless white people now present were awakened, or at least startled, seeing the power of God so prevalent among the Indians. I then made a particular address to them, which seemed to make some impression upon them, and excite some affection in them.

" There are some Indians in these parts who have always refused to hear me preach, and have been enraged against those who have attended on my preaching. But of late they are more bitter than ever; scoffing at christianity, and sometimes asking my hearers ' How often they have cried,' and ' whether they have not now cried enough to do their turn,' &c. So that they have already trial of cruel mockings.

Sept. 9.—" Left the Indians at the Forks of Delaware, and set out on a journey toward Susquehanna river, directing my course toward the Indian town more than an hundred and twenty miles westward from the Forks. Traveled about fifteen miles, and there lodged.

Shaumoking, Sept. 1745

Sept. 13.— After having lodged out three nights, arrived at the Indian town I aimed at, on the Susquehanna, called *Shaumoking ;* one of the places, and the largest of them, which I visited in May last. I was kindly received, and entertained by the Indians ; but had little satisfaction by reason of the heathenish dance and revel they then held in the house where I was obliged to lodge; which I could not suppress, though I often entreated them to desist, for the sake of one of their own friends, who was then sick in the house, and whose disorder was much aggravated by the noise. Alas ! how destitute of natural affection are these poor uncultivated pagans ! although they seem somewhat kind in their own way. Of a truth the dark corners of the earth are full of the habitations of cruelty. This town, as I observed in my Diary of May last, lies partly on the east side of the river, partly on the west, and partly on a large island in it, and contains upward of fifty houses, and nearly three hundred persons, though I never saw much more than half that number in it. They are of three different tribes of Indians, speaking three languages wholly unintelligible to each other. About one half of its inhabitants are *Delawares,* the others called *Senekas* and *Tutelas.* The Indians of this place are accounted the most drunken, mischievous, and ruffianlike fellows of any in these parts; and Satan seems to have his seat in this town in an eminent manner.

Sept. 14.—" Visited the Delaware King, who was supposed to be at the point of death when I was here in May last, but was now recovered ; discoursed with him and others respecting christianity ; spent the afternoon with them. and had more encouragement than I

expected. The king appeared kindly disposed, and
willing to be instructed. This gave me some encouragement that God would open an effectual door for
my preaching the Gospel here, and set up his kingdom
in this place. This was a support and refreshment to
me in the wilderness, and rendered my solitary circumstances comfortable and pleasant.

Lord's day, Sept. 15.—" Visited the chief of the
Delawares again; was kindly received by him, and
discoursed to the Indians in the afternoon. Still entertained hopes that God would open their hearts to
receive the Gospel, though many of them in the place
were so drunk from day to day that I could get no
opportunity to speak to them. Toward night discoursed with one who understood the languages of the
Six Nations, as they are usually called, who discovered
an inclination to hearken to christianity, which gave
me some hope that the Gospel might hereafter be sent
to those nations far remote.

Sept. 16.—" Spent the forenoon with the Indians,
endeavoring to instruct them from house to house, and
to engage them, as far as I could, to be friendly to
christianity. Toward night went to one part of the
town where they were sober, got together near fifty
of them, and discoursed to them, having first obtained
the king's cheerful consent. There was a surprising
attention among them, and they manifested a considerable desire of being further instructed. There were also
one or two that seemed to be touched with some concern for their souls, who appeared well pleased with
some conversation in private after I had concluded my
public discourse to them.

" My spirits were much refreshed with this appearance of things, and I could not but return with my

interpreter, having no other companion in this journey to my poor hard lodgings, rejoicing in hopes that God designed to set up his kingdom here, where satan now reigns in the most eminent manner; and found uncommon freedom in addressing the throne of grace for the accomplishment of so great and glorious a work.

Sept. 17.—" Spent the forenoon in visiting and discoursing to the Indians. About noon left Shaumoking (most of the Indians going out this day on their hunting design) and traveled down the river south-westward.

Juncauta, Sept. 1745.

Sept. 19.—" Visited an Indian town, called *Juncauta*, situate on an island in the Susquehanna. Was much discouraged with the temper and behavior of the Indians here ; although they appeared friendly when I was with them the last spring, and then gave me encouragement to come and see them again. But they now seemed resolved to retain their pagan notions, and persist in their idolatrous practices.

September 20.—" Visited the Indians again at Juncauta island, and found them almost universally very busy in making preparations for a great sacrifice and dance. Had no opportunity to get them together, in order to discourse with them about Christianity, by reason of their being so much engaged about their sacrifice. My spirits were much sunk with a prospect so very discouraging ; and especially seeing I had this day no interpreter but a pagan, who was as much attached to idolatry as any of them, and who could neither speak nor understand the language of these Indians ; so that I was under the greatest disadvantages imaginable. However, I attempted to discourse privately with some of them, but without any appearance of success: notwithstanding I still tarried with them.

"In the evening they met together, nearly a hundred of them, and danced around a large fire, having prepared ten fat deer for the sacrifice. The fat of the inwards they burnt in the fire while they were dancing, which sometimes raised the flame to a prodigious height; at the same time yelling and shouting in such a manner that they might easily have been heard two miles or more. They continued their sacred dance nearly all night, after which they ate the flesh of the sacrifice, and so retired each one to his own lodging.

"I enjoyed little satisfaction; being entirely alone on the island, as to any Christian company, and in the midst of this idolatrous revel; and having walked to and fro till body and mind were pained and much oppressed, I at length crept into a little crib made for corn, and there slept on the poles.

Lord's day, Sept. 21.—" Spent the day with the Indians on the island. As soon as they were well up in the morning I attempted to instruct them, and labored for that purpose to get them together; but soon found they had something else to do, for near noon they gathered together all their powaws, or conjurers, and set about half a dozen of them playing their juggling tricks, and acting their frantic distracted postures, in order to find out why they were then so sickly upon the island, numbers of them being at that time disordered with a fever and bloody flux. In this exercise they were engaged for several hours, making all the wild, ridiculous and distracted motions imaginable; sometimes singing, sometimes howling, sometimes extending their hands to the utmost stretch, and spreading all their fingers; they seemed to push with them as if they designed to push something away, or at least keep it off at arm's-end ; sometimes stroking their faces with their hands, then spurting water as fine as mist ; sometimes sitting flat on the earth, then bowing down their faces to the ground ; then wringing their sides as if in pain and anguish, twisting their faces, turning up their eyes, grunting, puffing, &c.

" Their monstrous actions tended to excite ideas of horror, and seemed to have something in them, as I thought, peculiarly suited to raise the devil, if he could be raised by any thing odd, ridiculous, and frightful. Some of them, I could observe, were much more fervent and devout in the business than others, and seemed to chant, peep, and mutter with a great degree of warmth and vigor, as if determined to awaken and engage the powers below. I sat at a small distance, not more than thirty feet from them, though undiscovered, with my Bible in my hand, resolving, if possible, to spoil their sport, and prevent their receiving any answers from the infernal world, and there viewed the whole scene. They continued their hideous charms and incantations for more than three hours, until they had all wearied themselves out; although they had in that space of time taken several intervals of rest ; and at length broke up, I apprehended, without receiving any answer at all.

" After they had done powawing, I attempted to discourse with them about Christianity ; but they soon scattered, and gave me no opportunity for any thing of that nature. A view of these things, while I was entirely alone in the wilderness, destitute of the society of any one who so much as 'named the name of Christ,' greatly sunk my spirits, and gave me the most gloomy turn of mind imaginable, almost stripped me of all resolution and hope respecting further attempts for pro-

pagating the Gospel and converting the pagans, and
rendered this the most burdensome and disagreeable
Sabbath which I ever saw. But nothing, I can truly
say, sunk and distressed me like the loss of my hope
respecting their conversion. This concern appeared
so great, and seemed to be so much my own, that I
seemed to have nothing to do on earth if this failed.
A prospect of the greatest success in the saving conversion of souls under Gospel light, would have done
little or nothing toward compensating for the loss of
my hope in this respect; and my spirits now were so
damped and depressed, that I had no heart nor power
to make any further attempts among them for that
purpose, and could not possibly recover my hope, resolution, and courage, by the utmost of my endeavors.

" The Indians of this island can, many of them, understand the English language considerably well; having formerly lived in some part of Maryland, among
or near the white people; but are very drunken, vicious,
and profane, although not so savage as those who have
less acquaintance with the English. Their customs,
in various respects, differ from those of the other Indians upon this river. They do not bury their dead
in a common form, but let their flesh consume above
the ground, in close cribs made for that purpose. At
the end of a year, or sometimes a longer space of time,
they take the bones, when the flesh is all consumed,
and wash and scrape them, and afterward bury them
with some ceremony. Their method of charming or
conjuring over the sick, seems somewhat different from
that of the other Indians, though in substance the same.
The whole of it among these and others, perhaps, is
an imitation of what seems, by Naaman's expression,
2 Kings, 5 : 11, to have been the custom of the ancient

heathen. It seems chiefly to consist in their ' striking their hands over the discased,' repeatedly stroking them, ' and calling upon their god ;' except the spurting of water like a mist, and some other frantic ceremonies common to the other conjurations which I have already mentioned.

" When I was in this region in May last I had an opportunity of learning many of the notions and customs of the Indians, as well as observing many of their practices. I then traveled more than an hundred and thirty miles upon the river, above the English settlements; and in that journey met with individuals of seven or eight distinct tribes, speaking as many different languages. But of all the sights I ever saw among them, or indeed any where else, none appeared so frightful, or so near a kin to what is usually imagined of *infernal powers,* none ever excited such images of terror in my mind, as the appearance of one who was a devout and zealous reformer, or rather restorer of what he supposed was the ancient religion of the Indians. He made his appearance in his *pontifical garb,* which was a coat of *bear skins,* dressed with the hair on, and hanging down to his toes; a pair of bear skin stockings; and a great *wooden* face painted, the one half black, the other half tawny, about the color of an Indian's skin, with an extravagant mouth, cut very much awry; the face fastened to a bear skin cap, which was drawn over his head. He advanced toward me with the instrument in his hand which he used for music in his idolatrous worship; which was a dry tortoise shell with some corn in it, and the neck of it drawn on to a piece of wood, which made a very convenient handle. As he came forward he beat his tune with the rattle, and danced with all his might, but did

not suffer any part of his body, not so much as his
fingers, to be seen. No one would have imagined,
from his appearance or actions, that he could have
been a human creature, if they had not had some intimation of it otherwise. When he came near me I
could not but shrink away from him, although it was
then noon day, and I knew who it was; his appearance
and gestures were so prodigiously frightful. He had
a house consecrated to religious uses, with divers
images cut upon the several parts of it. I went in, and
found the ground beat almost as hard as a rock, with
their frequent dancing upon it. I discoursed with him
about Christianity. Some of my discourse he seemed
to like, but some of it he disliked extremely. He told
me that God had taught him his religion, and that he
never would turn from it; but wanted to find some
who would join heartily with him in it; for the Indians,
he said, were grown very degenerate and corrupt. He
had thoughts, he said, of leaving all his friends, and
traveling abroad, in order to find some who would
join with him; for he believed that God had some
good people some where, who felt as he did. He had
not always, he said, felt as he now did; but had formerly been like the rest of the Indians, until about four or
five years before that time. Then, he said, his heart
was very much distressed, so that he could not live
among the Indians, but got away into the woods, and
lived alone for some months. At length, he said, God
comforted his heart, and showed him what he should
do; and since that time he had known God, and tried
to serve him; and loved all men, be they who they
would, so as he never did before. He treated me with
uncommon courtesy, and seemed to be hearty in it. I
was told by the Indians, that he opposed their drink-

ing strong liquor with all his power; and that, if at any time he could not dissuade them from it by all he could say, he would leave them, and go crying into the woods. It was manifest that he had a set of religious notions which he had examined for himself, and not taken for granted upon bare tradition; and he relished or disrelished whatever was spoken of a religious nature, as it either agreed or disagreed with *his standard.* While I was discoursing, he would sometimes say, ' Now that I like; so God has taught me;' &c. and some of his sentiments seemed very just. Yet he utterly denied the existence of a devil, and declared there was no such creature known among the Indians of old times, whose religion he supposed he was attempting to revive. He likewise told me, that departed souls went *southward,* and that the difference between the good and the bad was this: that the former were admitted into a beautiful town with spiritual walls; and that the latter would for ever hover around these walls, in vain attempts to get in. He seemed to be sincere, honest, and conscientious in his own way, and according to his own religious notions; which was more than I ever saw in any other Pagan. I perceived that he was looked upon and derided among most of the Indians, as a *precise zealot,* who made a needless noise about religious matters; but I must say that there was something in his temper and disposition which looked more like true religion than any thing I ever observed among other heathens.

"But alas! how deplorable is the state of the Indians upon this river! The brief representation which I have here given of their notions and manners, is sufficient to show that they are ' led captive by Satan at his will,' in the most eminent manner; and methinks might likewise be sufficient to excite the compassion, and engage the prayers, of God's children for these their fellow-men, who sit 'in the regions of the shadow of death.'

Sept. 22.—"Made some further attempts to instruct and Christianize the Indians on this Island, but all to no purpose. They live so near the white people that they are always in the way of strong liquor, as well as of the ill examples of nominal Christians; which renders it so unspeakably difficult to treat with them about Christianity."

Forks of Delaware, Oct. 1745.

Oct. 1.—" Discoursed to the Indians here, and spent some time in private conference with them about their souls' concerns, and afterward invited them to accompany, or if not, to follow me to Crossweeksung as soon as they could conveniently; which invitation numbers of them cheerfully accepted."

Crossweeksung, Oct. 1745

Oct. 5.—"Preached to my people from John, 14: 1–6. The divine presence seemed to be in the assembly. Numbers were affected with divine truth, and it was a comfort to some in particular. O what a difference is there between these, and the Indians with whom I had lately treated upon the Susquehanna! To be with those seemed to be like being banished from God and all his people; to be with these, like being admitted into his family, and to the enjoyment of his divine presence! How great is the change lately made upon numbers of those Indians; who, not many months ago, were as thoughtless and averse to Christianity as those upon the Susquehanna; and how astonishing is that grace which has made this change!

Lord's day, Oct. 6.—"Preached in the forenoon from John, 10 : 7–11. There was a considerable melting among my people; the dear young Christians were refreshed, comforted and strengthened; and one or two persons newly awakened. In the afternoon I discoursed on the story of the Jailor, Acts, 16; and in the evening expounded Acts, 20 : 1–12. There was at this time a very agreeable melting spread throughout the whole assembly. I think I scarce ever saw a more desirable affection among any people. There was scarcely a dry eye to be seen among them; and yet nothing boisterous or unseemly, nothing that tended to disturb the public worship; but rather to encourage and excite a Christian ardor and spirit of devotion. Those who I have reason to hope were savingly renewed were first affected, and seemed to rejoice much, but with brokenness of spirit and godly fear. Their exercises were much the same with those mentioned in my journal of August 26, evidently appearing to be the genuine effects of a spirit of adoption.

" After public service was over I withdrew, being much tired with the labors of the day; and the Indians continued praying among themselves for near two hours together; which continued exercises appeared to be attended with a blessed quickening influence from on high. I could not but earnestly wish that numbers of God's people had been present at this season to see and hear these things which I am sure must refresh the heart of every true lover of Zion. To see those who were very lately savage Pagans and idolaters, having no hope, and without God in the world, now filled with a sense of divine love and grace, and worshipping the Father in spirit and in truth, as numbers here appeared to do, was not a little affecting; and especially to see them appear so tender and humble, as well as lively, fervent, and devout in the divine service.

Oct. 24.—"Discoursed from John, 4 : 13, 14. There was a great attention, a desirable affection, and an unaffected melting in the assembly. It is surprising to see how eager they are to hear the word of God. I often times thought that they would cheerfully and diligently attend divine worship twenty-four hours together, if they had an opportunity so to do.

Oct. 25.—"Discoursed to my people respecting the Resurrection, from Luke, 20 : 27–36. When I came to mention the blessedness the godly shall enjoy at that season; their final freedom from death, sin and sorrow; their equality to the *angels* in their nearness to and enjoyment of Christ, some imperfect degree of which they are favored with in the present life, from whence springs their sweetest comfort; and their being the children of God, openly acknowledged by him as such; many of them were much affected and melted with a view of this blessed state.

Oct. 26.—"Being called to assist in the administration of the Lord's supper in a neighboring congregation, I invited my people to go with me. They in general embraced the opportunity cheerfully; and attended the several discourses of this solemnity with diligence and affection, most of them now understanding some thing of the English language.

Lord's day, Oct. 27.—"While I was preaching to a vast assembly of people abroad, who appeared generally easy and secure, there was one Indian woman, a stranger, who never had heard me preach before, nor ever regarded any thing about religion, who, having been now persuaded by some of her friends to come to meeting, though much against her will, was seized with distressing concern for her soul; and soon after expressed a great desire of going home, more than forty miles distant, to call her husband, that he also might be awakened to a concern for his soul. Some others of the Indians appeared to be affected with divine truth this day. The pious people of the English, numbers of whom I had opportunity to converse with, seemed refreshed with seeing the Indians worship God in that devout and solemn manner with the assembly of his people; and with those mentioned in Acts, 11:18, they could not but glorify God, saying, 'Then hath God also to the Gentiles granted repentance unto life.'

"Preached again in the afternoon, to a great assembly; at which time some of my people appeared affected; and when public worship was over, were inquisitive whether there would not be another sermon in the evening, or before the solemnity of the Lord's supper was concluded; being still desirous to hear God's word.

Oct. 28.—"Discoursed from Matt. 22:1-13. I was enabled to open the scriptures, and adapt my discourse and expression to the capacities of my people, *I know not how,* in a plain, easy, and familiar manner, beyond all that I could have done by the utmost study; and this without any special difficulty; yea, with as much freedom as if I had been addressing a common audience, who had been instructed in the doctrines of christianity all their days. The word of God at this time seemed to fall upon the assembly with a divine power and influence, especially toward the close of my discourse; there was both a sweet melting and bitter mourning in the audience. The dear christians were refreshed and comforted, convictions revived in others, and several persons newly awakened who had never been with us before. So much of the divine presence appeared in the assembly, that it seemed 'this was no other than the house of God and the gate of heaven.' All, who had any savor and relish of divine things, were even constrained by the sweetness of that season to say, 'Lord, it is good for us to be here.' If ever there was among my people an appearance of the New Jerusalem 'as a bride adorned for her husband,' there was much of it at this time; and so agreeable was the entertainment, where such tokens of the divine presence were, that I could scarcely be willing in the evening to leave the place and repair to my lodgings. I was refreshed with a view of the continuance of this blessed work of grace among them, and with its influence upon strangers among the Indians, who had of late from time to time providentially come into this part of the country.

Lord's day, Nov. 3.—"Preached to my people from Luke 16: 17. 'And it is easier for heaven and earth,' &c. more especially for the sake of several lately brought under deep concern for their souls. There was some apparent concern and affection in the assembly; though far less than has been usual of late.

"On this day *six* of the Indians made a profession of their faith. One of these was a woman near *fourscore* years of age. Two of the others were men *fifty* years old, who had been singular and remarkable among the Indians for their wickedness; one of them had been a murderer, and both notorious drunkards as well as excessively quarrelsome; but now I cannot but hope that both of them have become subjects of God's special grace. I kept them back for many weeks after they had given evidence of having passed a great

change, that I might have more opportunities to observe the fruits of the impressions which they had been
under, and apprehended the way was now clear to admit them to the ordinances.

Nov. 4.—Discoursed from John 11, briefly explaining most of the chapter. Divine truth made deep impressions upon many in the assembly. Numbers were
affected with a view of the power of Christ manifested
in his raising the dead; and especially when this instance of his power was improved to show his ability
to raise dead souls, such as many of them felt themselves to be, to a spiritual life; as also to raise the dead
at the last day, and dispense to them rewards and
punishments.

"There were numbers of those who had come here
lately from remote places, who were now brought under deep and pressing concern for their souls. One in
particular, who not long since came half drunk, and
railed on us, and attempted by all means to disturb us
while engaged in divine worship, was now so concerned and distressed for her soul, that she seemed unable to get any ease without an interest in Christ.
There were many tears and affectionate sobs and groans
in the assembly in general; some weeping for themselves; others for their friends. Although persons are
doubtless much more easily affected now than they
were in the beginning of this religious concern, when
tears and cries for their souls were things unheard of
among them; yet I must say that their affection in general appeared genuine and unfeigned; and especially
this appeared very conspicuous in those newly awakened. So that true and genuine convictions of sin seem
still to be begun and promoted in many instances.

Twenty three of the Indians in all have now pro-

fessed their faith in Christ.   Most of them belonged to
this region, a few to the Forks of Delaware.—Through
rich grace, none of them as yet have been left to disgrace their profession by any scandalous or unbecoming behavior.

"I might now properly make many REMARKS on a
work of grace so very remarkable as this has been in
various respects; but shall confine myself to a few general hints only.

1. "It is remarkable that God began this work
among the Indians at a time when I had *the least hope*,
and, to my apprehension, the least rational prospect of
seeing a work of grace propagated among them: my
bodily strength being then much wasted by a late tedious journey to the Susquehanna, where I was necessarily exposed to hardships and fatigues among the Indians; my mind being also exceedingly depressed with
a view of the unsuccessfulness of my labors. I had
little reason so much as to hope that God had made
me instrumental in the saving conversion of any of
the Indians, except my Interpreter and his wife.
Hence I was ready to look upon myself as a burden to
the Society which employed and supported me in this
business, and began to entertain serious thoughts of
giving up my *mission;* and almost resolved I would
do so at the conclusion of the present year, if I had
then no better prospect of success in my work than I
had hitherto had. I cannot say that I entertained these
thoughts because I was weary of the labors and fatigues which necessarily attended my present business,
or because I had light and freedom in my own mind
to turn any other way; but purely through dejection
of spirit, pressing discouragement, and an apprehen-

sion of its being unjust to spend money consecrated to religious uses, only to *civilize* the Indians, and bring them to an *external* profession of Christianity. This was all which I could then see any prospect of effecting, while God seemed, as I thought, evidently to frown upon the design of their saving conversion, by withholding the convincing and renewing influences of his blessed Spirit from attending the means which I had hitherto used with them for that end.

"In this frame of mind I first visited these Indians at Crossweeksung; apprehending that it was my indispensable duty, seeing I had heard there was a number in these parts, to make some attempts for their conversion to God, though I cannot say I had any hope of success, my spirits being now so extremely sunk. I do not know that my hopes respecting the conversion of the Indians were ever reduced to so low an ebb, since I had any special concern for them, as at this time. Yet *this* was the very season in which God saw fit to begin this glorious work! Thus he 'ordained strength out of weakness,' by making bare his almighty arm at a time when all hopes and human probabilities most evidently appeared to fail.—Whence I learn, that *it is good to follow the path of duty, though in the midst of darkness and discouragement.*

2. "It is remarkable how God providentially, and in a manner almost *unaccountable,* called these Indians together to be instructed in the great things that concerned their souls: and how he seized their minds with the most solemn and weighty concern for their eternal salvation, as fast as they came to the place where his word was preached. When I first came into these parts in June, I found not one man at the place I visited, but only four women and a few children; but

befcre I had been here many days, they gathered from
all quarters, some from more than twenty miles; and
when I made them a second visit in the beginning of
August, some came more than forty miles to hear me.
Many came without any intelligence of what was going on here, and consequently without any design of
theirs, so much as to gratify their curiosity.   Thus it
seemed as if God had summoned them together from
all quarters for nothing else but to deliver his message
to them; and that he did this, with regard to some of
them, without making use of any human means, although there was pains taken by some of them to give
notice to others at remote places.

"Nor is it less surprising that they were one after
another affected with a solemn concern for their souls,
almost as soon as they came upon the spot where divine truths were taught them.   I could not but think
often, that their coming to the place of our public worship, was like Saul and his messengers coming among
the prophets; they no sooner came but they prophesied;
and these were almost as soon affected with a sense of
their sin and misery, and with an earnest concern for
deliverance, as they made their appearance in our assembly.   After this work of grace began with power
among them, it was common for *strangers* of the Indians, before they had been with us one day, to be much
awakened, deeply convinced of their sin and misery,
and to inquire with great solicitude, 'What they should
do to be saved?'

3.   "It is likewise remarkable how God preserved
these poor ignorant Indians *from being prejudiced
against me*, and the truths I taught them, by those
means that were used with them for that purpose by
ungodly people.   There were many attempts made by

some ill-minded persons of the white people to prejudice them against, or frighten them from Christianity.
They sometimes told them, that the Indians were well
enough already;—that there was no need of all this
noise about Christianity;—that if they were Christians
they would be in no better, no safer, or happier state,
than they were already in.   Sometimes they told them,
that I was a knave, a deceiver, and the like; that I daily
taught them lies, and had no other design but to im-
pose upon them.   When none of these, and such like
suggestions, would avail to their purpose, they then
tried another expedient, and told the Indians, 'My design was to gather together as large a body of them as
I possibly could, and sell them to England for slaves;'
than which nothing could be more likely to terrify the
Indians, they being naturally of a jealous disposition,
and the most averse to a state of servitude perhaps of
any people living.

"But all these wicked insinuations, through divine
goodness over-ruling, constantly turned against the
authors of them, and only served to engage the affections of the Indians more firmly to me; for they, being
awakened to a solemn concern for their souls, could
not but observe, that the persons who endeavored to
embitter their minds against me, were altogether unconcerned about their own souls, and not only so, but
vicious and profane; and thence could not but argue,
that if they had no concern for their *own*, it was not
likely they should have for the souls of *others*.

"It seems yet the more wonderful that the Indians
were preserved from once harkening to these suggestions, inasmuch as I was an utter stranger among
them, and could give them no assurance of my sincere
affection to, and concern for them, by any thing that

was past,—while the persons who insinuated these
things were their old acquaintance, who had frequent
opportunities of gratifying their *thirsty appetites* with
strong drink, and consequently, doubtless had the
greatest interest in their affections. But from this instance of their preservation from fatal prejudices, I
have had occasion, with admiration, to say, 'If God
will work, who can hinder?'

4. "Nor is it less wonderful how God was pleased
to provide a *remedy* for my want of skill and freedom
in the Indian language, by remarkably fitting my Interpreter for, and assisting him in the performance of his
work. It might reasonably be supposed I must needs
labor under a vast disadvantage in addressing the Indians by an Interpreter; and that divine truths would
undoubtedly lose much of the *energy* and *pathos* with
which they might at first be delivered, by reason of
their coming to the audience from a second hand. But
although this has often, to my sorrow and discouragement, been the case in times past, when my Interpreter had little or no sense of divine things; yet now it
was quite otherwise. I cannot think my addresses to
the Indians ordinarily, since the beginning of this season of grace have lost any thing of the power or pungency with which they were made, unless it were sometimes for want of pertinent and pathetic terms and expressions in the Indian language; which difficulty
could not have been much redressed by my personal
acquaintance with their language. My Interpreter had
before gained some good degree of doctrinal knowledge, whereby he was rendered capable of understanding, and communicating, without mistakes, the intent
and meaning of my discourses, and that without being
confined strictly, and obliged to interpret verbatim.

He had likewise, to appearance, an experimental acquaintance with divine things; and it pleased God at this season to inspire his mind with longing desires for the conversion of the Indians, and to give him admirable zeal and fervency in addressing them in order thereto. It is remarkable, that, when I was favored with any special assistance in any work, and enabled to speak with more than common freedom, fervency, and power, under a lively and affecting sense of divine things, he was usually affected in the same manner almost instantly, and seemed at once quickened and enabled to speak in the same pathetic language, and under the same influence that I did. A *surprising ener-gy* often accompanied the word at such seasons; so that the face of the whole assembly would be apparently changed almost in an instant, and tears and sobs become common among them.

" He also appeared to have such a clear doctrinal view of God's usual methods of dealing with souls under a preparatory work of conviction and humiliation as he never had before; so that I could, with his help, discourse freely with the distressed persons about their internal exercises, their fears, discouragements, temptations, &c. He likewise took pains, day and night, to repeat and inculcate upon the minds of the Indians the truths which I taught them daily; and this he appeared to do, not from spiritual pride, and an affectation of setting himself up as a public teacher, but from a spirit of faithfulness, and an honest concern for their souls.

" His conversation among the Indians has likewise, so far as I know, been savory, as becomes a Christian, and a person employed in his work; and I may justly say, he has been a great comfort to me, and a great instrument of promoting this good work among the In-

dians; so that whatever be the state of his own soul, it
is apparent God has remarkably fitted him for this
work. Thus God has manifested that, without bestow-
ing on me the *gift of tongues*, he could find a way
wherein I might be as effectually enabled to convey
the truths of his glorious Gospel to the minds of these
poor benighted pagans.

5. " It is further remarkable, that God has carried on
his work here by *such means*, and in *such a manner*,
as tended to obviate, and leave no room for those prejudices and objections which have often been raised
against such a work. When persons have been awakened to a solemn concern for their souls, by hearing
the more awful truths of God's word, and the terrors·
of the divine law insisted upon, it has usually in such
cases been objected by some, that such persons were
only frighted with a fearful noise of hell and damnation; and that there was no evidence that their concern was the effect of a divine influence. But God
has left no room for this objection in the present case;
*this work of grace having been begun and carried on
by almost one continued strain of Gospel invitation to
perishing sinners.* This may reasonably be guessed,
from a view of the passages of Scripture I chiefly insisted upon in my discourses from time to time; which
I have for that purpose inserted in my diary.

" Nor have I ever seen so general an awakening in
any assembly in my life as appeared here while I was
opening and insisting upon the parable of the great
supper. Luke, 14. In which discourse I was enabled
to set before my hearers the unsearchable riches of
Gospel grace. Not that I would be understood here
that I never instructed the Indians respecting their
fallen state, and the sinfulness and misery of it; for

this was what I at first chiefly insisted upon with them, and endeavored to repeat and inculcate in almost every discourse, knowing that without this foundation I should but build upon the sand, and that it would be in vain to invite them to Christ unless I could convince them of their need of him. Mark, 2 : 17.

"But still this great awakening, this surprising concern, was never excited by any harangues of terror, but always appeared most remarkable when I insisted upon the compassion of a dying Savior, the plentiful provisions of the Gospel, and the free offers of divine grace to needy, distressed sinners. Nor would I be understood to insinuate, that such a religious concern might justly be suspected as not being genuine and from a divine influence, if produced from the preaching of terror; for this is perhaps God's more usual way of awakening sinners, and appears entirely agreeable to Scripture and sound reason. But what I meant here to observe is, that God saw fit to employ and bless milder means for the effectual awakening of these Indians, and thereby obviated the forementioned objection, which the world might otherwise have had a more plausible color of making.

"As there has been no room for any plausible objection against this work, with regard to the *means*, so neither with regard to the *manner* in which it has been carried on. It is true, persons' concern for their souls have been exceeding great; the convictions of their sin and misery have arisen to a high degree, and produced many tears, cries, and groans; but then they have not been attended with those disorders, either bodily or mental, which have sometimes prevailed among persons under religious impressions. There has here been no appearance of those convulsions, bodily agonies,

frightful screamings, swoonings, and the like, which
have been so much complained of in some places; although there have been some, who, with the jailer,
have been made to *tremble* under a sense of their sin
and misery, and have been made to cry out from a distressing view of their perishing state.

" Nor has there been any appearance of mental disorders here, such as *visions, trances, imaginations* of
being under prophetic inspiration, and the like; or
scarce any unbecoming disposition to appear remarkably affected either with concern or joy; though I must
confess I observed one or two persons, whose concern
I thought was in a considerable measure affected; and
one whose joy appeared to be of the same kind. But
these workings of spiritual pride I endeavored to crush
in their first appearances, and have not since observed
any affection, either of joy or sorrow, but what appeared genuine and unaffected. But,

Lastly. The *effects* of this work have likewise been
very remarkable. I doubt not but that many of these
people have gained more *doctrinal* knowledge of divine
truths since I first visited them in June last, than could
have been instilled into their minds by the most diligent use of proper and instructive means for whole
years together, without such a divine influence. Their
pagan notions and idolatrous practices seem to be entirely abandoned in these parts. They are regulated,
and appear regularly disposed in the affairs of marriage; an instance whereof I have given in my journal
of August 14. They seem generally divorced from
drunkenness, their darling vice, the ' sin that easily
besets them;' so that I do not know of more than two
or three, who have been my *steady hearers*, that have
drank to excess since I first visited them; although be-

fore it was common for some or other of them to be
drunk almost every day: and some of them seem now
to fear this sin in particular, more than death itself. A
principle of honesty and justice appears in many of
them ; and they seem concerned to discharge their old
debts, which they have neglected, and perhaps scarcely thought of for years past. Their manner of living
is much more decent and comfortable than formerly,
having now the benefit of that money which they used
to consume upon strong drink. Love seems to reign
among them, especially those who have given evidences of having passed a saving change: and I never
saw any appearance of bitterness or censoriousness in
these, nor any disposition to 'esteem themselves better
than others,' who had not received the like mercy.

"As their sorrows under convictions have been great
and pressing, so many of them have since appeared to
'rejoice with joy unspeakable, and full of glory ;' and
yet I never saw any thing ecstatic or flighty in their
joy. Their consolations do not incline them to light-
ness ; but, on the contrary, are attended with solemnity, and often times with tears, and an apparent brokenness of heart, as may be seen in several passages of my
diary. In this respect some of them have been surprised at themselves, and have with concern observed
to me, that ' when their hearts have been glad,' which
is a phrase they commonly make use of to express
spiritual joy, ' they could not help crying for all.'

"And now, upon the whole, I think I may justly
say, that here are all the symptoms and evidences of a
remarkable work of grace among these Indians, which
can reasonably be desired or expected. May the *great
Author* of this work maintain and promote the same
here, and propagate it *every where*, till 'the whole earth
be filled with his glory !' Amen.

"I have now rode more than three thousand miles, of which I have kept an exact account, since the beginning of March last, and almost the whole of it has been in my own proper business as a *missionary*, upon the design, either immediately or more remotely, of propagating *Christian knowledge* among the Indians. I have taken pains to look out for a colleague or companion, to travel with me; and have likewise used endeavors to procure something for his support, among religious persons in New-England, which cost me a journey of several hundred miles; but have not, as yet, found any person qualified and disposed for this good work, although I had some encouragement from ministers and others, that it was hoped a maintenance might be procured for one, when *the man* should be found.

"I have likewise of late represented to the gentlemen concerned with this mission, the necessity of having an English *school* speedily set up among these Indians, who are now willing to be at the pains of gathering together in a body, for this purpose. In order thereto, I have humbly proposed to them the collecting of money for the maintenance of a schoolmaster, and the defraying of other necessary charges, in the promotion of this good work; which they are now attempting in the several congregations of Christians to which they respectively belong.

"The several companies of Indians to whom I have preached in the summer past, live at *great distances* from each other. It is more than *seventy miles* from Crossweeksung, in New-Jersey, to the Forks of Delaware in Pennsylvania; and thence to sundry of the Indian settlements which I visited on the Susquehanna, is more than an *hundred and twenty* miles. So much of my time is necessarily consumed in journeying, that I can have but little for *any* of my necessary studies, and consequently for the study of the Indian languages in particular; and especially seeing I am obliged to discourse so frequently to the Indians at each of these places while I am with them, in order to redeem time to visit the rest. I am, at times, almost discouraged from attempting to gain any acquaintance with the Indian languages, they are so very numerous; some account of which I gave in my diary of May last; and especially, seeing my other labors and fatigues engross almost the whole of my time, and bear exceedingly hard upon my *constitution*, so that my health is much impaired. However, I have taken considerable pains to learn the Delaware language, and propose still to do so, as far as my other business and bodily health will admit. I have already made some proficiency in it, though I have labored under many and great disadvantages in my attempts of that nature. It is but just to observe here, that all the pains I took to acquaint myself with the language of the Indians with whom I spent my first year, were of little or no service to me here among the Delawares; so that my work, when I came among these Indians, was all to be begun anew.

"As these poor ignorant pagans stood in need of having 'line upon line, and precept upon precept,' in order to their being instructed and grounded in the principles of Christianity; so I preached 'publicly, and taught from house to house,' almost every day for whole weeks together, when I was with them. My *public* discourses did not then make up the one half of my work, while there were so many constantly coming to me with that important inquiry, 'What must we do to be saved ?' and opening to me the various exercises of their minds. Yet I can say, to the praise of divine grace, that the apparent success, with which my labors were crowned, unspeakably more than compensated for the labor itself, and was likewise a great means of supporting and carrying me through the business and fatigues under which, it seems, my nature would have sunk without such an encouraging prospect. But although this success has afforded matter of support, comfort, and thankfulness; yet in this season I have found great need of assistance in my work, and have been much oppressed for want of one to bear a part of my labors and hardships. ' May the Lord of the harvest send forth *other laborers* into this part of his harvest, that those who sit in darkness may see great light; and that the whole earth may be filled with the knowledge of himself! Amen.' "

CHAPTER VIII

Being part 2d of his public journal of " the Continuance and Progress of a remarkable work of grace among the Indians in New-Jersey and Pennsylvania, kept by order of the Society in Scotland for propagating Christian knowledge."—Renewal of labor at Crossweeksung—outpouring of the spirit—remarkable case—signal displays of divine power—a convert—a number of Christian Indians accompany him to the Forks of Delaware—striking conversion at Crossweeksung—day of fasting—Lord's supper—conversion of a Conjurer—general remarks on the preceding narrative.

Nov. 5, 1745.—June 19, 1746

Crossweeksung, New-Jersey, 1745

Lord's day, Nov. 24.—" Preached both parts of the day from the story of Zaccheus. Luke, 19 : 1-9. In the latter exercise, when I opened and insisted upon the salvation that comes to a sinner upon his becoming a son of Abraham, or a true believer, the word seemed to be attended with divine power to the hearts of the hearers. Numbers were much affected with divine truth; former convictions were revived; one or two persons newly awakened; and a most affectionate engagement in divine service appeared among them universally. The impressions they were under appeared to be the genuine effect of God's word brought home to their hearts by the power and influence of the Divine Spirit.

Nov. 26.—" After having spent some time in private conferences with my people, I discoursed publicly among them from John, 5 : 1–9. I was favored with some special freedom and fervency in my discourse, and a powerful energy accompanied divine truth. Many wept and sobbed affectionately, and scarcely any appeared unconcerned in the whole assembly. The influence which seized the audience appeared gentle, and yet pungent and efficacious. It produced no boisterous commotion of the passions; but seemed deeply to affect the heart, and excite in the persons under convictions of their lost state, heavy groans and tears; and in others, who had obtained comfort, a sweet and humble melting. It seemed like the gentle but steady showers which effectually water the earth, without violently beating upon the surface. The persons lately awakened were some of them deeply distressed for their souls, and appeared earnestly solicitous to obtain an interest in Christ; and some of them, after public worship was over, in anguish of spirit, said 'they knew not what to do, nor how to get their wicked hearts changed,' &c.

Nov. 28.—" Discoursed to the Indians publicly, after
having used some private endeavors to instruct and
excite some in the duties of Christianity. Opened and
made remarks upon the sacred story of our Lord's
transfiguration. Luke, 9 : 28–36. Had a principal view
in insisting upon this passage of Scripture to the edification and consolation of God's people. Observed
some, that I have reason to think are truly such, exceedingly affected with an account of the glory of Christ
in his transfiguration, and filled with longing desires of
being with him, that they might with open face behold
his glory.

" After public service was over, I asked one of them,
who wept and sobbed most affectionately, what she
now wanted ? She replied, ' O, to be with Christ.
She did not know how to stay,' &c. This was a
blessed refreshing season to the religious people in general. The Lord Jesus Christ seemed to manifest his
divine glory to them, as when transfigured before his
disciples; and they were ready, with the disciples, universally to say, ' Lord it is good for us to be here.'

" The influence of God's word was not confined to
those who had given evidence of being truly gracious:
though at this time I calculated my discourse for and
directed it chiefly to such. But it appeared to be a
season of divine power in the whole assembly; so that
most were in some measure affected. One aged man,
in particular, lately awakened, was now brought under
a deep and pressing concern for his soul, was now
earnestly inquisitive ' how he might find Jesus Christ.'
God seems still to vouchsafe his divine presence, and
the influence of his blessed Spirit to accompany his
word, at least in some measure, in all our meetings for
divine worship.

Nov. 30.—" Preached near night, after having spent some hours in private conference with some of my people about their souls' concerns. Explained the story of the rich man and Lazarus. Luke, 16 : 19–26. The word made powerful impressions upon many in the assembly, especially while I discoursed of the blessedness of Lazarus in Abraham's bosom. This I could perceive affected them much more than what I spoke of the rich man's misery and torments; and thus it has been usually with them. They have almost always appeared much more affected with the comfortable than the dreadful truths of God's word. That which has distressed many of them under conviction is, that they found they wanted and could not obtain the happiness of the godly; at least they have often appeared to be more affected with this than with the terrors of hell. But whatever be the means of their awakening, it is plain, numbers are made deeply sensible of their sin and misery, the wickedness and stubbornness of their own hearts, their utter inability to help themselves, or to come to Christ for help without divine assistance, and so are brought to see their perishing need of Christ to do all for them, and to lie at the foot of sovereign mercy.

Lord's day, Dec. 1.—" Discoursed to my people in the forenoon from Luke, 16 : 27–31. There appeared an unfeigned affection in many, and some seemed deeply impressed with divine truth. In the afternoon preached to a number of white people; at which time the Indians attended with diligence, and many of them were able to understand a considerable part of the discourse. At night discoursed to my people again, and gave them particular cautions and directions relating to their conduct in divers respects, and pressed them to watchfulness in their deportment, seeing they were encompassed with those who waited for their halting, and who stood ready to draw them into temptations of every kind, and then to expose religion by their missteps.

Lord's day, Dec. 8.—" Discoursed on the story of the blind man. John, 9. There appeared no remarkable effect of the word upon the assembly at this time. The persons who have lately been much concerned for their souls seemed now not so affected or solicitous to obtain an interest in Christ as has been usual, although they attended divine service with seriousness and diligence. Such have been the doings of the Lord here in awakening sinners, and affecting the hearts of those who are brought to solid comfort, with a fresh sense of divine things from time to time, that it is now strange to see the assembly sit with dry eyes, and without sobs and groans.

Dec. 12.—" Preached from the parable of the *Ten Virgins.* Matt. 25. The divine power seemed in some measure to attend this discourse; in which I was favored with uncommon freedom and plainness of address, and enabled to open divine truths, and explain them to the capacities of my people in a manner beyond myself. There appeared in many persons an affectionate concern for their souls, although the concern in general seemed not so deep and pressing as it had formerly done. Yet it was refreshing to see many melted into tears and unaffected sobs; some with a sense of divine love, and some for the want of it.

Dec. 15.—" Preached to the Indians from Luke, 13 : 24-28. Divine truth fell with weight and power upon the audience, and seemed to reach the hearts of many. Near night discoursed to them again from

Matt. 25 : 31–46. At this season also the word appeared to be accompanied with a divine influence, and made powerful impressions upon the assembly in general, as well as upon numbers in a very special and particular manner. This was an amazing season of grace. The word of the Lord this day ' was quick and powerful, sharper than a two-edged sword,' and pierced the hearts of many. The assembly was greatly affected and deeply wrought upon; yet without so much apparent commotion of the passions as appeared in the beginning of this work of grace. The impressions made by the word of God upon the audience appeared solid, rational, and deep ; worthy of the solemn truths by means of which they were produced, and far from being the effects of any sudden fright, or groundless perturbation of mind. O how did the hearts of the hearers seem to bow under the weight of divine truth, and how evident did it now appear that they received and felt them, ' not as the word of man, but as the word of God.' None can form a just idea of the appearance of our assembly at this time, but those who have seen a congregation solemnly awed, and deeply impressed by the special power and influence of divine truths delivered to them in the name of God.

Dec. 16.—" Discoursed to my people in the evening from Luke, 11 : 1–13. After having insisted some time upon the ninth verse, wherein there is a command and encouragement to ask for the divine favor, I called upon them to ask for a new heart with the utmost importunity, as the man mentioned in the parable, on which I was discoursing, pleaded for loaves of bread at midnight. There was much affection and concern in the assembly, and especially one woman appeared in great distress for her soul. She was brought to such an agony in seeking after Christ, that the sweat ran off her face for a considerable time, though the evening was very cold; and her bitter cries were the most affecting indications of her heart.

Dec. 21.—" My people having now attained to a considerable degree of knowledge in the principles of christianity; I thought it proper to set up a catechetical lecture among them, and this evening attempted something in that form, proposing questions to them agreeably to the Assembly's Shorter Catechism, receiving their answers, and then explaining and insisting, as appeared necessary and proper upon each question. After this I endeavored to make some practical improvement of the whole. This was the method I entered upon. They were able readily and rationally to answer many important questions which I proposed to them; so that upon trial I found their doctrinal knowledge to exceed my own expectations. In the improvement of my discourse, when I came to infer and open the blessedness of those who have so great and glorious a God as had before been spoken of, ' for their everlasting friend and portion,' several were much affected; and especially when I exhorted, and endeavored to persuade them to be reconciled to God through his dear Son, and thus to secure an interest in his everlasting favor. So that they appeared not only enlightened and instructed, but affected, and engaged in their soul's concerns by this method of discoursing.

Lord's day, Dec. 22.—" Discoursed upon the story of the young man in the Gospel. Matt. 9 : 16–22. God made it a seasonable word, I am persuaded, to some souls, and in particular to one, the same mentioned in my journal of the 16th instant, who never before obtained any settled comfort, though I have abundant reason to think she had passed a saving change some days before. She now appeared in a heavenly frame of mind, composed and delighted with the divine will. When I came to discourse particularly with her, and to inquire of her how she obtained relief and deliverance from the spiritual distresses which she had lately suffered, she answered, in broken English, '*Me try, me try save myself; last, my strength be all gone;* (meaning her ability to save herself;) *could not me stir bit further. Den last me forced let Jesus Christ alone send me hell, if he please.*' I said, 'But you was not willing to go to hell, was you?' She replied, '*Could not me help it. My heart, he would wicked for all. Could not me make him good,*' (meaning, she saw it was right she should go to hell, because her heart was wicked, and would be so after all she could do to mend it.) I asked her how she got out of this case. She answered still in the same broken language, '*By by, my heart be glad desperately.*' I asked her why her heart was glad? She replied, '*Glad my heart, Jesus Christ do what he please with me. Did not me care where he put me; love him for all,*' &c. She could not readily be convinced but that she was willing to go to hell if Christ was pleased to send her there; although the truth evidently was, that her will was so swallowed up in the divine will that she could not frame any hell in her imagination which would be dreadful or undesirable, provided it was the will of God to send her to it. Toward night discoursed to them again in the catechetical method which I entered upon the evening before. When I came to improve the truth which I had explained to them, and to answer that question, 'But how shall I know whether God has chosen me to everlasting life?' by pressing them to come and give up their hearts to Christ, and thereby ' to make their election sure,' they then appeared much affected, and the persons under concern were afresh engaged in seeking after an interest in him; while some others, who had obtained comfort before, were refreshed to find that love to God in themselves which was an evidence of his electing love to them.

Dec. 25.—" The Indians having been used on Christmas days to drink and revel among some of the white people in these parts, I thought it proper this day to call them together and discourse to them upon divine things; which I accordingly did from the parable of the barren fig-tree. Luke, 13 : 6–9. A divine influence, I am persuaded, accompanied the word at this season. The power of God appeared in the assembly, not by producing any remarkable cries, but by rousing several stupid creatures who were scarcely ever moved with any concern before. The power attending divine truth seemed to have the influence of the earthquake rather than of the whirlwind upon them. Their passions were not so much alarmed as has been common here in times past, but their judgments appeared to be powerfully convinced by the masterly and conquering influence of divine truth. The impressions made upon the assembly in general, seemed not superficial, but deep, and heart affecting. O how ready did they now appear universally to embrace and comply with every thing which they heard, and were convinced was their duty. God was in the midst of us, of a truth, bowing and melting stubborn hearts! How many tears and sobs were then to be seen and heard among us! What liveliness and strict attention! What eagerness and intenseness of mind appeared in the whole assembly, in the time of divine service. They seemed to watch and wait for the droppings of God's word, as the thirsty earth, for the 'former and latter rain.'

"Afterward I discoursed to them on the duty of husbands and wives, from Eph. 5 : 22–33, and have reason to think this was a word in season. Spent some time further in the evening in inculcating the truths on which I had insisted in my former discourse, respecting the barren fig-tree; and observed a powerful influence still accompany what was spoken.

Dec. 26.—" This evening was visited by a person under great spiritual distress; the most remarkable instance of this kind I ever saw. She was, I believe, more than *fourscore* years old; and appeared to be much broken and very childish, through age; so that it seemed impossible for man to instil into her any notions of divine things; not so much as to give her any doctrinal instruction, because she seemed incapable of being taught. She was led by the hand into my house, and appeared in extreme anguish. I asked her what ailed her? She answered, '*her heart was distressed, and she feared she should never find Christ.*' I asked her when she began to be concerned, with divers other questions relating to her distress. To all which she answered, for substance, to this effect : '*That she had heard me preach many times, but never knew any thing about it, never felt it in her heart, till the last Sabbath, and then it came,*' she said, '*as if a needle had been thrust into her heart; since which time she had no rest day nor night.*' She added, '*that on the evening before Christmas, a number of Indians being together, at the house where she was, and discoursing about Christ, their talk pricked her heart so that she could not set up, but fell down in her bed; at which time she went away,*' as she expressed it, '*and felt as if she dreamed, and*

*yet is confident she did not dream. When she was thus
gone, she saw two paths; one appeared very broad
and crooked; and that turned to the left hand. The
other appeared straight and very narrow; and that
went up the hill to the right hand. She traveled,'* she
said, *'for some time up the narrow right hand path, till
at length something seemed to obstruct her journey.
She sometimes called it darkness; and then described it
otherwise, and seemed to compare it to a block or bar.
She then remembered what she had heard me say about
striving to enter in at the straight gate, although she
took little notice of it at the time when she heard me discourse upon that subject; and thought she would climb
over this bar. But just as she was thinking of this, she
came back again,'* as she termed it, meaning that she
came to herself; *'whereupon her soul was extremely
distressed, apprehending that she had now turned back,
and forsaken Christ, and that there was therefore no
hope of mercy for her.'*

"As I was sensible that trances, and imaginary views
of things are of dangerous tendency in religion, where
sought after and depended upon; so I could not but be
much concerned about this exercise, especially at first;
apprehending this might be a design of satan to bring
a blemish upon the work of God here, by introducing
visionary scenes, imaginary terrors, and all manner of
mental disorders and delusions, in the room of genuine
convictions of sin, and the enlightening influences of
the blessed Spirit; and I was almost resolved to declare,
that I looked upon this to be one of satan's devices,
and to caution my people against this and similar exercises of that nature. However, I determined first to
inquire into her knowledge, to see whether she had
any just views of things, that might be the occasion of

her present distressing concern, or whether it was a
mere fright, arising only from imaginary terrors. I
asked her numerous questions respecting man's primitive, and more especially, his present state, and respecting her own heart; which she answered rationally,
and to my surprise. I thought it next to impossible, if
not altogether so, that a Pagan, who was become a
child through age, should in that state gain so much
knowledge by any mere human instruction, without
being remarkably enlightened by a divine influence.
I then proposed to her the provision made in the gospel for the salvation of sinners, and the ability and
willingness of Christ 'to save to the uttermost all, old
as well as young, that come to him.' To this she
seemed to give a hearty assent; but instantly replied,
'Ay, but I cannot come; my wicked heart will not come
to Christ; I do not know how to come,' &c. This she
spoke in anguish of spirit, striking on her breast, with
tears in her eyes, and with such earnestness in her
looks as was indeed piteous and affecting. She seems
to be really convinced of her sin and misery, and her
need of a change of heart. Her concern is abiding
and constant, so that nothing appears why this exercise may not have a saving issue. Indeed there seems
reason to hope such an issue, seeing she is so solicitous
to obtain an interest in Christ, that her heart, as she
expresses it, *prays day and night*.

"How far God may make use of the imagination in
awakening some persons under these, and similar circumstances, I cannot pretend to determine. Or, whether this exercise be from a divine influence, I shall leave
others to judge. But this I must say, that its effects
hitherto bespeak it to be such; nor can it, as I see, be
accounted for in any rational way, but from the influ-

ence of some spirit either good or evil. The woman, I am sure never heard divine things in the manner in which she now viewed them; and it would seem strange that she should get such a rational notion of them from the mere working of her own fancy, without some superior, or at least foreign aid. Yet I must say, I have looked upon it as one of the glories of this work of grace among the Indians, and a special evidence of its being from a divine influence, that there has, till now, been no appearance of such things, no visionary notions, trances, and imaginations, intermixed with those rational convictions of sin, and solid consolations, of which numbers have been made the subjects. And might I have had my desire, there had been no appearance of any thing of this nature at all.

Dec. 28. "Discoursed to my people in the catechetical method on which I lately entered. In the improvement of my discourse, wherein I was comparing man's present with his primitive state, and showing from what he had fallen, and the miseries in which he is now involved, and to which he is exposed in his natural estate; and pressing sinners to take a view of their deplorable circumstances without Christ, as also to strive that they might obtain an interest in him; the Lord, I trust, granted a remarkable influence of his blessed Spirit to accompany what was spoken; and a great concern appeared in the assembly. Many were melted into tears and sobs; and the impressions made upon them seemed deep and heart-affecting. In particular, there were two or three persons who appeared to be brought to the last exercises of a preparatory work, and reduced almost to extremity; being in a great measure convinced of the impossibility of their helping themselves, or of mending their own hearts; and seemed to be upon the point of giving up all hope in themselves, and of venturing upon Christ, as poor, helpless, and undone. Yet they were in distress and anguish because they saw no safety in so doing, unless they could do something toward saving themselves. One of these persons was the very aged woman above-mentioned, who now appeared 'weary and heavy laden' with a sense of her sin and misery, and her perishing need of an interest in Christ.

Lord's day, Dec. 29.—"Preached from John, 3: 1–5. A number of white people were present, as is usual upon the Sabbath. The discourse was accompanied with power, and seemed to have a silent, but deep and piercing influence upon the audience. Many wept and sobbed affectionately. There were some tears among the white people as well as the Indians. Some could not refrain from crying out; though there were not many so exercised. But the impressions made upon their hearts appeared chiefly by the extraordinary earnestness of their attention, and their heavy sighs and tears.

"After public worship was over I went to my house, proposing to preach again after a short season of intermission. But they soon came in, one after another, with tears in their eyes, to know '*what they should do to 'e saved.*' The divine Spirit in such a manner set home upon their hearts what I spake to them that the house was soon filled with cries and groans. They all flocked together upon this occasion; and those, whom I had reason to think in a Christless state, were almost universally seized with concern for their souls. It was an amazing season of power among them; and seemed as if God had bowed the heavens and come down. So astonishingly prevalent was the operation upon old as

well as young, that it seemed as if none would be left
in a secure and natural state, but that God was now
about to convert all the world. I was ready to think,
then, that I should never again despair of the conversion of any man or woman living, be they who or what
they would.

"It is impossible to give a just and lively description
of the appearance of things at this season; at least such
as to convey a bright and adequate idea of the ef
fects of this influence. A number might now be seen
rejoicing that God had not taken away the powerful
influence of his blessed Spirit from this place; refreshed
to see so many striving to enter in at the strait gate;
and animated with such concern for them, that they
wanted to push them forward, as some of them expressed it. At the same time numbers both of men and women, old and young, might be seen in tears; and some
in anguish of spirit, appearing in their very countenances like condemned malefactors bound toward the
place of execution, with a heavy solicitude sitting in
their faces; so that there seemed here, as I thought, a
lively emblem of the solemn day of account: a mixture of heaven and hell; of joy and anguish inexpressible.

"The concern and religious affection was such, that
I could not pretend to have any formal religious exercise among them; but spent the time in discoursing to
one and another, as I thought most proper and seasonable for each; and sometimes addressed them altogether; and finally concluded with prayer. Such were their
circumstances at this season, that I could scarcely have
half an hour's rest from speaking, from about half an
hour before twelve o'clock, at which time I began public worship, till after seven at night. There appeared

to be four or five persons newly awakened this day and the evening before; some of whom but very lately came among us.

Dec. 30. "Was visited by four or five young persons under concern for their souls; most of whom were very lately awakened. They wept much while I discoursed with them and endeavored to press upon them the necessity of flying to Christ without delay for salvation.

Dec. 31.—"Spent some hours this day in visiting my people from house to house, and conversing with them about their spiritual concerns; endeavoring to press upon Christless souls the necessity of a renovation of heart; and scarce left a house without leaving some or other of its inhabitants in tears, appearing solicitously engaged to obtain an interest in Christ.

"The Indians are now gathered together from all quarters to this place, and have built them little cottages, so that more than *twenty families* live within a quarter of a mile from me. A very convenient situation with regard both to public and private instruction.

Jan. 1, 1746.—Spent considerable time in visiting my people again. Found scarcely one but what was under some serious impressions respecting their spiritual concerns.

Jan. 2.—"Visited some persons newly come among us, who had scarce ever heard any thing of Christianity before, except the empty name. Endeavored to instruct them, particularly in the first principles of religion, in the most easy and familiar manner I could. There are strangers from remote parts, almost continually dropping in among us, so that I have occasion repeatedly to open and inculcate the first principles of Christianity.

Jan. 4.—"Prosecuted my catechetical method of instructing. Found my people able to answer questions
with propriety, beyond what could have been expected
from persons so lately brought out of heathenish darkness. In the improvement of my discourse there appeared some concern and affection in the assembly;
and especially in those of whom I entertained hopes
as being truly gracious, at least several of them were
much affected and refreshed.

Lord's day, Jan. 5.—" Discoursed from Matt. 12 : 10
–13. There appeared not so much liveliness and affection in divine service as usual. The same truths which
have often produced many tears and sobs in the assembly seemed now to have no special influence upon
any in it. Near night I proposed to have proceeded
in my usual method of catechising; but while we were
engaged in the first prayer, the power of God seemed
to descend upon the assembly in such a remarkable
manner, and so many appeared under pressing concern for their souls, that I thought it much more expedient to insist upon the plentiful provision made by
divine grace for the redemption of perishing sinners,
and to press them to a speedy acceptance of the great
salvation, than to ask them questions about doctrinal
points. What was most practical seemed most seasonable to be insisted upon, while numbers appeared
so extraordinarily solicitous to obtain an interest in
the great Redeemer.

" This day the woman mentioned in my journal of
December 22, made a public profession of her faith.
She has discovered a very sweet and heavenly frame
of mind from time to time, since her first reception of
comfort. One morning in particular, she came to see
me, discovering an unusual joy and satisfaction in her

countenance; and when I inquired into the reason of it, she replied, 'that God had made her feel that it was right for him to do what he pleased with all things; and that it would be right if he should cast her husband and son both into hell; and she saw it was so right for God to do what he pleased with them, that she could not but rejoice in God even if he should send them into hell;' though it was apparent she loved them dearly. She moreover inquired whether I was not sent to preach to the Indians by some good people a great way off. I replied, 'Yes, by the good people in Scotland.' She answered, 'that her heart loved those good people so the evening before, that she could scarce help praying for them all night, her heart would go to God for them.' Thus, the blessing of those ready to perish, is like to come upon those pious persons who have communicated of their substance to the propagation of the Gospel.

Lord's day, Jan. 12.—" Preached from Isaiah, 55 : 6. The word of God seemed to fall upon the audience with a divine weight and influence, and evidently appeared to be 'not the word of man.' The blessed Spirit, I am persuaded, accompanied what was spoken to the hearts of many; so that there was a powerful revival of conviction in numbers who were under spiritual exercises before.

" Toward night catechised in my usual method. Near the close of my discourse there appeared a great concern, and much affection in the audience; which increased while I continued to invite them to come to an all-sufficient Redeemer for eternal salvation. The Spirit of God seems, from time to time, to be striving with souls here. They are so frequently and repeatedly roused, that they seem unable at present to lull themselves asleep.

Jan. 13.—" Was visited by several persons under deep concern for their souls; one of whom was newly awakened. It is a most agreeable work to treat with souls who are solicitously inquiring ' what they shall do to be saved.' As we are never to be ' weary in well doing,' so the obligation seems to be peculiarly strong when the work is so very desirable. Yet I must say, my health is so much impaired, and my spirits so wasted with my labors and solitary manner of living; there being no human creature in the house with me; that their repeated and almost incessant applications to me for help and direction, are sometimes exceedingly burdensome, and so exhaust my spirits that I become fit for nothing at all, entirely unable to prosecute my business, sometimes for days together. What contributes much toward this difficulty is, that I am obliged to spend much time in communicating a little matter to them ; there being oftentimes many things to be premised before I can speak directly to what I principally aim at; which things would readily be taken for granted where there was a competency of doctrinal knowledge.

Jan. 14.—" Spent some time in private conference with my people, and found some disposed to take comfort, as I thought, upon slight grounds. They are now generally awakened, and it is become so disgraceful, as well as terrifying to the conscience, to be destitute of religion, that they are in imminent danger of taking up with an appearance of grace, rather than to live under the fear and disgrace of an unregenerated state.

Jan. 18.—" Prosecuted my catechetical method of discoursing. There appeared a great solemnity, and some considerable affection in the assembly. This method of instruction I find very profitable. When I first entered upon it I was exercised with fears, lest my discourses would unavoidably be so doctrinal that they would tend only to enlighten the head, but not to affect the heart. But the event proved quite otherwise; for these exercises have hitherto been remarkably blessed in the latter, as well as the former respects.

Lord's day, Jan. 19.—" Discoursed to my people from Isaiah, 55 : 7. Toward night catechised in my ordinary method; and this appeared to be a powerful season of grace among us. Numbers were much affected. Convictions were powerfully revived, and Christians refreshed and strengthened; and one weary, heavy laden soul, I have abundant reason to hope, brought to true rest and solid comfort in Christ; who afterward gave me such an account of God's dealing with his soul as was abundantly satisfying, as well as refreshing to me.

" He told me he had often heard me say that persons must see and feel themselves utterly helpless and undone—that they must be emptied of a dependence upon themselves, and of all hope of saving themselves, in order to their coming to Christ for salvation. He had long been striving after this view of things; supposing that this would be an excellent frame of mind, to be thus emptied of a dependence upon his own goodness; that God would have respect to this frame, would then be well pleased with him, and bestow eternal life upon him. But when he came to feel himself in this helpless, undone condition, he found it quite contrary to all his thoughts and expectations; so that it was not the same frame, nor indeed any thing like the frame after which he had been seeking. Instead of its being a good frame of mind, he now found nothing but badness in himself, and saw it was for ever impossible for him to make himself any better. He wondered, he said, that he had ever hoped to mend his own heart. He was amazed that he had never before seen that it was utterly impossible for him, by all his contrivances and endeavors, to do any thing in that way, since the matter now appeared to him in so clear a light. Instead of imagining now that God would be pleased with him for the sake of this frame of mind, and this view of his undone estate, he saw clearly, and felt that it would be just with God to send him to eternal misery; and that there was no goodness in what he then felt; for he could not help seeing that he was naked, sinful, and miserable, and that there was nothing in such a sight to deserve God's love or pity.

" He saw these things in a manner so clear and convincing, that it seemed to him, he said, he could convince every body of their utter inability to help themselves, and their unworthiness of any help from God. In this frame of mind he came to public worship this evening; and while I was inviting sinners to come to Christ naked and empty, without any goodness of their own to recommend them to his acceptance, then he thought with himself that he had often tried to come and give up his heart to Christ, and he used to hope that some time or other he should be able to do so; but now he was convinced that he could not, and it seemed utterly vain for him ever to try any more; and he could not, he said, find a heart to make any further attempt, because he saw it would signify nothing at all; nor did he now hope for a better opportunity or more ability hereafter, as he had formerly done, because he saw and was fully convinced that his own strength would for ever fail.

While he was musing in this manner he saw, he

said, with his heart, (which is a common phrase among
them,) something that was unspeakably good and lovely, and what he had never seen before; and 'this stole
away his heart whether he would or no.' He did not,
he said, know what it was he saw. He did not say
'this is Jesus Christ;' but it was such glory and beauty
as he never saw before. He did not now give away
his heart, as he had formerly intended and attempted
to do; but *it went away of itself* after that glory he
then discovered. He used to make a bargain with
Christ to give up his heart to him that he might have
eternal life for it. But now he thought nothing about
himself or what would become of him hereafter; but
was pleased, and his mind wholly taken up with the
unspeakable excellency of what he then beheld. After
some time he was wonderfully pleased with the way
of salvation by Christ; so that it seemed unspeakably
desirable to be saved altogether by the mere free grace
of God in him. The consequence of this exercise is,
that he appears to retain a sense and relish of divine
things, and to maintain a life of seriousness and true
religion.

Jan. 28.—"The Indians in these parts have, in times
past, run themselves in debt by their excessive drinking; and some have taken the advantage of them, and
put them to trouble and charge, by arresting some of
them; whereby it was supposed their hunting lands in
great part were much endangered, and might speedily
be taken from them. Being sensible that they could
not subsist together in these parts, in order to their
being a Christian congregation, if these lands should
be taken, which was thought very likely; I thought it
my duty to use my utmost endeavors to prevent so unhappy an event. Having acquainted the gentlemen

concerned in this mission with the affair, according to the best information I could get of it, they thought it proper to expend the money which they had been and still were collecting for the religious interest of the Indians, at least a part of it, for discharging their debts, and securing these lands, that there might be no entanglement lying upon them to hinder the settlement and hopeful enlargement of a Christian congregation of Indians in these parts. Having received orders from them, I answered in behalf of the Indians, *eighty-two pounds, five shillings*, New-Jersey currency, at *eight shillings per ounce ;* and so prevented the danger or difficulty in this respect.

" As God has wrought a wonderful work of grace among these Indians, and now inclines others from remote places to fall in among them almost continually ; and as he has opened a door for the prevention of the difficulty now mentioned, which seemed greatly to threaten their religious interests as well as worldly comforts ; it is to be hoped that he designs to establish a church for himself among them, and hand down true religion to their posterity.

Jan. 30.—" Preached to the Indians from John, 3 : 16, 17.   There was a solemn attention and some affection visible in the audience ; especially several persons who had long been concerned for their souls, seemed afresh excited and engaged in seeking after an interest in Christ. One, with much concern, afterward told me 'his heart was so pricked with my preaching he knew not where to turn or what to do.'

Jan. 31.—"This day the person whom I had made choice of and engaged for a school master among the Indians arrived among us, and was heartily welcomed by my people universally. Whereupon I distributed several dozen of primers among the children and young people.

Feb. 1—"My schoolmaster entered upon his business among the Indians. He has generally about thirty children and young persons in his school in the day time, and about fifteen married people in the evening school. The number of married persons being less than it would be if they could be more constantly at home, and could spare time from their necessary employments for an attendance upon these instructions.

"In the evening catechised in my usual method. Toward the close of my discourse a surprising power seemed to attend the word, especially to some persons. One man considerably in years, who had been a remarkable drunkard, a conjurer and murderer, and was awakened some months before, was now brought to great extremity under his spiritual distress; so that he trembled for hours together, and apprehended himself just dropping into hell, without any power to rescue or relieve himself. Divers others appeared under great concern, as well as he, and solicitous to obtain a saving change.

Lord's day, Feb. 2.—" Preached from John, 5 : 24, 25. There appeared, as usual, some concern and affection in the assembly. Toward night proceeded in my usual method of catechising. Observed my people more ready in answering the questions proposed to them than ever before. It is apparent they advance daily in doctrinal knowledge. But what is still more desirable, the Spirit of God is yet operating among them; whereby experimental as well as speculative knowledge is propagated in their minds.

Feb. 5.—" Discoursed to a considerable number of Indians in the evening; at which time numbers of them appeared much affected and melted with divine things.

Feb. 8.—"Spent a considerable part of the day in

visiting my people from house to house, and conversing
with them about their souls concerns. Many persons
wept, while I discoursed to them, and appeared concerned for nothing so much as for an interest in the
great Redeemer. In the evening catechised as usual.
Divine truth made some impressions upon the audience; and were attended with an affectionate *engagement* of soul in some.

Lord's day, Feb. 9.—"Discoursed to my people from
the story of the blind man. Matt. 10 : 46–52. The
word of God seemed weighty, and powerful upon the
assembly at this time, and made considerable impressions upon many; several in particular, who have
generally been remarkably stupid and careless under
the means of grace, were now awakened, and wept affectionately. The most earnest attention, as well as
tenderness and affection, appeared in the audience universally. Two persons publicly professed Christ.

"Toward night catechised. God made this a powerful season to some. There were many affected. Former convictions appeared to be powerfully revived.
There was likewise one, who had been a vile drunkard,
remarkably awakened. He appeared to be in great
anguish of soul, wept, and trembled, and continued to
do so till near midnight. There was also a poor heavy
laden soul, who had been long under heavy distress, as
constant and pressing as I ever saw, who was now
brought to a comfortable calm, and seemed to be
bowed and reconciled to the divine sovereignty, and
told me she now felt and saw that it was right for
God to do with her as he pleased; and that her heart
felt pleased and satisfied it should be so; although of
late she had often found her heart rise and quarrel with
God because he would, *if he pleased*, send her to hell

after all she had done. She added that the heavy
burden she had lain under was now removed; that she
had tried to recover her concern and distress again,
fearing that the Spirit of God was departing from her,
and would leave her wholly careless, but that she could
not recover it; that she felt she never could do any
thing to save herself, but must perish for ever if Christ
did not do all for her; that she did not deserve he
should help her; and that it would be right if he should
leave her to perish. But Christ could save her though
she could do nothing to save herself, &c. and here she
seemed to rest."

Forks of Delaware, February, 1746

Lord's day, Feb. 16.—"Knowing that numbers of
the Indians in these parts were obstinately set against
Christianity; and that some of them had refused to
hear me preach in times past; I thought it might be
proper and beneficial to the Christian interest here to
have a number of my religious people from Crossweeksung with me, to converse with them about religious matters; hoping it might be a means to convince
them of the truth and importance of Christianity, to
see and hear some of their own nation discoursing of
divine things, and manifesting earnest desires that
others might be brought out of heathenish darkness,
as themselves were. For this purpose I selected half
a dozen of the most serious and intelligent of those
Indians, and having brought them to the Forks of Delaware, I this day met with them and the Indians of
this place. Numbers of the latter probably could not
have been prevailed upon to attend this meeting, had
it not been for these religious Indians who accompanied me hither, and preached to them   Some of those

who had in times past been extremely averse to Christianity, now behaved soberly; and some others laughed and mocked. However, the word of God fell with such weight and power, that numbers seemed to be stunned, and expressed a willingness to hear me again of these matters.

"Afterward prayed with, and made an address to the white people present; and could not but observe some visible effects of the word, such as tears and sobs among them. After public worship, spent some time, and took pains to convince those that mocked of the truth and importance of what I had been insisting upon; and so endeavored to awaken their attention to divine truth. Had reason to think, from what I observed then and afterward, that my endeavors took considerable effect upon one of the worst of them.

" Those few Indians then present, who used to be my hearers in these parts, some having removed hence to Crossweeksung, seemed somewhat kindly disposed toward me, and glad to see me again. They had been so much attacked, however, by some of the opposing Pagans, that they were almost ashamed or afraid to manifest their friendship.

Feb. 17.—" After having spent much time in discoursing to the Indians in their respective houses, I got them together and repeated and inculcated what I had before taught them. Afterward discoursed to them from Acts, 8 : 5–8. A divine influence seemed to attend the word. Several of the Indians here appeared to be somewhat awakened, and manifested earnest tears and sobs. My people of Crossweeksung continued with them day and night repeating and inculcating the truths I had taught them; and sometimes prayed and sung psalms among them ; discoursing with each other in their hearing, of the great things God had done for them and for the Indians from whence they came. This seemed, as my people told me, to have more effect upon them than when they directed their discourse immediately to them.

Feb. 18.—" Preached to an assembly of Irish people, nearly fifteen miles distant from the Indians.

Feb. 19.—" Preached to the Indians again, after having spent considerable time in conversing with them more privately. There appeared a great solemnity, and some concern and affection among the Indians belonging to these parts, as well as a sweet melting among those who came with me. Numbers of the Indians here seemed to have their prejudices and aversion to Christianity removed; and appeared well disposed, and inclined to hear the word of God.

Feb. 20.—" Preached to a small assembly of High Dutch people, who had seldom heard the Gospel preached, and were some of them, at least, very ignorant; but numbers of them have lately been put upon an inquiry after the way of Salvation with thoughtfulness. They gave wonderful attention; and some of them were much affected under the word, and afterward said, as I was informed, that they never had been so much enlightened about the way of Salvation in their whole lives before. They requested me to tarry with them, or come again and preach to them. It grieved me that I could not comply with their request. I could not but be affected with their circumstances: for they were as ' sheep not having a shepherd,' and some of them appeared under some degree of distress for sin; standing in peculiar need of the assistance of an experienced spiritual guide.

Feb. 21.—Preached to a number of people, many of

them Low Dutch. Several of the fore-mentioned High
Dutch people attended the sermon, though eight or ten
miles distant from their houses. Numbers of the Indians also belonging to these parts came of their own
accord with my people from Crossweeksung, to the
meeting. There were two in particular who, though
the last Sabbath they opposed and ridiculed Christianity, now behaved soberly. May the present encouraging appearances continue!

Feb. 22.—" Preached to the Indians. They appeared
more free from prejudice and more cordial to Christianity than before; and some of them appeared affected with divine truth.

Lord's day, Feb. 23.—" Preached to the Indians
from John, 6 : 35–37. After public service discoursed
particularly with several of them, and invited them to
go down to Crossweeksung and tarry there at least for
some time; knowing that they would then be free
from the scoffs and temptations of the opposing Pagans, as well as in the way of hearing divine truths
discoursed of, both in public and private. Obtained a
promise of some of them that they would speedily pay
us a visit, and attend some farther instructions. They
seemed to be considerably enlightened, and much
freed from their prejudices against Christianity. But
it is much to be feared that their prejudices will revive
again, unless they can enjoy the means of instruction
here, or be removed where they may be under such
advantages, and out of the way of their Pagan ac-
quaintances.

Crossweeksung, March, 1746

March, 1.—" Catechised in my ordinary method.
Was pleased and refreshed to see them answer the
questions proposed to them with such remarkable

readiness, discretion, and knowledge. Toward the close of my discourse divine truth made considerable impression upon the audience, and produced tears and sobs in some under concern; and more especially a sweet and humble melting in several, who, I have reason to hope, were truly gracious.

Lord's day, March 2.—Preached from John, 15 : 16. The assembly appeared not so lively in their attention as usual, nor so much affected with divine truth in general as has been common. Some of my people who went up to the Forks of the Delaware with me, being now returned, were accompanied by two of the Indians belonging to the Forks who had promised me a speedy visit. May the Lord meet with them here. They can scarcely go into a house now but they will meet with Christian conversation, whereby it is to be hoped they may be both instructed and awakened.

" Discoursed to the Indians again in the afternoon, and observed among them some animation and engagedness in divine service, though not equal to what has often appeared here. I know of no assembly of Christians where there seems to be so much of the presence of God, where brotherly love so much prevails, and where I should take so much delight in the public worship of God in general, as in *my own congregation ;* although not more than nine months ago, they were worshipping *devils* and *dumb idols* under the power of Pagan darkness and superstition. Amazing change this ! effected by nothing less than divine power and grace. This is the doing of the Lord, and it is justly marvellous in our eyes.

March 5.—" Spent some time just at evening in prayer, singing and discoursing to my people upon divine things; and observed some agreeable tenderness and affection among them. Their present situation is so compact and commodious, that they are easily and quickly called together with only the sound of a conch-shell, (a shell like that of a periwinkle,) so that they have frequent opportunities of attending religious exercises publicly. This seems to be a great means, under God, of keeping alive the impression of divine things in their minds.

March 8.—" Catechised in the evening. My people answered the questions proposed to them well. I can perceive their knowledge in religion increases daily. And, what is still more desirable, the divine influence, which has been so remarkable among them, appears still to continue, in some good measure. The divine presence seemed to be in the assembly this evening. "Some, who I have good reason to think are Christians indeed, were melted with a sense of divine goodness and their own barrenness and ingratitude, and seemed to *hate themselves*, as one of them afterward expressed it. Convictions also appeared to be revived in several instances; and divine truth was attended with such influence upon the assembly in general, that it might justly be called an evening of divine power.

Lords' day, March 9.—" Preached from Luke, 10 : 38–42. The word of God was attended with power and energy upon the audience. Numbers were affected, and concerned to obtain the one thing needful. Several, who have given good evidence of being truly gracious, were much affected with a sense of their want of spirituality, and saw the need they stood in of growing in grace. The greater part of those who had been under any impressions of divine things in times past, seemed now to have those impressions revived.

" In the afternoon proposed to have catechised in

my usual method: but, while we were engaged in the first prayer in the Indian language, as usual, a great part of the assembly was so much moved and affected with divine things that I thought it seasonable and proper to omit the proposing of questions for that time, and to insist upon the most practical truths. I accordingly did so; making a further improvement of the passage of Scripture on which I had discoursed in the former part of the day. There appeared to be a powerful divine influence in the congregation. Several who, as I have reason to think, are truly pious, were so deeply affected with a sense of their own barrenness, and their unworthy treatment of the blessed Redeemer, that they *looked on him as pierced* by themselves, and *mourned,* yea, some of them were *in bitterness, as for a first-born.*

" Some poor awakened sinners, also, appeared to be in anguish of soul to obtain an interest in Christ; so that there was a *geat mourning* in the assembly: many heavy groans, sobs, and tears! and one or two, newly come among us, were considerably awakened.

" Methinks it would have refreshed the heart of any, who truly love Zion's interests, to have been in the midst of this divine influence, and seen the effects of it upon saints and sinners. The place of divine worship appeared both solemn and sweet; and was so endeared by a display of the divine presence and grace that those who had any relish for divine things could not but cry, ' How amiable are thy tabernacles, O Lord of Hosts!' After public worship was over, numbers came to my house, where we sang and discoursed of divine things; and the presence of God seemed here also to be in the midst of us.

" While we were singing there was one individual,

the woman mentioned in my journal of February 9, who, I may venture to say, if I may be allowed to say so much of any person I ever saw, was ' filled with joy unspeakable and full of glory;' and could not but burst forth in prayer and praises to God before us all, with many tears; crying, sometimes in English and some-times in Indian, ' *O blessed Lord! do come, do come! O do take me away; do let me die, and go to Jesus Christ! I am afraid if I live I shall sin again. O do let me die now! O dear Jesus, do come! I cannot stay, I cannot stay! O how can I live in this world; do take my soul away from this sinful place! O let me never sin any more! O what shall I do, what shall I do, dear Je-sus. O dear Jesus!*' In this ecstacy she continued some time, uttering these and similar expressions in-cessantly. The grand argument she used with God to take her away immediately was, that 'if she lived, she should sin against him.' When she had a little recov-ered herself, I asked her if Christ was now sweet to her soul? Whereupon, turning to me with tears in her eyes, and with all the tokens of deep humility I ever saw in any person, she said, 'I have many times heard you speak of the goodness and the sweetness of Christ, that he was better than all the world. But O I knew nothing what you meant. I never believed you, I nev-er believed you! But now I know it is true;' or words to that effect. I answered, 'And do you see enough in Christ for the greatest of sinners?' She replied, 'O enough, enough for all the sinners in the world, if they would but come.' When I asked her, 'If she could not tell them of the goodness of Christ.' Turning herself about to some Christless souls, who stood by, and were much affected, she said, 'O there is enough in Christ for you if you would but come. O strive.

strive to give up your hearts to him,' &c. On hearing
something of the glory of heaven mentioned, that
there was no sin in that world; she again fell into the
same ecstacy of joy and desire of Christ's coming; repeating her former expressions, 'O dear Lord, do let
me go! O what shall I do; what shall I do. I want
to go to Christ. I cannot live. O do let me die," &c.
"She continued in this sweet frame for more than two
hours before she was able to get home. I am very
sensible that there may be great joys, arising even to
an ecstasy, where there is still no substantial evidence
of their being well grounded. But in the present case
there seemed to be no evidence wanting in order to
prove this joy to be divine; either in regard to its pre-
paratives, attendants, or consequents.

"Of all the persons whom I have seen under spiritual
exercise I scarcely ever saw one appear more bowed
and broken under convictions of sin and misery, or
what is usually called a preparatory work, than this
woman; nor scarcely any who seemed to have a
greater acquaintance with their own heart than she
had. She would frequently complain to me of the
hardness and rebellion of her heart. Would tell me
that her heart rose and quarrelled with God, when
she thought he would do with her as he pleased, and
send her to hell, notwithstanding her prayers, good
frames, &c., and that her heart was not willing to
come to Christ for Salvation, but tried every where
else for help. As she seemed to be remarkably sensible of her stubbornness and contrariety to God, under
conviction, so she appeared to be no less remarkably
bowed and reconciled to his sovereignty, before she
obtained any relief or comfort; something of which I
have noticed in my journal of Feb. 9. Since that time

she has seemed constantly to breathe the temper and
spirit of the new creature; crying after Christ, not
through fear of hell as before, but with strong desires
after him as her only satisfying portion; and has many
times wept and sobbed bitterly because, as she apprehended, she did not and could not love him.   When I
have sometimes asked her why she appeared so sorrowful, and whether it was because she was afraid of
hell; she would answer 'No, I be not distressed about
that; but my heart is so wicked I cannot love Christ;'
and thereupon burst into tears.   But although this has
been the habitual frame of her mind for several weeks
together, so that the exercise of grace appeared evident
to others; yet she seemed wholly insensible to it herself, and never had any remarkable comfort and sensible satisfaction until this evening.

"This sweet and surprising ecstasy appeared to
spring from a true spiritual discovery of the glory,
ravishing beauty, and excellency of Christ; and not
from any gross imaginary notions of his human nature,
such as that of seeing him in such a place, or posture,
as hanging on the cross, as bleeding and dying, as gent-
ly smiling, and the like; which delusions some have
been carried away with.   Nor did it rise from sordid
selfish apprehensions of her having any benefit whatsoever conferred on her; but from a view of his personal excellency and transcendant loveliness; which
drew forth those vehement desires of enjoying him
which she now manifested, and made her long 'to be
absent from the body, that she might be present with
the Lord.'

"The *attendants* of this ravishing comfort were such
as abundantly discovered its spring to be divine; and
that it was truly 'a joy in the Holy Ghost.'   Now she

viewed divine truths as living realities, and could say, 'I know these things are so; I feel that they are true!' Now her soul was resigned to the divine will in the most tender point; so that when I said to her, 'What if God should take away your husband from you, who was then very sick, how do you think you could bear that?' She replied, 'He belongs to God, and not to me; he may do with him just as he pleases.' Now she had the most tender sense of the evil of sin, and discovered the utmost aversion to it, longing to die, that she might be delivered from it. Now she could freely trust her all with God for time and eternity. When I questioned her, 'How she would be willing to die and leave her little infant; and what she thought would become of it in that case?' she answered, 'God will take care of it. It belongs to him. He will take care of it.' Now she appeared to have the most humbling sense of her own meanness and unworthiness, her weakness and inability to preserve herself from sin, and to persevere in the way of holiness, crying, 'If I live I shall sin.' I then thought that I had never seen such an appearance of ecstacy and humility meeting in any one person in all my life before.

"The *consequents* of this joy are no less desirable and satisfactory than its attendants. She since appears to be a most tender, broken-hearted, affectionate, devout, and humble Christian; as exemplary in life and conversation as any person in my congregation. May she still ' grow in grace and in the knowledge of Christ.'

March 10. "Toward night the Indians met together, of their own accord, and sang, prayed, and discoursed of divine things among themselves; at which time there was much affection among them. Some, who are hopefully pious, appeared to be melted with divine

things; and some others seemed much concerned for
their souls. Perceiving their engagement and affection in religious exercises, I went among them, and
prayed, and gave a word of exhortation ; and observed
two or three somewhat affected and concerned, who
scarce ever appeared to be under any religious impressions before. It seemed to be a day and evening of divine power. Numbers retained the warm impressions
of divine things which had been made upon their minds
the day before.

March 14.—"Was visited by a considerable number of
my people, and spent some time in religious exercises
with them.

March 15. "In the evening catechised. My people answered the questions put to them with surprising readiness and judgment. There appeared some
warmth, and a feeling sense of divine things among
those who I have reason to hope are real Christians,
while I was discoursing upon peace of conscience and
joy in the Holy Ghost. These seemed quickened and
enlivened in divine service, though there was not so
much appearance of concern among those whom I
have reason to think in a Christless state.

Lord's day, March 16.—"Preached to my congregation from Hebrews, 2 : 1–3. Divine truth seemed to
have some considerable influence upon some of the
hearers, and produced many tears, as well as heavy
sighs and sobs, among those who have given evidence
of being real Christians, and others also. The impressions made upon the audience appeared in general
deep and heart-affecting ; not superficial, noisy and affected.

"Toward night discoursed again on the Great Salvation. The word was again attended with some pow-

er upon the audience. Numbers wept affectionately, and to appearance unfeignedly; so that the Spirit of God seemed to be moving upon the face of the assembly. The woman mentioned in my journal of last Lord's day made a profession of her faith, and appeared to be in a devout, humble, and excellent frame of mind.

"My house being thronged with my people in the evening; I spent the time in religious exercises with them until my nature was almost spent. They are so unwearied in religious exercises, and insatiable in their thirsting after Christian knowledge, that I can sometimes scarcely avoid laboring so as greatly to exhaust my strength and spirits.

March 19.—"Several of the persons who went with me to the Forks of Delaware in February last, having been detained there by the dangerous illness of one of their company, returned home but this day. Whereupon my people generally met together of their own accord, in order to spend some time in religious exercises; and especially to give thanks to God for his preserving goodness to those who had been absent from them for several weeks, and recovering mercy to him who had been sick; and that he had now returned them all in safety. As I was then absent; they desired my school-master to assist them in carrying on their religious solemnity; who tells me that they appeared engaged and affectionate in repeated prayer, singing, &c.

March 22.—"Catechised in my usual method in the evening. My people answered questions to my great satisfaction. There appeared nothing very remarkable in the assembly, considering what has been common among us. Although I may justly say the strict attention, the tenderness and affection, the many tears and heart-affecting sobs, appearing in numbers in the assembly, would have been very remarkable, were it not that God has made these things common among us, and even with strangers soon after their coming among us, from time to time. I am far from thinking that every appearance and particular instance of affection that has been among us, has been truly genuine, and purely from a divine influence   I am sensible of the contrary; and doubt not but there has been some corrupt mixture, some *chaff* as well as *wheat;* especially since religious concern has become so common and prevalent here.

Lord's day, March 23.—" There being about *fifteen strangers,* adult persons, come among us in the week past, several of whom had never been in any religious meeting till now; I thought it proper to discourse this day in a manner peculiarly suited to their circumstances and capacities; and accordingly attempted it from Hosea, 13:9. ' O Israel, thou hast destroyed thyself.' In the forenoon I opened, in the plainest manner I could, man's apostacy and ruined state, after having spoken some things respecting the being and perfections of God, and his creation of man in a state of uprightness and happiness.   In the afternoon endeavored to open the glorious provision God has made for the redemption of apostate creatures, by giving his own dear Son to suffer for them and satisfy divine justice on their behalf. There was not that affection and concern in the assembly which has been common among us; although there was a desirable attention appearing in general, and even in most of the strangers.

" Near sun-set I felt an uncommon concern upon my mind, especially for the poor *strangers;* that God had so much withheld his presence and the powerful influence of his Spirit from the assembly in the exercises of the day; and thereby withheld from them that degree of conviction which I hoped they might have had. In this frame I visited several houses, and discoursed with some concern and affection to several persons particularly; but without much appearance of success till I came to a house where several of the strangers were. There the solemn truths on which I discoursed appeared to take effect; first upon some children; then upon several adult persons who had been somewhat awakened before; and afterward upon several of the Pagan strangers.

"I continued my discourse, with some fervency, until almost every one in the house was melted into tears, and many wept aloud, and appeared earnestly concerned to obtain an interest in Christ. Upon this, numbers soon gathered from all the houses round about; and so thronged the place that we were obliged to remove to the house where we usually met for public worship. The congregation gathered immediately, and many appearing remarkably affected, I discoursed some time from Luke, 19 : 10; endeavoring to open the mercy, compassion, and concern of Christ for lost, helpless, and undone sinners. There was much visible concern and affection in the assembly; and I doubt not but that a divine influence accompanied what was spoken to the hearts of many. There were five or six of the strangers, men and women, who appeared to be considerably awakened; and, in particular, one very rugged young man, who seemed as if nothing would move him, was now brought to tremble like the jailor, and weep for a long time.

"The Pagans who were awakened, seemed at once to put off their savage roughness and Pagan manners, and became sociable, orderly and humane in their carriage. When they first came, I exhorted my religious people to take pains with them as they had done with other strangers from time to time, to instruct them in Christianity. But when some of them attempted something of that nature, the strangers wou.d soon rise up and walk to other houses in order to avoid the hearing of such discourses. Whereupon some of the serious persons agreed to disperse themselves into the several parts of the settlement; so that wherever the strangers went, they met with some instructive discourse, and warm addresses respecting their salvation. But now there was no need of using policy, in order to get an opportunity of conversing with some of them about their spiritual concerns; for they were so far touched with a sense of their perishing state, as made them voluntarily yield to the closest addresses which were made them, respecting their sin and misery, their need of an acquaintance with, and interest in the great Redeemer.

March 24.—"Numbered the Indians to see how many souls God had gathered together here since my coming into these parts; and found there were now about *an hundred and thirty* persons together, old and young. Several of those, who are my stated hearers, perhaps to the number of *fifteen* or *twenty*, were absent at this season. If all had been together the number would now have been very considerable; especially considering how few were together at my first coming into this part of the country: the whole number not amounting to *ten* persons at that time.

"My people went out this day with the design of clearing some of their land, above fifteen miles distant from this settlement, in order to their settling there in a compact form, where they might be under the advantages of attending the public worship of God, of having their children taught in a school, and at the same time have a conveniency for planting: their land, in the place of our *present* residence, being of little or no value for that purpose. The design of their settling thus in a body, and cultivating their lands, of which they have done very little in their Pagan state, being of such necessity and importance to their religious interest as well as worldly comfort; I thought it proper to call them together, and show them the duty of laboring with faithfulness and industry, and that they must not now 'be slothful in business,' as they had ever been in their Pagan state. I endeavored to press the importance of their being laborious, diligent, and vigorous in the prosecution of their business; especially at the present juncture, the season of planting being now near, in order to their being in a capacity of living together, and enjoying the means of grace and instruction. Having given them directions for their work, which they very much wanted, as well as for their behavior in divers respects; I explained, sang, and endeavored to inculcate upon them Dr. Watts' Psalm,

If God to build the house deny &c.

and having recommended them, and the design of their going forth, to God, by prayer with them, I dismissed them to their business.

"In the evening read and expounded to those of my people who were yet at home, and to the *strangers* newly come, the substance of the 3d chapter of the Acts. Numbers seemed to melt under the word; especially while I was discoursing upon verse 19. 'Repent ye, therefore, and be converted,' &c. Several of the strangers also were affected. When I asked them after ward, whether they did not now feel that their hearts were wicked, as I had taught them; one of them replied, ‘ Yes, she felt it now.’   Although before she came here, upon hearing that I taught the Indians that their hearts were all bad by nature, and needed to be changed and made good by the power of God; she had said, ‘ Her heart was not wicked, and she had never done any thing that was bad in her life.’ This, indeed, seems to be the case with them, I think universally, in their pagan state.   They seem to have no consciousness of sin and guilt, unless they can charge themselves with some gross acts of sin contrary to the commands of the *second table.*’

March 27.—“ Discoursed to a number of my people in one of their houses in a more private manner. Inquired particularly into their spiritual states, in order to see what impressions they were under. Laid before them the marks of a regenerate, as well as of an unregenerate state; and endeavored to suit and direct my discourse to them severally, according as I apprehended their states to be.   There were a considerable number gathered together before I finished my discourse; and several seemed much affected while I was urging the necessity and infinite importance of getting into a renewed state.   I find particular and close dealing with souls in private is often very successful.

March 29.—“ In the evening catechised, as usual upon Saturday. Treated upon the benefits which believers receive from Christ at death. The questions were answered with great readiness and propriety; and those who I have reason to think are the dear people of God were in general sweetly melted. There appeared such a liveliness and vigor in their attendance upon the word of God, and such eagerness to be made partakers of the benefits mentioned, that they seemed not only to be ' looking for,' but ' hasting to, the coming of the day of God.' Divine truths seemed to distil upon the audience with a gentle but melting efficacy, as the refreshing ' showers upon the new mown grass.' The assembly in general, as well as those who appear truly religious, were affected with some brief accounts of the blessedness of the godly at death; and most of them then discovered an affectionate inclination to cry ' Let me die the death of the righteous, and let my last end be like his;' although many were not duly engaged to obtain the change of heart that is necessary to that blessed end.

Lord's day, March 30.—" Discoursed from Matt. 25 : 31–40. There was a very considerable moving, and affectionate melting, in the assembly. I hope that there were some real, deep, and abiding impressions of divine things made upon the minds of many. There was one aged man, newly come among us, who appeared to be considerably awakened that never was touched with any concern for his soul before. In the evening catechised. There was not that tenderness and melting engagement among God's people which appeared the evening before, and many other times. They answered the *questions* distinctly, and well, and were devout and attentive in divine service.

March 31.—" Called my people together, as I had done the Monday evening before, and discoursed to them again on the necessity and importance of laboring industriously in order to their living together, and enjoying the means of grace, &c. Having engaged in a solemn prayer to God among them for a blessing upon their attempts, I dismissed them to their work. Numbers of them, both men and women, seemed to offer themselves willingly to this service; and some appeared affectionately concerned that God might go with them, and begin their little town for them; that by his blessing it might be a place comfortable for them and theirs, with regard both to procuring the necessaries of life and to attending on the worship of God.

April 5.—" Catechised in the evening. There appeared to be some affection and fervent engagement in divine service through the assembly in general; especially toward the conclusion of my discourse. After public worship a number of those who I have reason to think are truly religious came to my house, and seemed eager for some farther entertainment upon divine things. While I was conversing with them about their scriptural exercises; observing to them, that God's work in the hearts of all his children was, for substance the same; and that their trials and temptations were also alike; and showing the obligations such were under to love one another in a peculiar manner, they seemed to be melted into tenderness and affection toward each other. I thought that that particular token of their being the disciples of Christ, viz. of their having love one toward another, had scarcely ever appeared more evident than at this time.

Lord's day, April 6.—" Preached from Matt. 7 : 21– 23. There were considerable effects of the word visible in the audience, and such as were very desirable; an earnest attention, a great solemnity, many tears and heavy sighs, which were modestly suppressed in a considerable measure, and appeared unaffected and without any indecent commotion of the passions. Numbers of the religious people were put upon serious and close examination of their spiritual state by hearing that 'not every one that saith to Christ, Lord, Lord, shall enter into his kingdom.' Some expressed fears lest they had deceived themselves, and taken up a false hope, because they found they had done so little of the will of his Father who is in heaven.

" There was one man brought under a very great and pressing concern for his soul; which appeared more especially after his retirement from public worship. That which he says gave him his great uneasiness was, not so much any particular sin, as that he had never done the will of God at all, but had sinned continually, and so had no claim to the kingdom of heaven. In the afternoon I opened to them the discipline of Christ in his Church, and the method in which offenders are to be dealt with; at which time the religious people were much affected; especially when they heard that the offender, continuing obstinate, must finally be esteemed and treated 'as an heathen man,' as a pagan, who has no part nor lot among God's visible people. Of this they seemed to have the most awful apprehensions; a state of heathenism, out of which they were so lately brought, appearing very dreadful to them.

"After public worship I visited several houses to see how they spent the remainder of the Sabbath, and to treat with them solemnly on the great concerns of their souls. The Lord seemed to smile upon my private endeavors, and to make these particular and personal addresses more effectual upon some than my public discourses.

April 7.—" Discoursed to my people in the evening, from 1 Cor. 11 : 23–26. Endeavored to open to them the institution, nature, and ends of the Lord's Supper, as well as of the qualifications and preparations necessary to the right participation of that ordinance. Numbers appeared much affected with the love of Christ, manifested in his making this provision for the comfort of his people, at a season when himself was just entering upon his sharpest sufferings.

Lord's day, April 20.—" Discoursed, both forenoon and afternoon, from Luke, 24; explaining most of the chapter, and making remarks upon it. There was a desirable attention in the audience; though there was not so much appearance of affection and tenderness among them as had been usual. Our meeting was very full; there being sundry strangers present who had never been with us before.

" In the evening catechised. My people answered the questions proposed to them readily and distinctly; and I could perceive that they advanced in their knowledge of the principles of Christianity. There appeared an affectionate melting in the assembly at this time. Several, who I trust are truly religious, were refreshed and quickened, and seemed by their discourse and behavior after public worship to have their 'hearts knit together in love.' This was a sweet and blessed season, like many others with which my poor people have been favored in months past. God has caused *this little fleece* to be repeatedly wet with the blessed dew of his divine grace, while all the earth around has been comparatively dry.

April 25 —" Set apart this day, as preparatory to the administration of the Lord's Supper, for solemn fasting and prayer. The design was to implore the blessing of God upon our renewing covenant with him, and with one another, to walk together in the fear of God, in love and christian fellowship, and to entreat that his presence might be with us in our designed approach to

his table ; as well as to humble ourselves before God on
account of the apparent withdrawment, at least in a
measure, of that blessed influence which has been so
prevalent upon persons of all ages among us ; as also
on account of the rising appearance of carelessness,
vanity, and vice, among some who once appeared to
be touched and affected with divine truth, and brought
to some sensibility of their miserable and perishing
state by nature. It was also designed that we might
importunately pray for the peaceable settlement of the
Indians together in a body ; that they might be a commodious congregation for the worship of God ; and
that God would defeat all the attempts that were, or
might be, made against that pious design.*

" The solemnity was observed and seriously attended, not only by those who proposed to commune at
the Lord's table, but by the whole congregation. In
the former part of the day I endeavored to open to
my people the nature and design of a fast, as I had
attempted more briefly to do before, and to instruct
them in the duties of such a solemnity. In the afternoon I insisted on the special reasons there were for
our engaging in these solemn exercises at this time ;
both in regard to the need we stood in of divine assistance, in order to a due preparation for that sacred
ordinance, upon which some of us were proposing,

* There was at this time a terrible clamor raised against the
Indians in various places in the country, and insinuations as
though I was training them up to cut people's throats. Numbers wished to have them banished from these parts, and some
gave out great words in order to fright and deter them from
settling upon the best and most convenient tract of their own
lands; threatening to trouble them in the law; pretending a
claim to these lands themselves, although never purchased of
the Indians.

with leave of divine Providence, speedily to attend; and also in respect of the manifest decline of God's work here, as to the effectual conviction and conversion of sinners; there having been few of late deeply awakened out of a state of security. The worship of God was attended with great solemnity and reverence, with much tenderness and many tears, by those who appeared to be truly religious; and there was some appearance of divine power upon those who had been awakened some time before, and who were still under concern.

"After repeated prayer, and attendance upon the word of God, I proposed to the religious people, with as much brevity and plainness as I could, the substance of the doctrine of the christian faith, as I had formerly done; and had their renewed cheerful assent to it. I then led them to a solemn renewal of their covenant, wherein they had explicitly and publicly given up themselves to God the Father, Son, and Holy Ghost, avouching him to be their God; and at the same time renouncing their heathenish vanities, their idolatrous and superstitious practices; solemnly engaging to take the Word of God, so far as it was or might be made known to them, for the rule of their lives; promising to walk together in love, to watch over themselves and one another, to lead lives of seriousness and devotion, and to discharge the relative duties incumbent on them respectively, &c. This solemn transaction was attended with much gravity and seriousness; and at the same time with the utmost readiness, freedom and cheerfulness; and a religious union and harmony of soul seemed to crown the whole solemnity. I could not but think in the evening, that there had been manifest tokens of the divine presence with us in all the several services of the day; though it was also manifest that there was not that concern among Christless souls which has often appeared here.

April 26.—"Toward noon prayed with a dying child, and gave a word of exhortation to the bystanders to prepare for death; which seemed to take effect upon some. In the afternoon discoursed to my people from Matthew, 26 : 26–30; of the author, the nature, and designs of the Lord's supper; and endeavored to point out the worthy receivers of that ordinance. The religious people were affected, and even melted with divine truth,—with a view of the dying love of Christ. Several others, who had been for some months under convictions of their perishing state, appeared now to be much moved with concern, and afresh engaged in seeking after an interest in Christ; although I cannot say that the word of God appeared so quick and powerful, so sharp and piercing to the assembly, as it had sometimes formerly done.

"In the evening I catechised those who were designed to partake of the Lord's supper the next day, upon the institution, nature and end of that ordinance; and had abundant satisfaction respecting their doctrinal knowledge and fitness in that respect for an attendance upon it. They likewise appeared in general to have an affecting sense of the solemnity of this sacred ordinance, and to be humbled under a sense of their own unworthiness to approach to God in it; and to be earnestly concerned that they might be duly prepared for an attendance upon it. Their hearts were full of love one toward another, and that was the frame of mind they seemed concerned to maintain and bring to the Lord's table with them. In the singing and prayer a.ter catechising, there appeared an agreeable tender-

ness and melting among them; and such tokens of
brotherly love and affection as would even constrain
one to say, 'Lord, it is good to be here;' it is good to
dwell where such an heavenly influence distills.

Lord's day, April 27.—"Preached from Tit. 2: 14;
'Who gave himself for us,' &c. The word of God, at
this time, was attended with some appearance of divine
power upon the assembly; so that the attention and
gravity of the audience were remarkable; and especially toward the conclusion of the exercise, many persons were much affected. Administered the Lord's
supper to *twenty three* persons of the Indians, the number of the men and women being nearly equal; several others, to the number of *five* or *six*, being now absent at the Forks of Delaware, who would otherwise
have communed with us. The ordinance was attended with great solemnity, and with a most desirable tenderness and affection. It was remarkable that during
the administration of the ordinance, especially in the
distribution of the bread, they seemed to be affected in
a most lively manner, as if Christ had been really crucified before them. The words of the institution, when
repeated and enlarged upon in the season of the administration, seemed to meet with the same reception,
to be entertained with the same free and full belief and
affectionate engagement of soul, as if the Lord Jesus
Christ himself had been present, and had personally
spoken to them. The affections of the communicants,
although considerably raised, were, notwithstanding,
agreeably regulated and kept within proper bounds.
So that there was a sweet, gentle, and affectionate melting, without any indecent or boisterous commotion of
the passions.

" Having rested sometime after the administration

of the Supper, being extremely tired with the necessary prolixity of the work, I walked from house to house, and conversed particularly with most of the communicants, and found they had been almost universally refreshed at the Lord's table, 'as with new wine.' Never did I see such an appearance of Christian love among any people in all my life. It was so remarkable, that one might well have cried with an agreeable surprise, ' Behold how they love one another.' I think there could be no greater tokens of mutual affection among the people of God, in the early days of Christianity, than what now appeared here. The sight was so desirable, and so well becoming the gospel, that nothing less could be said of it than it was ' the doing of the Lord,' the genuine operation of Him, ' who is Love.'

"Toward night discoursed again on the forementioned text, Tit. 2 : 14; and insisted on the immediate end and design of Christ's death: viz. That he might redeem his people from all iniquity, &c. This appeared to be a season of divine power among us. The religious people were much refreshed, and seemed remarkably tender and affectionate, full of love, joy, and peace, and desirous of being completely ' redeemed from all iniquity;' so that some of them afterward told me that ' they had never felt the like before.' Convictions also appeared to be revived in many instances; and several persons were awakened whom I had never observed under any religious impressions before.

"Such was the influence which attended our assembly, and so unspeakably desirable the frame of mind which many enjoyed in divine service, that it seemed almost grievous to conclude the public worship. The congregation, when dismissed, although it was then almost dark, appeared loth to leave the place and employments which had been rendered so dear to them by the benefits enjoyed, while a blessed quickening influence distilled upon them. Upon the whole, I must say, I had great satisfaction relative to the administration of this ordinance in various respects. I have abundant reason to think, that those who came to the Lord's table had a good degree of doctrinal knowledge of the nature and design of the ordinance, and that they acted with understanding in what they did.

" In the preparatory services I found, I may justly say, uncommon freedom in opening to their understandings and capacities, the covenant of grace, and in showing them the *nature* of this ordinance. They were likewise thoroughly sensible that it was no more than a *sign*, and not the *real* body and blood of Christ; that it was designed for the refreshment and edification of the *soul*, and not for the feasting of the *body*. They were also acquainted with the end of the ordinance, that they were therein called to commemorate the dying love of Christ.

" This competency of doctrinal knowledge, together with their grave and decent attendance upon the ordinance, their affectionate melting under it, and the sweet and Christian frame of mind which they discovered after it, gave me great satisfaction respecting my administration of it to them. O, what a sweet and blessed season was this! God himself, I am persuaded, was in the midst of his people. I doubt not but many, in the conclusion of the day, could say with their whole hearts, ' Verily, a day thus spent in God's house is better than a thousand elsewhere.' There seemed to be but *one heart* among the pious people. The sweet union, harmony and endearing love and tenderness subsisting among them was, I thought, the most lively emblem of the heavenly world which I had ever seen.

April 28.—" Concluded the solemnity of the Lord's supper with a discourse upon John, 14 : 15. ' If ye love me, keep my commandments.' At this time there appeared a very agreeable tenderness in the audience in general, but especially in the communicants. O, how free, how engaged and affectionate did these appear in the service of God ! they seemed willing to have their ears bored to the door posts of God's house, and to be his servants for ever.

" Observing numbers in this excellent frame, and the assembly in general affected, and that by a divine influence, I thought it proper to improve this advantageous season as Hezekiah did the desirable season of his great passover, 2 Chron. 31, in order to promote the blessed reformation begun among them ; and to engage those that appeared serious and religious to persevere therein. Accordingly I proposed to them, that they should renewedly enter into covenant before God, that they would watch over themselves and one another, lest they should dishonor the name of Christ by falling into sinful and unbecoming practices ; and especially that they would watch against the sin of drunkenness, ' the sin that easily besets them,' and the temptations leading thereto, as well as the appearance of evil in that respect. They cheerfully complied with the proposal, and explicitly joined in that covenant ; whereupon I proceeded in the most solemn manner of which I was capable, to call God to witness respecting their sacred engagements, and reminded them of the greatness of the guilt they would contract to themselves in the violation of it, as well as observed to them that God would be a terrible witness against those, who should presume to do so in the great and notable day of the

Lord. It was a season of amazing solemnity; and a divine awe appeared upon the face of the whole assembly in this transaction. Affectionate sobs, sighs and tears were now frequent in the audience; and I doubt not but that many silent cries were then sent up to the Fountain of grace for supplies of grace sufficient for the fulfilment of these solemn engagements.

Lord's day, May 4.—" My people being now remov ed to their lands, mentioned in my diary of March 24, where they were then and have since been making provision for a compact settlement, in order to their more convenient enjoyment of the Gospel and other means of instruction, as well as of the comforts of life; I this day visited them; being now obliged to board with an English family at some distance from them; and preached to them in the forenoon from Mark, 4 : 5. Endeavored to show them the reason there was to fear, lest many promising appearances and hopeful beginnings in religion might prove abortive, like the seed dropped upon stony places.

" In the afternoon discoursed upon Rom. 8 : 9. 'Now, if any man have not the spirit of Christ, he is none of his.' I have reason to think this discourse was peculiarly seasonable, and that it had a good effect upon some of the hearers. Spent some hours afterward in private conference with my people, and labored to regulate some things which I apprehended amiss among some of them.

May 5.—" Visited my people again, and took care of their worldly concerns; giving them directions relating to their business. I daily discover more and more of what importance it is likely to be to their religious interests, that they become laborious and industrious, acquainted with the affairs of husbandry, and able in a good measure to raise the necessaries and comforts of life within themselves; for their present method of living greatly exposes them to temptations of various kinds.

May 9.—" Preached from John, 5 : 40, in the open wilderness; the Indians having as yet no house for public worship in this place, nor scarcely any shelters for themselves. Divine truths made considerable impressions upon the audience, and it was a season of great solemnity, tenderness, and affection.

" This day received into communion the conjurer, murderer, &c. mentioned in my diary of August 8, 1745, and February 1, 1746, who appears to be such a remarkable instance of divine grace that I cannot omit to give some brief account of him here. He lived near, and sometimes attended my meeting at the Forks of Delaware, for more than a year; but was, like many others of them, extremely attached to strong drink, and seemed to be in no degree reformed by the means which I used with them for their instruction and conversion. At this time he likewise murdered a likely young Indian, which threw him into some kind of horror and desperation, so that he kept at a distance from me, and refused to hear me preach for several months together, until I had an opportunity of conversing freely with him, and giving him encouragement, that his sin might be forgiven, for Christ's sake. After this he again attended my meeting sometimes.

" But that which was the worst of all his conduct, was his *conjuration*. He was one of those who are sometimes called powaws among the Indians; and, notwithstanding his frequent attendance upon my preaching, he still followed his old charms and juggling tricks, ' giving out that himself was some great

one, and to him they gave heed,' supposing him to be
possessed of great power. When I have instructed
them respecting the miracles wrought by Christ in
healing the sick, &c. and mentioned them as evidence
of his divine mission, and the truths of his doctrine;
they have quickly observed the wonders of that kind
which this man had performed by his magic charms.
Hence they had a high opinion of him and his superstitious notions; which seemed to be a fatal obstruc-
tion to some of them in regard to their receiving the
Gospel. I had often thought that it would be a great
favor to the design of evangelizing these Indians, if
God would take that wretch out of the world; for I had
scarcely any hope of his ever becoming good. But
God, whose thoughts are not as man's thoughts, has
been pleased to take a much more desirable method
with him; a method agreeable to his own merciful
nature, and I trust advantageous to his own interest
among the Indians, as well as effectual to the salvation
of his poor soul. To God be the glory of it.

" The first genuine concern for his soul was excited
by seeing my interpreter and his wife publicly profess
Christ, at the Forks of Delaware, July 21, 1745; which
so prevailed upon him, that with the invitation of an
Indian who was a friend to Christianity, he followed
me down to Crossweeksung, in the beginning of August, in order to hear me preach; and there continued
for several weeks in the season of the most remarkable
and powerful awakening among the Indians; at which
time he was more effectually awakened, and brought
under great concern for his soul. And then, he says,
upon his ' feeling the word of God in his heart,' as he
expresses it, his spirit of *conjuration* left him entirely,
so that he has had no more power of that nature since.

than any other man living. He also declares, that he does not now so much as know how he used to charm and conjure, and that he could not now do any thing of that nature if he were ever so desirous of it.

"He continued under convictions of his sinful and perishing state, and a considerable degree of concern for his soul, all the fall and the former part of the winter past; but was not so deeply exercised until some time in January. Then the word of God took such hold upon him that he was brought into deep distress, and knew not what to do, nor where to turn himself. He then told me, that when he used to hear me preach from time to time in the fall of the year, my preaching pricked his heart, and made him very *uneasy*, but did not bring him to so great distress, because he still hoped he could do something for his own relief; but now, he said, I drove him up in such a sharp corner, that he had no way to turn, and could not avoid being in distress. He continued constantly under the heavy burden and pressure of a wounded spirit, until at length he was brought into the acute anguish and utmost agony of soul, mentioned in my Journal of February 1, which continued that night and part of the next day. After this he was brought to the utmost calmness and composure of mind; his trembling and heavy burden were removed; and he appeared perfectly sedate, although he had to his apprehensions scarcely any hope of salvation.

"I observed him to appear remarkably composed; and therefore asked him how he did? He replied, 'It is done, it is done, it is all done now.' I asked him what he meant? He answered, 'I can never do any more to save myself; it is all done for ever. I can do no more.' I queried with him, whether he could not

do a little more, rather than go to hell? He replied,
'my heart is dead. I can never help myself.' I asked
him what he thought would become of him then?
He answered, 'I must go to hell.' I asked him if he
thought it was right that God should send him to hell?
He replied, 'O it is right. The devil has been in me
ever since I was born.' I asked him if he felt this when
he was in such great distress the evening before? He
answered, 'No; I did not then think it was right. I
thought God would send me to hell, and that I was
then dropping into it; but my heart quarrelled with
God, and would not say it was right he should send
me there. But now I know it is right; for I have always served the devil; and my heart has no goodness
in it now, but it is as bad as ever it was,' &c. I thought
I had scarcely ever seen any person more effectually
brought off from a dependance upon his own contrivances and endeavors for salvation, or more apparently
to lie at the foot of sovereign mercy, than this man
did under these views of things.

"In this frame of mind he continued for several
days, passing sentence of condemnation upon himself,
and constantly owning that it would be right he should
be damned, and that he expected this would be his
portion for the greatness of his sins. Yet it was plain
that he had a secret hope of mercy, though impercep-
tible to himself, which kept him not only from despair
but from any pressing distress: so that, instead of being sad and dejected, his very countenance appeared
pleasant and agreeable.

"While he was in this frame he several times asked
me 'When I would preach again?' and seemed desirous to hear the word of God every day. I asked,
'Why he wanted to hear me preach, seeing his heart

was dead, and all was done; that he could never help himself, and expected that he must go to hell?' He replied, 'I love to hear you speak about Christ for all.' I added, 'But what good will that do you, if you must go to hell at last?'—using now his own language with him, having before from time to time labored in the best manner I could to represent to him the excellency of Christ, his all-sufficiency and willingness to save lost sinners, and persons just in his case; although to no purpose, as to yielding him any special comfort. He answered, 'I would have others come to Christ, if I must go to hell myself.' It was remarkable, that he seemed to have a great love for the people of God; and nothing affected him so much as the thought of being separated from them. This seemed to be a very dreadful part of the hell to which he saw himself doomed. It was likewise remarkable, that in this season he was most diligent in the use of all the means for the soul's salvation; although he had the clearest view of the inefficiency of means to afford him help. He would frequently say, that all he did signified nothing at all; and yet was never more constant in doing; attending secret and family prayer daily, and surprisingly diligent and attentive in hearing the word of God; so that he neither despaired of mercy, nor yet presumed to hope upon his own doings, but used means because appointed of God in order to salvation; and because he would wait upon God in his own way.

"After he had continued in this frame of mind more than a week, while I was discoursing publicly, he seemed to have a lively soul-refreshing view of the excellency of Christ and the way of salvation by him, which melted him into tears, and filled him with admiration, comfort, satisfaction and praise to God.

Since then he has appeared to be a humble, devout and affectionate christian ; serious and exemplary in his conversation and behavior, frequently complaining of his barrenness, his want of spiritual warmth, life and activity, and yet frequently favored with quickening and refreshing influences. In all respects, so far as I am capable of judging, he bears the marks of one 'created anew in Christ Jesus to good works.'

"His zeal for the cause of God was pleasing to me when he was with me at the Forks of Delaware in February last. There being an old Indian at the place where I preached who threatened to bewitch me, and my religious people who accompanied me there ; this man presently challenged him to do his worst, telling him that himself had been as great a conjurer as he ; and that notwithstanding, as soon as he felt that word in his heart which these people loved, meaning the word of God, his power of conjuring immediately left him. 'And so it would you,' said he, 'if you did but once feel it in your heart; and you have no power to hurt them, nor so much as to touch one of them,' &c. So that I may conclude my account of him by observing, in allusion to what was said of St. Paul, that he now zealously 'defends and practically preaches the faith which he once destroyed,' or at least was instrumental in obstructing. May God have the glory of the amazing change which he has wrought in him.

Lord's day, May 18.—"Discoursed both parts of the day from Rev. 3: 20, 'Behold I stand at the door and knock.' There appeared some affectionate melting toward the conclusion of the forenoon exercise, and one or two instances of fresh awakening. In the intermission of public worship I took occasion to discourse to numbers in a more private way, on the kindness and patience of the blessed Redeemer in standing and knocking, in continuing his gracious calls to sinners, who had long neglected and abused his grace; which seemed to take some effect upon several.

"In the afternoon divine truth was attended with solemnity, and with some tears; although there was not that powerful awakening and quickening influence which in times past has been common in our assemblies. The appearance of the audience was comparatively discouraging, and I was ready to fear that God was about to withdraw the blessed influence of his Spirit from us.

May 19.—"Visited and preached to my people from Acts, 20: 18, 19, and endeavored to rectify their notions about religious affections; showing them on the one hand the desirableness of religious affection, tenderness and fervent engagement in the worship and service of God, when such affection flows from a true spiritual discovery of divine glories, from a just sense of the transcendant excellence and perfections of the blessed God, and a view of the glory and loveliness of the great Redeemer; and that such views of divine things will naturally excite us to 'serve the Lord with many tears, with much affection and fervency, and yet with all humility of mind.' On the other hand, I observed the sinfulness of seeking after high affections immediately and for their own sakes; that is, of making them the object which our eye and heart is first and principally set upon, when the glory of God ought to be that object. Showed them, that, if the heart be directly and chiefly fixed on God, and the soul engaged to glorify him, some degree of religious affection will be the effect and attendant of it. But to seek after affection directly and chiefly; to have the heart principally set upon that; is to place it in the room of God and his

glory. If it be sought, that others may take notice of
it, and admire us for our spirituality and forwardness
in religion, it is then abominable pride; if for the sake
of feeling the pleasure of being affected, it is then idolatry and self-gratification.   Labored also to expose the
disagreeableness of those affections which are sometimes wrought up in persons by the power of fancy, and
their own attempts for that purpose, while I still endeavored to recommend to them that religious affection, fervency and devotion which ought to attend all
our religious exercises, and without which religion will
be but an empty name and lifeless carcase.   This appeared to be a seasonable discourse, and proved very
satisfactory to some of the religious people who before
were exercised with some difficulties relating to this
point.   Afterward took care of, and gave my people
directions about their worldly affairs.

May 24.—"Visited the Indians, and took care of
their secular business; which they are not able to man-
age themselves without the constant care and advice
of others.   Afterward discoursed to some of them particularly about their spiritual concerns.—Enjoyed this
day somewhat of the same frame of mind which I felt
the day before.

Lord's day, May 25.—"Discoursed both parts of the
day from John, 12:44-48.   There was some degree of
divine power attending the word of God.   Several
wept, and appeared considerably affected, and one, who
had long been under spiritual trouble, now obtained
clearness and comfort, and appeared to rejoice in God
her Savior.   It was a day of grace and divine goodness; a day wherein something I trust was done for
the cause of God among my people; a season of comfort and sweetness to numbers of the religious people;

although there was not that influence upon the congregation which was common some months ago.

Lord's day, June 1.—" Preached both forenoon and afternoon from Matt. 11 : 27, 28. The presence of God seemed to be in the assembly ; and numbers were considerably melted and affected under divine truth. There was a desirable appearance in the congregation in general, an earnest attention and an agreeable tenderness ; and it seemed as if God designed to visit us with further showers of divine grace. I then received into communion *five* persons ; and was not a little refreshed with this addition made to the church of such as I hope will be saved. I have reason to hope that God has lately, at and since our celebration of the Lord's supper, brought home to himself several persons who had long been under spiritual trouble and concern ; although there have been few instances of persons lately awakened out of a state of security. Those comforted of late seem to be brought in, in a more *silent* way ; neither their concern, nor consolation being so powerful and remarkable as appeared among those more suddenly wrought upon in the beginning of this work of grace.

June 7.—"Being desired by the Rev. WILLIAM TENNENT to be his assistant in the administration of the Lord's Supper, I this morning rode to Freehold to render that assistance. My people also being invited to attend at that solemnity, they cheerfully embraced the opportunity, and this day attended the preparatory services with me.

Lord's day, June 8.—"Most of my people, who had been *communicants* at the Lord's table, before being present on this occasion, communed with others in the holy ordinance, at the desire, and I trust to the satisfaction and comfort of numbers of God's people, who

had longed to see *this day*, and whose hearts had rejoiced in *this* work of grace among the Indians, which
prepared the way for what appeared so agreeable at
this time.   Those of my people who communed, seemed in general agreeably affected at the Lord's table,
and some of them considerably melted with the love
of Christ, although they were not so remarkably refreshed and feasted at this time, as when I administered
this ordinance to them in our own congregation only.
Some of the *by-standers* were affected with seeing those
who had been 'aliens from the commonwealth of Israel, and strangers to the covenant of promise,' who
of all men had lived 'without hope and without God
in the world,' now brought near to God, as his professing people, by a solemn and devout attendance upon
this sacred ordinance.   As numbers of God's people
were refreshed at this sight, and thereby excited to
bless God for the enlargement of his kingdom in the
world; so some others, I was told, were awakened by
it, apprehending the danger they were in of being
themselves finally *cast out ;* while they saw others
from the east and west preparing, and hopefully prepared in some good measure, to sit down in the kingdom of God.   At this season others of my people also,
who were not communicants, were considerably affected; convictions were revived in several instances; and
one, the man particularly mentioned in my journal of
the 6th instant, obtained comfort and satisfaction; and
has since given me such an account of his spiritual
exercises, and the manner in which he obtained relief,
as appears very hopeful.   It seems as if He, who commanded the light to shine out of darkness, had now
'shined into his heart, and given him the light of,' and

experimental 'knowledge of the glory of God in the face of Jesus Christ.'

June 9.—"A considerable number of my people met together early in a retired place in the *woods*, and prayed, sang, and conversed of divine things; and were seen by some religious persons of the white people to be affected and engaged, and some of them in tears in these religious exercises.

"After they had attended the concluding exercises of the Lord's Supper they returned home; many of them rejoicing for all the goodness of God which they had seen and felt: so that this appeared to be a profitable as well as comfortable season to numbers of my congregation. Their being present at this occasion, and a number of them communing at the Lord's table with other Christians, was, I trust, for the honor of God and the interest of religion in these parts; as numbers, I have reason to think, were quickened by means of it.

June 13.—"Preached to my people upon the *new creature*, from 2 Cor. 5:17. The presence of God appeared to be in the assembly. It was a sweet and agreeable meeting, wherein the people of God were refreshed and strengthened; beholding their faces in the glass of God's word, and finding in themselves the marks and lineaments of the new creature. Some sinners under concern were also renewedly affected; and afresh engaged for the securing of their eternal interests.

" *Three* Indians were at this time received into communion. One of them was the very *aged woman* of whose exercises I gave an account in my diary of Dec. 26. She now gave me a very punctual, rational, and satisfactory account of the remarkable change which she experienced some months after the beginning of her concern, which I must say, appeared to be the genuine operations of the Divine Spirit, so far as I am capable of judging. Although she was become so childish, through age, that I could do nothing in a way of questioning her, nor scarcely make her understand any thing that I asked her; yet when I let her alone to go on with her own story, she could give a very distinct and particular relation of the many and various exercises of soul she had experienced; so deep were the impressions left upon her mind by that influence and those exercises which she had experienced. I have great reason to think that she is born anew in her old age: she being, I presume, upward of *eighty*.

June 19.—"Visited my people with two of the Reverend correspondents. Spent some time in conversation with some of them upon spiritual things; and took some care of their worldly concerns.

"This day makes up a complete year from the first time of my preaching to these Indians in New-Jersey. What amazing things has God wrought, in this space of time, for this poor people! What a surprising change appears in their tempers and behavior! How are morose and savage Pagans, in this short period, transformed into agreeable, affectionate, and humble Christians! and their drunken and Pagan howlings turned into devout and fervent praises to God! They 'who were sometimes in darkness are now become light in the Lord.' May they 'walk as children of the light and of the day!' And now to Him that is of power to establish them according to the gospel, and the preaching of Christ—to God only wise, be glory through Jesus Christ, for ever and ever, Amen."

"AT the close of this Narrative I would make a few GENERAL REMARKS upon what, to me, appears worthy of notice, relating to the continued work of grace among my people.

I."I cannot but take notice, that I have in general, ever since my first coming among the Indians in New-Jersey, been favored with that assistance which to me is uncommon, in preaching *Christ crucified*, and making him the *centre* and *mark* to which all my discourses among them were directed.

"It was the principal scope and drift of all my discourses to this people, for several months together, (after having taught them something of the being and perfections of God, his creation of man in a state of rectitude and happiness, and tne obligations mankind were thence under to love and honor him,) to lead them into an acquaintance with their deplorable state by nature, as fallen creatures; their inability to extricate and deliver themselves from it; the utter insufficiency of any external reformations and amendments of life, or of any religious performances, of which they were capable, while in this state, to bring them into the favor of God, and interest them in his eternal mercy; thence to show them their absolute need of Christ to redeem and save them from the misery of their fallen state;—to open his all-sufficiency and willingness to save the chief of sinners;—the freeness and riches of divine grace, proposed 'without money, and without price,' to all that will accept the offer; thereupon to press them without delay to betake themselves to him,

under a sense of their misery and undone state, for relief and everlasting salvation;—and to show them the
abundant encouragement the gospel proposes to needy,
perishing, and helpless sinners, in order to engage them
so to do.   These things, I repeatedly and largely insisted upon from time to time.

"I have oftentimes remarked with admiration, that
whatever subject I have been treating upon, after having spent time sufficient to explain and illustrate the
truths contained therein, I have been naturally and
easily led to Christ as the substance of every subject.
If I treated on the being and glorious perfections of
God; I was thence naturally led to discourse of Christ,
as the only 'way to the Father.'—If I attempted to
open the deplorable misery of our fallen state; it was
natural from thence to show the necessity of Christ to
undertake for us, to atone for our sins, and to redeem
us from the power of them.—If I taught the commands
of God, and showed our violation of them; this brought
me, in the most easy and natural way, to speak of, and
recommend the Lord Jesus Christ as one who had
'magnified the law' which we had broken, and who
was 'become the end of it, for righteousness, to every
one that believes.'   Never did I find so much freedom
and assistance in making all the various lines of my
discourses meet together, and centre in Christ, as I
have frequently done among these Indians.

"Sometimes when I have had thoughts of offering
but a few words upon some particular subject, and saw
no occasion, nor indeed much room, for any considerable enlargement, there has appeared such a fountain
of gospel-grace shining forth in, or naturally resulting
from a just explication of it; and Christ has seemed
in such a manner to be pointed out as the substance

of what I was considering and explaining; that I have been drawn in a way not only easy and natural, proper and pertinent, but almost unavoidable, to discourse of him, either in regard to his undertaking, incarnation, satisfaction, admirable fitness for the work of man's redemption, or the infinite need that sinners stand in of an interest in him; which has opened the way for a continued strain of gospel invitation to perishing souls, to come empty and naked, weary and heavy laden, and cast themselves upon him.

"As I have been remarkably influenced and assisted to dwell upon the Lord Jesus Christ, and the way of salvation by him, in the general current of my discourses here, and have been, at times, surprisingly furnished with pertinent matter relating to him, and the design of his incarnation; so I have been no less assisted oftentimes in an advantageous manner of opening the mysteries of divine grace, and representing the infinite excellencies, and 'unsearchable riches of Christ,' as well as of recommending him to the acceptance of perishing sinners. I have frequently been enabled to represent the divine glory, the infinite preciousness and transcendant loveliness of the great Redeemer, the suitableness of his person and purchase to supply the wants, and answer the utmost desires of immortal souls; —to open the infinite riches of his grace, and the wonderful encouragement proposed in the gospel to unworthy, helpless sinners;—to call, invite, and beseech them to come and give up themselves to him, and be reconciled to God through him;—to expostulate with them respecting their neglect of one so infinitely lovely, and freely offered;—and this in such a manner, with such freedom, pertinency, pathos, and application to the conscience, as, I am sure, I never could have made myself master of, by the most assiduous application of mind. Frequently, at such seasons, I have been surprisingly helped in adapting my discourses to the capacities of my people, and bringing them down into such easy, and familiar methods of expression, as has rendered them intelligible even to Pagans.

"I do not mention these things as a recommendation of my own performances; for I am sure I found, from time to time, that I had no skill or wisdom for my great work; and knew not how 'to choose out acceptable words' proper to address to poor benighted Pagans. But thus God was pleased to help me, 'not to know any thing among them, save Jesus Christ and him crucified.' Thus I was enabled to show them their misery without him, and to represent his complete fitness to redeem and save them.

"This was the preaching God made use of for awakening sinners, and the propagation of this 'work of grace among the Indians.' It was remarkable, from time to time, that when I was favored with any special freedom, in discoursing of the 'ability and willingness of Christ to save sinners,' and 'the need in which they stood of such a Savior;' there was then the greatest appearance of divine power in awakening numbers of secure souls, promoting convictions begun, and comforting the distressed.

"I have sometimes formerly, in reading the Apostle's discourse to Cornelius, (Acts, 10,) wondered to see him so quickly introduce the Lord Jesus Christ into his sermon, and so entirely dwell upon him through the whole of it, observing him in this point very widely to differ from many of our modern preachers; but latterly this has not seemed strange, since Christ has appeared to be the substance of the gospel and the centre in which

the several lines of divine revelation meet. Still I am
sensible that there are many things necessary to be spoken to persons under Pagan darkness, in order to make
way for a proper introduction of the name of Christ,
and his undertaking in behalf of fallen man.

II. "It is worthy of remark, that numbers of these
people are brought to a strict compliance with the rules
of morality and sobriety, and to a conscientious performance of the external duties of Christianity, by the
internal power and influence of divine truth—the peculiar doctrines of grace upon their minds; without their
having these moral duties frequently repeated and inculcated upon them, and the contrary vices particularly
exposed and spoken against. What has been the general strain and drift of my preaching among these Indians, what were the truths I principally insisted upon,
and how I was influenced and enabled to dwell from
time to time, upon the peculiar doctrines of grace, I
have already stated. Those doctrines, which had the
most direct tendency to humble the fallen creature;
to show him the misery of his natural state; to bring
him down to the foot of sovereign mercy, and to exalt
the great Redeemer—discover his transcendant excellency and infinite preciousness, and so recommend him
to the sinner's acceptance—were the subject-matter of
what was delivered in public and private to them, and
from time to time repeated and inculcated.

"God was pleased to give these divine truths such
a powerful influence upon the minds of these people,
and so to bless them for the effectual awakening of
numbers of them, that their lives were quickly reformed, without my insisting upon the precepts of morality, and spending time in repeated harangues upon external duties. There was indeed no room for any kind

of discourses but those which respected the essentials
of religion, and the experimental knowledge of divine
things, while there were so many inquiring daily—not
how they should regulate their external conduct, for
that, persons who are honestly disposed to comply with
duty, when known, may in ordinary cases be easily
satisfied about, but—how they should escape from the
wrath they feared, and felt that they deserved,—obtain
an effectual change of heart,—get an interest in Christ,
—and come to the enjoyment of eternal blessedness?
So that my great work still was to lead them into a
further view of their utter undoneness in themselves,
the total depravity and corruption of their hearts; that
there was no manner of goodness in them; no good
dispositions nor desires; no love to God, nor delight
in his commands; but, on the contrary, hatred, enmity,
and all manner of wickedness reigning in them:—and
at the same time to open to them the glorious and complete remedy provided in Christ for perishing sinners,
and offered freely to those who have no goodness of
their own, no works of righteousness which they have
done, to recommend them to God.

"This was the continued strain of my preaching;
this my great concern and constant endeavor, so to enlighten the mind, as thereby duly to affect the heart,
and, as far as possible, give persons a *sense* and *feeling*
of these precious and important doctrines of grace, at
least so far as means might conduce to it.   These were
the doctrines, and this the method of preaching, which
were blessed of God for the awakening, and I trust,
the saving conversion of numbers of souls; and which
were made the means of producing a remarkable reformation among the hearers in general.

"When these truths were felt at heart, there was

now no vice unreformed—no external duty neglected. Drunkenness, the darling vice, was broken off, and scarce an instance of it known among my hearers for months together. The abusive practice of *husbands and wives* in putting away each other, and taking others in their stead, was quickly reformed; so that there are three or four couples who have voluntarily dismissed those whom they had wrongfully taken, and now live together again in love and peace. The same might be said of all other vicious practices. The reformation was general; and all springing from the *internal* influence of divine truth upon their hearts, and not from any *external* restraints, or because they had heard these vices particularly exposed, and repeatedly spoken against. Some of them I never so much as mentioned; particularly that of the parting of men and their wives, till some, having their conscience awakened by God's word, came, and *of their own accord* confessed themselves guilty in that respect. When I at any time mentioned their wicked practices, and the sins they were guilty of contrary to the *light of nature*, it was not with a design, nor indeed with any hope, of working an effectual reformation in their external manners by this means, for I knew, that while the tree remained corrupt, the fruit would naturally be so. My design was to lead them, by observing the wickedness of their lives, to a view of the corruption of their hearts, and so to convince them of the necessity of a renovation of nature, and to excite them, with the utmost diligence to seek after that great change, which, if once obtained, I was sensible, would of course produce a reformation of external manners in every respect.

"And as all vice was reformed upon their feeling the

power of these truths upon their hearts, so the external duties of Christianity were complied with, and conscientiously performed from the same internal influence; family prayer set up, and constantly maintained, unless among a few who had more lately come, and had felt little of this divine influence. This duty was constantly performed, even in some families where there were none but females, and scarce a prayerless person was to be found among near an hundred of them. The Sabbath was seriously and religiously observed, and care taken by parents to keep their children orderly upon that sacred day; and this, not because I had driven them to the performance of these duties by frequently inculcating them, but because they had felt the power of God's word upon their hearts,—were made sensible of their sin and misery, and thence could not but pray, and comply with every thing which they knew to be their duty, from what they felt within themselves. When their hearts were touched with a sense of their eternal concerns, they could pray with great freedom, as well as fervency, without being at the trouble first to learn set forms for that purpose. Some of them, who were suddenly awakened at their first coming among us, were brought to pray and cry for mercy with the utmost importunity, without ever being instructed in the duty of prayer, or so much as once directed to a performance of it.

"The happy effects of these peculiar doctrines of grace upon this people, show, even to demonstration, that, instead of their opening a door to licentiousness, as many vainly imagine, and slanderously insinuate, they have a directly contrary tendency; so that a close application, a *sense* and *feeling* of them, will have the most powerful influence toward the renovation, and *effectual* reformation both of heart and life.

"Happy experience, as well as the word of God and the example of Christ and his apostles, has taught me, that the very method of preaching which is best suited to awaken in mankind a sense and lively apprehension of their depravity and misery in a fallen state, —to excite them so earnestly to seek after a change of heart, as to fly for refuge to free and sovereign grace in Christ as the only hope set before them,—is likely to be most successful in the reformation of their external conduct. I have found that close addresses, and solemn applications of divine truth to the conscience, strike at the root of all vice; while smooth and plausible harangues upon moral virtues and external duties, at best are like to do no more than lop off the branches of corruption, while the root of all vice remains still untouched.

"A view of the blessed effect of honest endeavors to bring home divine truths to the conscience, and duly to affect the heart with them, has often reminded me of those words of our Lord, which I have thought might be a proper exhortation for ministers in respect to their treatment of others, as well as for persons in general with regard to themselves. 'Cleanse first the inside of the cup and platter, that the outside may be clean also.' Cleanse, says he, the inside that the outside may be clean. As if he had said, the only effectual way to have the outside clean, is to begin with what is within; and if the fountain be purified, the streams will naturally be pure. Most certain it is, if we can awaken in sinners a lively sense of their inward pollution and depravity—their need of a change of heart—and so engage them to seek after inward cleansing, their external defilement will naturally be cleansed, their vicious ways of course be reformed and their conversation and behavior become regular.

"Now, although I cannot pretend that the reformation among my people does, in every instance, spring from a saving change of heart; yet I may truly say, it flows from some *heart-affecting* view and sense of divine truths which all have had in a greater or less degree. I do not intend, by what I have observed here, to represent the preaching of morality and pressing persons to the external performance of duty; to be altogether unnecessary and useless, especially at times when there is less of divine power attending the means of grace, when, for want of internal influences, there is need of external restraints. It is doubtless among the things that ought to be done, while others are not to be left undone. But what I principally designed by this remark, was to discover a plain matter of fact, viz. That the reformation, the sobriety, and the external compliance with the rules and duties of Christianity, appearing among my people, are not the effect of any mere doctrinal instruction, or merely rational view of the beauty of morality, but from the internal power and influence which the soul-humbling doctrines of grace have had upon their hearts.

III. "It is remarkable, that God has so *continued and renewed* the showers of his grace here; so *quickly* set up his visible kingdom among these people; and so smiled upon them in relation to their acquirement of knowledge, both divine and human. It is now nearly a year since the beginning of this gracious outpouring of the divine Spirit among them ; and although it has often seemed to decline and abate for some short space of time—as may be observed by several passages of my Journal, where I have endeavored to note things just as from time to time they appeared to me—yet the shower has seemed to be renewed, and the work of grace revived again. A divine influence seems still apparently to attend the means of grace, in a greater or less degree, in most of our meetings for religious exercises; whereby religious persons are refreshed, strengthened, and established,—convictions revived and promoted in many instances, and some few persons newly awakened from time to time. It must be acknowledged, that for some time past there has, in general, appeared a more manifest decline of this work; and the divine Spirit has seemed, in a considerable measure, withdrawn, especially with regard to his awakening influence; so that the *strangers* who come latterly, are not seized with concern as formerly; and some few who have been much affected with divine truths in time past, now appear less concerned. Yet, blessed be God, there is still an appearance of divine power and grace, a desirable degree of tenderness, religious affection and devotion in our assemblies.

"As God has continued and renewed the showers of his grace among this people for some time, so he has with uncommon *quickness* set up his visible kingdom, and gathered himself a church in the midst of them. *Fifteen* individuals, since the conclusion of my last Journal, have made a public profession of their faith, making *thirty-eight* within the space of *eleven* months, all of whom appear to have had a work of special grace wrought in their hearts; I mean, to have had the experience not only of the awakening, but, in a judgment of charity, of the renewing influences of the divine Spirit. There are many others under solemn concern for their souls, and deep convictions of their sin and misery, but who do not yet give that decisive evidence which could be desired, of a saving change.

"From the time when, as I am informed, some of them were attending an *idolatrous feast* and *sacrifice* in honor to *devils*, to the time when they sat down at the Lord's table, I trust to the honor of God, was not more than a *full year.* Surely Christ's little flock here, so suddenly gathered from among Pagans, may justly say, in the language of the church of old, 'The Lord hath done great things for us, whereof we are glad.'

"Much of the goodness of God has also appeared in relation to their acquisition of knowledge, both in religion and in the affairs of common life. There has been a wonderful thirst after *Christian knowledge* prevailing among them in general, and an eager desire of being instructed in Christian doctrines and manners. This has prompted them to ask many pertinent as well as important questions; the answers to which have tended much to enlighten their minds and promote their knowledge in divine things. Many of the doctrines which I have delivered, they have queried with me about, in order to gain further light and insight into them; and have from time to time manifested a good understanding of them, by their answers to the questions proposed to them in my catechetical lectures.

"They have likewise queried with me respecting a proper *method*, as well as proper *matter of prayer*, and expressions suitable to be used in that religious exercise; and have taken pains in order to the performance of this duty with understanding.—They have likewise taken pains, and appeared remarkably apt in learning to sing *psalm-tunes*, and are now able to sing with a good degree of decency in the worship of God. —They have also acquired a considerable degree of useful knowledge in the affairs of common life; so that they now appear like rational creatures, fit for human society, free of that savage roughness and brutish stupidity which rendered them very disagreeable in their Pagan state.

"They seem ambitious of a thorough acquaintance with the English language, and for that end frequently speak it among themselves. Many of them have made good proficiency in acquiring it, since my coming among them; so that most of them can understand a considerable part, and some the substance of my discourses, without an *Interpreter*, being used to my simple and familiar methods of expression, though they could not well understand other ministers.

"As they are desirous of instruction, and surprisingly apt in the reception of it, so divine Providence has smiled upon them with regard to the *proper means* in order to it. The attempts made for establishing a *school* among them have succeeded, and a kind Providence has sent them a *schoolmaster*, of whom I may justly say, I know of 'no man like minded, who will naturally care for their state.' He has generally *thirty* or *thirty-five* children in his school; and when he kept an evening school, as he did while the length of the evenings would admit of it, *fifteen* or *twenty* grown people, married and single, attended.

"The children learn with surprising readiness; so that their master tells me, he never had an English school which learned, in general, so fast. There were not above two in thirty, although some of them were very small, but learned all the letters in the alphabet within three days after his entrance upon his business; and several in that space of time learned to spell considerably. Some of them, in less than five months, have learned to read with ease in the Psalter or Testament.

"They are instructed twice a week in the *Catechism*, on Wednesday and Saturday. *Some* of them, since the latter end of February, when they began, have committed more than half of it to memory; and *most* of them have made some proficiency in it.

"They are likewise instructed in the duty of *secret prayer*, and most of them constantly attend it night and morning, and are very careful to inform their master, if they apprehend that any of their little schoolmates neglect that religious exercise.

IV. "It is worthy to be noted, to the praise of sovereign grace, that amidst so great a work of conviction —so much concern and religious affection—there has been *no prevalence, nor indeed any considerable appearance of false religion*—heats of imagination, intemperate zeal, or spiritual pride; and that there have been very few instances of irregular and scandalous behavior among those who have appeared serious.

"This work of grace has, in the main, been carried on with a surprising degree of purity, and freedom from corrupt mixture. Their religious concern has generally been rational and just; arising from a sense of their sins, and exposure to the divine displeasure on account of them; as well as their utter inability to deliver themselves from the misery they felt and feared. If there has been, in any instance, an appearance of concern and perturbation of mind, when the subjects of it knew not why; yet there has been no prevalence of any such thing; and indeed I scarcely know of any instance of that nature at all.—It is very remarkable, that, although the concern of many persons under convictions of their perishing state has been very great and pressing, yet I have never seen any thing like desperation attending it in any one instance. They have had the most lively sense of their undoneness in themselves; have been brought to give up all hopes of deliverance from themselves; have experienced great distress and anguish of soul; and yet, in the seasons of the greatest extremity, there has been no appearance of despair in any of them,—nothing that has discouraged, or in any wise hindered them from the most diligent use of all proper means for their conversion and salvation. Hence it is apparent, that there is not that danger of persons being driven into despair under spiritual trouble, unless in cases of deep and habitual melancholy, which the world in general is ready to imagine.

"The comfort which persons have obtained after their distresses, has likewise in general appeared solid, well grounded, and scriptural; arising from a spiritual and supernatural illumination of mind,—a view of divine things, in a measure, as they are,—a complacency of soul in the divine perfections,—and a peculiar satisfaction in the way of salvation by free sovereign grace in the great Redeemer.

"Their joys have seemed to rise from a variety of views and considerations of divine things, although for substance the same. Some, who, under conviction, seemed to have the hardest struggles and heart-risings against the divine sovereignty, have seemed, at the first dawn of their comfort, to rejoice in a peculiar manner in that divine perfection:—and have been delighted to think that themselves, and all things else, were in the hand of God, and that he would dispose of them 'just as he pleased.'

"Others, who, just before their reception of comfort, have been remarkably oppressed with a sense of their undoneness and poverty, who have seen themselves, as

It were, falling down into remediless perdition, have been at first more peculiarly delighted with a view of the freeness and riches of divine grace, and the offer of salvation made to perishing sinners 'without money and without price.'

"Some have at first appeared to rejoice especially in the *wisdom* of God, discovered in the way of salvation by Christ; it then appearing to them 'a new and living way,' a way of which they had never thought, nor had any just conceptions, until opened to them by the special influence of the divine Spirit. Some of them, upon a lively spiritual view of this way of salvation, have wondered at their past folly in seeking salvation in other ways, and that they never saw this way of salvation before, which now appeared so plain and easy, as well as excellent to them.

"Others, again, have had a more general view of the beauty and excellency of Christ, and have had their souls delighted with an apprehension of his divine glory, as unspeakably exceeding all they had ever conceived before; yet, without singling out any one of the divine perfections in particular; so that, although their comforts have seemed to arise from a variety of views and considerations of divine glories, still they were *spiritual* and *supernatural* views of them, and not groundless fancies, which were the spring of their joys and comforts.

"Yet it must be acknowledged that, when this work became so universal and prevalent, and gained such general credit and esteem among the Indians that Satan seemed to have little advantage of working against it in his own proper garb, he then transformed himself 'into an angel of light,' and made some vigorous attempts to introduce turbulent commotions of the pas-

sions in the room of genuine convictions of sin, imaginary and fanciful notions of Christ, as appearing to the
mental eye in a human shape, and in some particular
postures, &c. in the room of spiritual and supernatural
discoveries of his divine glory and excellency, as well
as many other delusions. I have reason to think, that,
if these things had met with countenance and encouragement, there would have been a very considerable
harvest of this kind of converts here.

" *Spiritual pride* also discovered itself in various instances. Some persons, whose feelings had been greatly excited, seemed very desirous from thence of being
thought truly gracious; who, when I could not but express to them my fears respecting their spiritual state,
discovered their resentments to a considerable degree.
There also appeared in one or two of them, an unbecoming ambition of being teachers of others. So that
Satan has been a busy adversary here as well as elsewhere. But, blessed be God, though something of this
nature has appeared, yet nothing of it has prevailed,
nor indeed made any considerable progress at all. My
people are now apprised of these things, are made acquainted, that Satan in such a manner 'transformed
himself into an angel of light,' in the first season of
the great outpouring of the divine Spirit in the days of
the apostles; and that something of this nature, in a
greater or less degree, has attended almost every revival and remarkable propagation of true religion ever
since. They have learned so to distinguish between
the gold and dross, that the credit of the latter ' is trod-
den down like the mire of the streets;' and, as it is natural for this kind of stuff to die with its credit, there
is now scarce any appearance of it among them.

" As there has been no prevalence of irregular heats,

imaginary notions, spiritual pride, and satanical delusions among my people ; so there have been very few
instances of scandalous and irregular behavior among
those who have made a profession, or even an appearance of seriousness. I do not know of more than
three or four such persons who have been guilty of
any open misconduct, since their first acquaintance
with Christianity ; and I know of no one who persists
in any thing of that nature. Perhaps the remarkable
purity of this work in the *latter* respect, its freedom
from frequent instances of scandal, is very much owing
to its purity in the *former* respect, its freedom from
corrupt mixtures of spiritual pride, wild-fire, and delu-
sion, which naturally lay a foundation for scandalous
practices.

"May this blessed work, in the power and purity of it,
prevail among the poor Indians here, as well as spread
elsewhere, till their remotest tribes shall see the salvation of God ! Amen."

CHAPTER IX

*From the close of his Public Journal, June 19, 1746, to his death
—continuance of labor at Crossweeksung and Cranberry—
journey with six Christian Indians to the Susquehanna, and
labors there—return to Crossweeksung—compelled by prostra-
tion of health to leave the Indians—confinement by sickness at
Elizabethtown—farewell visit to the Indians—his brother John
succeeds him as a Missionary—arrival among his friends in
Connecticut—visit to President Edwards in Northampton—
journey to Boston, where he is brought near to death—usefulness in Boston—returns to Northampton—triumphs of grace
in his last sickness—death.*

[June 19, 1746—October 9, 1747.]

Lord's day, June 29, 1746.—" Preached both parts of
the day, from John, 14 : 19. God was pleased to assist

me, to afford me both freedom and power, especially toward the close of my discourses forenoon and afternoon. God's power appeared in the assembly, in both exercises. Numbers of God's people were refreshed and melted with divine things; one or two comforted, who had been long under distress; convictions, in divers instances, were powerfully revived; and one man in years was much awakened, who had not long frequented our meeting, and appeared before as stupid as a stock. God amazingly renewed and lengthened out my strength. I was so spent at noon that I could scarcely walk, and all my joints trembled so that I could not sit, nor so much as hold my hand still; and yet God strengthened me to preach with power in the afternoon, although I had given out word to my people, that I did not expect to be able to do it. Spent some time afterward in conversing, particularly, with several persons, about their spiritual state; and had some satisfaction concerning one or two. Prayed afterward with a sick child, and gave a word of exhortation. Was assisted in all my work. Blessed be God! Returned home with more health than I had in the morning, although my linen was wringing wet upon me, from a little after ten, till past five in the afternoon. My spirits also were considerably refreshed; and my soul rejoiced in hope, that I had through grace done something for God. In the evening walked out, and enjoyed a sweet season in secret prayer and praise. But O I found the truth of the Psalmist's words, 'My goodness extendeth not to thee!' I could not make any returns to God; I longed to live only to him, and to be in tune for his praise and service for ever. Oh for spirituality and holy fervency, that I might spend and be spent for God to my latest moment

July 10.—" Spent most of the day in writing. Toward night rode to Mr. Tennent's; enjoyed some
agreeable conversation; went home in the evening, in
a solemn, sweet frame of mind; was refreshed in secret
duties, longed to live wholly and only for God, and
saw plainly there was nothing in the world worthy of
my affection—my heart was dead to all below; yet not
through dejection, as at some times, but from views of
a better inheritance.

July 12.—" This day was spent in fasting and prayer
by my congregation, as preparatory to the Lord's supper. I discoursed, both parts of the day, from Rom.
4 : 25, ' Who was delivered for our offences,' &c.
God gave me some assistance, and something of divine
power attended the word; so that this was an agreeable season. Afterward led them to a solemn renewal
of their covenant, and fresh dedication of themselves
to God. This was a season both of solemnity and
sweetness, and God seemed to be ' in the midst of us.'
Returned to my lodgings in the evening, in a comfortable frame of mind.

Lord's day, *July* 13.—" In the forenoon, discoursed
on the ' bread of life,' from John, 6 : 35. God gave me
some assistance, in a part of my discourse especially;
and there appeared some tender affection in the assembly under divine truth; my soul also was somewhat
refreshed. Administered the Lord's supper to thirty-
one of the Indians. God seemed to be present in this
ordinance; the communicants were sweetly melted and
refreshed. O how they melted, even when the elements were first uncovered! There was scarcely a
dry eye among them, when I took off the linen, and
showed them the symbols of Christ's *broken body*.
Having rested a little, after the administration of the

ordinance, I visited the communicants, and found them generally in a sweet loving frame; not unlike what appeared among them on the former sacramental occasion, April 27. In the afternoon, discoursed upon *coming to Christ*, and the *satisfaction* of those who do so, from the same verse I insisted on in the forenoon. This was likewise an agreeable season, one of much tenderness, affection, and enlargement in divine service; and God, I am persuaded, crowned our assembly with his presence. I returned home much spent, yet rejoicing in the goodness of God.

July 14.—" Went to my people, and discoursed to them from Psalm 119 : 106, ' I have sworn, and I will perform it,' &c. Observed, (1.) that all God's judgments or commandments are righteous. (2.) That God's people have sworn to keep them ; and this they do especially at the Lord's table. There appeared to be a powerful divine influence on the assembly, and considerable melting under the word. Afterward I led them to a renewal of their covenant before God, that they would watch over themselves and one another, lest they should fall into sin, and dishonor the name of Christ. This transaction was attended with great solemnity ; and God seemed to own it by exciting in them a fear and jealousy of themselves, lest they should sin against God ; so that the presence of God seemed to be among us in this conclusion of the sacramental solemnity.

July 21.—" Preached to the Indians, chiefly for the sake of some *strangers;* proposed my design of taking a journey speedily to the Susquehanna ; exhorted my people to pray for me, that God would be with me in that journey ; and then chose divers persons of the congregation to travel with me. Afterward spent some time in discoursing to the strangers, and was somewhat encouraged with them. Took care of my people's secular business, and was not a little exercised with it. Had some degree of composure and comfort in secret retirement.

July 22.—"Was in a dejected frame most of the day; wanted to wear out life, and have it at an end; but had some desires of *living to God*, and wearing out life *for him*. Oh that I could indeed do so!"

July 29.—"My mind was cheerful, and free from the melancholy with which I am often exercised; had freedom in looking up to God at various times in the day. In the evening I enjoyed a comfortable season in secret prayer; was helped to plead with God for my own dear people, that he would carry on his own blessed work among them; and assisted in praying for the divine presence to attend me in my intended journey to the Susquehanna. I scarce knew how to leave the throne of grace, and it grieved me that I was obliged to go to bed; I longed to do something for God, but knew not how. Blessed be God for this freedom from dejection!

July 30.—"Was uncommonly comfortable, both in body and mind; in the forenoon especially, my mind was solemn; I was assisted in my work, and God seemed to be near to me; so that the day was as comfortable as most I have enjoyed for some time. In the evening was favored with assistance in secret prayer, and felt much as I did the evening before. Blessed be God for that freedom I then enjoyed at the throne of grace, for myself, my people, and my dear friends!

August 1.—"In the evening enjoyed a sweet season in secret prayer; clouds of darkness and perplexing care were sweetly scattered, and nothing anxious re-

mained. O how serene was my mind at this season!
how free from that distracting concern I have often
felt! 'Thy will be done,' was a petition sweet to my
soul; and if God had bid me choose for myself in any
affair, I should have chosen rather to have referred
the choice to him; for I saw he was infinitely wise,
and could not do any thing amiss, as I was in danger
of doing. Was assisted in prayer for my dear flock,
that God would promote his own work among them,
and go with me in my intended journey to the Susquehanna; was helped to remember my dear friends
in New-England, and my dear brethren in the ministry. I found enough in the sweet duty of prayer to
have engaged me to continue in it the whole night,
would my bodily state have admitted of it. O how
sweet it is, to be enabled heartily to say, 'Lord, not
my will, but thine be done.'

August 2.—"Near night, preached from Matt. 11.
29. 'Take my yoke upon you,' &c. Was considerably
helped, and the presence of God seemed to be somewhat remarkably in the assembly; divine truth made
powerful impressions, both upon saints and sinners.
Blessed be God for such a revival among us! In the
evening was very weary, but found my spirits supported and refreshed.

August 7.—"Rode to my house where I spent the
last winter, in order to bring some things I needed for
my Susquehanna journey; was refreshed to see that
place, which God so marvellously visited with the
showers of his grace. O how amazing did the *power
of God* often appear there! 'Bless the Lord, O my
soul, and forget not all his benefits.'

August 9.—"In the afternoon visited my people; set
their affairs in order as much as possible, and contrived

for them the management of their worldly business; discoursed to them in a solemn manner, and concluded with prayer. Was composed and comfortable in the evening, and somewhat fervent in secret prayer; had some sense and view of the eternal world; and found a serenity of mind. O that I could magnify the Lord for any freedom which he affords me in prayer!

Lord's day, Aug. 10.—" Discoursed to my people both parts of the day, from Acts, 3 : 19, 'Repent ye, therefore,' &c. In discoursing of repentance, in the forenoon, God helped me, so that my discourse was searching; some were in tears, both of the Indians and white people, and the word of God was attended with some power. In the intermission I was engaged in conversing on their spiritual state, one of whom had very recently found comfort, after spiritual trouble and distress. In the afternoon was somewhat assisted again, though weak and weary. Three persons this day made a public profession of their faith. Was in a comfortable frame in the evening, and enjoyed some satisfaction in secret prayer. I have rarely felt myself so full of tenderness as this day.

August 11.—" Being about to set out on a journey to the Susquehanna the next day, with leave of Providence, I spent some time this day in prayer with my people, that God would bless and succeed my intended journey, that he would send forth his blessed Spirit with his word, and set up his kingdom among the poor Indians in the wilderness. While I was opening and applying part of the 110th and 111th Psalms, the *power of God* seemed to descend on the assembly in some measure ; and while I was making the first prayer, numbers were melted, and I found some affectionate enlargement of soul myself. Preached from Acts. 4 : 31,

'And when they had prayed, the place was shaken,' &c. God helped me, and my interpreter also; there was a shaking and melting among us; and several, I doubt not, were in some measure 'filled with the Holy Ghost.' Afterward, Mr. Macnight prayed; and I then opened the two last stanzas of the 72d Psalm; at which time God was present with us; especially while I insisted upon the promise of *all nations blessing* the great *Redeemer*. My soul was refreshed, to think that this day this blessed, glorious season, should surely come; and I trust numbers of my dear people were also refreshed. Afterward prayed; had some freedom, but was almost spent; then walked out, and left my people to carry on religious exercises among themselves. They prayed repeatedly, and sung, while I rested and refreshed myself. Afterward went to the meeting, prayed with, and dismissed the assembly. Blessed be God, this has been a day of grace. There were many tears and affectionate sobs among us this day. In the evening my soul was refreshed in prayer; enjoyed liberty at the throne of grace, in praying for my people and friends, and the church of God in general. 'Bless the Lord, O my soul.'"

The next day he set out on his journey toward the Susquehanna, and six of his Christian Indians with him, whom he had chosen out of his congregation, as those he judged most fit to assist him in the business upon which he was going. He took his way through Philadelphia; intending to go to the Susquehanna, far down, where it is settled by the white people, below the country inhabited by the Indians; and so to travel up the river to the Indian habitations. For although this was much farther, yet hereby he avoided the mountains and hideous wilderness that must be crossed in the nearer way; which in time past he found to be extremely difficult and fatiguing.

Aug. 19.—"Lodged by the side of the Susquehanna. Was weak and disordered both this and the preceding day, and found my spirits considerably damped, meeting with none that I thought godly people.

Aug. 20.—"Having lain in a cold sweat all night, I coughed up much bloody matter this morning, and was under great disorder of body, and not a little melancholy; but what gave me some encouragement, was, I had a secret hope that I might speedily get a dismission from earth, and all its toils and sorrows. Rode this day to one Chambers', upon the Susquehanna, and there lodged. Was much afflicted in the evening with an ungodly crew, drinking, swearing, &c. O what a *hell* would it be, to be numbered with the *ungodly!* Enjoyed some agreeable conversation with a traveller, who seemed to have some relish of true religion.

Aug. 21.—"Rode up the river about fifteen miles, and there lodged, in a family which appeared quite destitute of God. Labored to discourse with the man about the life of religion, but found him very artful in evading such conversation. O what a death it is to some, to hear of the things of God! Was out of my element; but was not so dejected as at some times.

Aug. 22.—"Continued my course up the river; my people now being with me, who before were parted from me; travelled above all the English settlements; at night lodged in the open woods, and slept with more comfort than while among an ungodly company of white people. Enjoyed some liberty in secret prayer this evening; and was helped to remember dear friends, as well as my dear flock, and the church of God in general.

Aug. 23.—"Arrived at the Indian town, called *Shaumoking*, near night; was not so dejected as formerly, but yet somewhat exercised. Felt composed in the evening, and enjoyed some freedom in leaving my *all* with God.

Lord's day, Aug. 24.—"Toward noon, visited some of the Delawares, and conversed with them about Christianity. In the afternoon discoursed to the *King*, and others, upon divine things; who seemed disposed to hear. Spent most of the day in these exercises. In the evening enjoyed some comfort and satisfaction; and especially had some sweetness in secret prayer. This duty was made so agreeable to me, that I loved to walk abroad, and repeatedly engage in it. O how comfortable is a little glimpse of God!

Aug. 25.—"Spent most of the day in writing. Sent out my people that were with me, to talk with the Indians, and contract a friendship and familiarity with them, that I might have a better opportunity of treating with them about Christianity. Some good seemed to be done by their visit this day, many appeared willing to hearken to Christianity. My spirits were a little refreshed this evening, and I found some liberty and satisfaction in prayer.

Aug. 26.—"About noon, discoursed to a considerable number of Indians. God helped me, I am persuaded; for I was enabled to speak with much plainness, and some warmth and power; and the discourse had impression upon some, and made them appear very serious. I thought things now appeared as encouraging as they did at Crossweeks. At the time of my first visit to those Indians, I was a little encouraged; I pressed things with all my might, and called out my people, who were then present, to give in *their testimony* for God; which they did. Toward night, was refreshed; had a heart to pray for the setting up of God's kingdom here, as well as for my dear congregation below, and my dear friends elsewhere.

Aug. 28.—"In the forenoon, I was under great concern of mind about my work. Was visited by some who desired to hear me preach; discoursed to them in the afternoon with some fervency, and labored to persuade them to turn to God. Was full of concern for the kingdom of Christ, and found some enlargement of soul in prayer, both in secret and in my family. Scarce ever saw more clearly, than this day, that it is God's work to convert souls, and especially poor Heathens. I knew I could not touch them; I saw I could only speak to dry bones, but could give them no sense of what I said. My eyes were up to God for help: I could say the work was his; and if done, the glory would be his.

Lord's day, Aug. 31.—"Spent much time, in the morning, in secret duties; found a weight upon my spirits, and could not but cry to God with concern and engagement of soul. Spent some time also in reading and expounding God's word to my dear family which was with me, as well as in singing and prayer with them. Afterwards spake the word of God to some few of the Susquehanna Indians. In the afternoon, felt very weak and feeble. Near night was somewhat refreshed in mind, with some views of things relating to my great work. O how heavy is my work, when *faith* cannot take hold of an *almighty arm* for the performance of it! Many times have I been ready to sink in this case. Blessed be God, that I may repair to a full fountain!

Sept. 1.—"Set out on a journey toward a place

called *The great Island*, about fifty miles distant from
Shaumoking, on the north-western branch of the Susquehanna. Travelled some part of the way, and at
night lodged in the woods. Was exceedingly feeble
this day, and sweat much the night following.

Sept. 2.—"Rode forward, but no faster than my people went on foot. Was very weak, on this as well as
the preceding days. I was so feeble and faint, that I
feared it would kill me to lie out in the open air; and
some of our company being parted from us, so that we
had now no axe with us, I had no way but to climb
into a young pine-tree, and with my knife to lop the
branches, and so make a shelter from the dew. But
the evening being cloudy, with a prospect of rain, I
was still under fears of being extremely exposed:
sweat much, so that my linen was almost wringing
wet all night. I scarcely ever was more weak and
weary than this evening, when I was able to sit up at
all. This was a melancholy situation; but I endeavored to quiet myself with considerations of the possibility
of my being in much worse circumstances amongst
enemies, &c.

Sept. 3.—"Rode to the Delaware-town; found many drinking and drunken. Discoursed with some of
the Indians about Christianity; observed my Interpreter much engaged, and assisted in his work; a few persons seemed to hear with great earnestness and engagement of soul. About noon, rode to a small town of
Shauwaunoes, about eight miles distant; spent an hour
or two there, and returned to the Delaware-town, and
lodged there. Was scarce ever more confounded with
a sense of my own unfruitfulness and unfitness for my
work than now. O what a dead, heartless, barren, un-
profitable wretch did I now see myself to be! My

spirits were so low, and my bodily strength so wasted, that I could do nothing at all. At length, being much overdone, lay down on a buffalo-skin; but sweat much the whole night.

Sept. 4.—"Discoursed with the Indians, in the morning, about Christianity; my Interpreter, afterward, carrying on the discourse to a considerable length. Some few appeared well disposed, and somewhat affected. Left this place, and returned toward Shaumoking; and at night lodged in the place where I lodged the Monday night before: was in very uncomfortable circumstances in the evening, my people being late, and not coming to me till past ten at night; so that I had no fire to dress any victuals, or to keep me warm, or keep off wild beasts; and I was scarce ever more weak and exhausted. However, I lay down and slept before my people came up, expecting nothing else but to spend the whole night alone, and without fire.

Sept. 5.—"Was exceeding weak, so that I could scarcely ride; it seemed sometimes as if I must fall from my horse, and lie in the open woods: however, got to Shaumoking toward night: felt somewhat of a spirit of thankfulness, that God had so far returned me: was refreshed to see one of my Christians, whom I left here in my late excursion.

Sept. 6.—"Spent the day in a very weak state; coughing and spitting blood, and having little appetite for any food I had with me; was able to do very little, except discourse a while of divine things to my own people, and to some few I met with. Had, by this time, very little life or heart to speak for God, through feebleness of body. Was scarcely ever more ashamed and confounded in myself than now. I was sensible that there were numbers of God's people who knew I was then out upon a design, or at least the pretence, of doing something for God, and in his cause, among the poor Indians; and they were ready to suppose that I was *fervent in spirit;* but O the heartless frame of my mind filled me with confusion! O, methought, if God's people knew me as God knows, they would not think so highly of my zeal and resolution for God as perhaps now they do! I could not but desire they should see how heartless and irresolute I was, that they might be undeceived, and 'not think of me above what they ought to think.' And yet I thought, if they saw the utmost of my unfaithfulness, the smallness of my courage and resolution for God, they would be ready to shut me out of their doors, as unworthy of the company or friendship of Christians.

Lord's day, Sept. 7.—"Was much in the same weak state of body, and afflicted frame of mind, as in the preceding day: my soul was grieved, and mourned that I could do nothing for God. Read and expounded some part of God's word to my own dear family, and spent some time in prayer with them; discoursed also a little to the Pagans; but spent the Sabbath with a little comfort.

Sept. 8.—"Spent the forenoon among the Indians; in the afternoon, left Shaumoking, and returned down the river a few miles. Had proposed to tarry a considerable time longer among the Indians upon the Susquehanna, but was hindered from pursuing my purpose by the sickness that prevailed there, the feeble state of my own people that were with me, and especially my own extraordinary weakness, having been exercised with great nocturnal sweats, and a coughing up of blood, almost the whole of the journey. I was a great part of the time so feeble and faint, that it seem-

ed as though I never should be able to reach home;
and at the same time very destitute of the comforts,
and even the necessaries of life; at least, what was necessary for one in so weak a state. In this journey I
sometimes was enabled to speak the word of God with
some power, and divine truth made some impression
on those who heard me; so that several, both men and
women, old and young, seemed to cleave to us, and be
well disposed toward Christianity; but *others mocked*
and shouted, which damped those who before seemed
friendly, at least some of them. Yet God, at times, was
evidently present, assisting me, my Interpreter, and
other dear friends who were with me. God gave sometimes a good degree of freedom in prayer for the ingathering of souls there; and I could not but entertain
a strong hope, that the journey would not be wholly
fruitless. Whether the issue of it would be the setting
up of Christ's kingdom there, or only the drawing of
some few persons down to my congregation in New-
Jersey; or whether they were now only preparing for
some farther attempts that might be made among them,
I did not determine; but I was persuaded the journey
would not be lost. Blessed be God, that I had any
encouragement and hope.

Sept. 9.—" Rode down the river near thirty miles.
Was extremely weak, much fatigued, and wet with a
thunder storm. Discoursed with some warmth and
closeness to some poor ignorant souls, on the *life* and
power of *religion :* what were, and what were not the
evidences of it. They seemed much astonished when
they saw my Indians ask a blessing and give thanks at
dinner, concluding *that* a very high evidence of grace
in them; but were equally astonished when I insisted
that neither that, nor yet secret prayer, was any sure

evidence of grace. O the ignorance of the world! How are some empty outward forms, that may all be entirely selfish, mistaken for true religion, infallible evidences of it! The Lord pity a deluded world!

Sept. 11.—" Rode homeward; but was very weak, and sometimes scarce able to ride. Had a very importunate invitation to preach at a meeting-house I came by, the people being then gathered, but could not by reason of weakness. Was resigned and composed under my weakness; but was much exercised with concern for my companions in travel, whom I had left with much regret, some lame, and some sick.

Sept. 20.—" Arrived among my own people, (near Cranberry,) just at night: found them praying together; went in, and gave them some account of God's dealings with me and my companions in the journey; which seemed affecting to them. I then prayed with them, and thought the divine presence was among us; several were melted into tears, and seemed to have a sense of divine things. Being very weak, I was obliged soon to repair to my lodgings, and felt much worn out in the evening. Thus God has carried me through the fatigues and perils of another journey to the Susquehanna, and returned me again in safety, though under a great degree of bodily indisposition. O that my soul were truly thankful for renewed instances of mercy! Many hardships and distresses I endured in this journey; but the Lord supported me under them all."

Hitherto BRAINERD had kept a constant *diary*, giving an account of what passed from day to day, with very little interruption; but henceforward his diary is very much interrupted by his illness; under which he was often brought so low, as either not to be capable of writing, or not well able to bear the burden of a care

so constant as was requisite to recollect every evening
what had passed in the day, and digest it, and put on
paper an orderly account of it. However, his diary
was not wholly neglected; but he took care, from time
to time, to take some notice in it of the most material
things concerning himself and the state of his mind,
even till within a few days of his death.

Lord's day, Sept. 21, 1746.—" I was so weak that I
could not preach, nor pretend to ride over to my people
in the forenoon. In the afternoon rode out; sat in my
chair, and discoursed to them from Rom. 14 : 7, 8. I
was strengthened and helped in my discourse, and
there appeared something agreeable in the assembly.
I returned to my lodgings extremely tired, but thankful that I had been enabled to speak a word to my
poor people, from whom I had been so long absent.
Was enabled to sleep very little this night, through
weariness and pain. O how blessed should I be, if the
little I do were all done with right views! O that,
' whether I live, I might live to the Lord; or whether I
die, I might die unto the Lord; that, whether living or
dying, I might be the Lord's !'

Sept. 27.—" Spent this day, as well as the whole
week past, under a great degree of bodily weakness,
exercised with a violent cough and a considerable
fever. I had no appetite for any kind of food, could
not retain it on my stomach, and frequently had little
rest in my bed, owing to pains in my breast and back.
I was able, however, to ride over to my people, about
two miles, every day, and take some care of those who
were then at work upon a small house for me to reside
in among the Indians.* I was sometimes scarce able

* This was the *fourth* house he built for his residence among
the Indians. Beside that at *Kaunaumeek*, and that at the

to walk, and never able to sit up the whole day, through the week. Was calm and composed, and but little exercised with melancholy, as in former seasons of weakness. Whether I should ever recover or no, seemed very doubtful; but this was many times a comfort to me, that *life* and *death* did not depend upon *my* choice. I was pleased to think, that He who is infinitely wise, had the determination of this matter; and that I had no trouble to consider and weigh things upon all sides, in order to make the choice whether I should live or die. Thus my time was consumed; I had little strength to pray, none to write or read, and scarce any to meditate; but, through divine goodness, I could with great composure look death in the face, and frequently with sensible joy. O how blessed it is to be *habitually prepared* for death!

Lord's day, Sept. 28.—" Rode to my people, and, though under much weakness, attempted to preach from 2 Cor. 13 : 5. Discoursed about half an hour, at which season divine power seemed to attend the word ; but being extremely weak, I was obliged to desist; and after a turn of faintness, with much difficulty rode to my lodgings, where, betaking myself to my bed, I lay in a burning fever, and almost delirious for several hours, till, toward morning, my fever went off with a violent sweat. I have often been feverish and unable to rest quietly after preaching; but this was the most severe, distressing turn, that ever preaching brought upon me. Yet I felt perfectly at rest in my own mind, because I had made my utmost attempts to speak for God, and knew I could do no more.

Forks of Delaware, and another at *Crossweeksung*, he built one now at *Cranberry*

Oct. 4.—" Spent the former part of this week under a great degree of infirmity and disorder, as I had done several weeks before; was able, however, to ride a little every day, although unable to sit up half the day, till Thursday. Took some care daily of some persons at work upon my house. On Friday afternoon found myself wonderfully revived and strengthened. Having some time before given notice to my people, and those of them at the Forks of Delaware in particular, that I designed, with the leave of Providence, to administer the Lord's supper upon the first Sabbath in October, on Friday afternoon I preached preparatory to the ordinance, from 2 Cor. 13 : 5; finishing what I had proposed to offer upon the subject the Sabbath before. The sermon was blessed of God to the stirring up religious affection and a spirit of devotion in his people, and greatly affected one who had *backslidden* from God, which caused him to judge and condemn himself. I was surprisingly strengthened in my work while I was speaking; but was obliged immediately after to repair to bed, being now removed into my own house among the Indians. Spent some time in conversing with my people about divine things as I lay upon my bed, and found my soul refreshed, though my body was weak.—This being Saturday, I discoursed particularly with divers of the communicants; and this afternoon preached from Zech. 12 : 10. There seemed to be a tender melting and hearty mourning for sin, in numbers in the congregation. My soul was in a comfortable frame, and I enjoyed freedom and assistance in public service; was myself, as well as most of the congregation, much affected with the humble confession and apparent broken-heartedness of the forementioned backslider, and could not but rejoice that God had given him such a sense of his sin and unworthiness. Was extremely tired in the evening, but lay on my bed, and discoursed to my people.

Lord's day, Oct. 5.—"Was still very weak; and in the morning considerably afraid I should not be able to go through the work of the day; having much to do, both in private and public. Discoursed before the administration of the Lord's supper, from John, 1 : 29, 'Behold the Lamb of God, that taketh away the sins of the world.' Where I considered (1.) in what respects Christ is called the 'Lamb of God;' and observed that he is so called, from the purity and innocency of his nature—from his meekness and patience under sufferings—from his being that atonement which was pointed out in the sacrifice of lambs, and in particular by the paschal lamb. (2.) Considered how and in what sense he 'takes away the sin of the world;' and observed, that the means and manner in and by which he takes away the sins of men, was his 'giving himself for them,' doing and suffering in their room and stead, &c. And he is said to take away the sin of the world, not because all the world shall actually be redeemed from sin by him, but because he has done and suffered sufficient to answer for the sins of the world, and so to redeem all mankind;—he actually does take away the sins of the elect world. And (3.) considered how we are to behold him, in order to have our sins taken away. Not with our bodily eyes; nor by imagining him on the cross, &c.; but by a spiritual view of his glory and goodness, engaging the soul to rely on him, &c.—The divine presence attended this discourse; and the assembly was considerably melted with divine truth. After sermon, two made a public profession, and I administered the Lord's supper to

near forty communicants of the Indians, besides divers dear Christians of the white people. It seemed
to be a season of divine power and grace; and numbers
seemed to rejoice in God. O the sweet union and harmony then appearing among the religious people!
My soul was refreshed, and my religious friends of
the white people with me. After the ordinance, could
scarcely get home, though it was not more than twenty
rods; but was supported and led by my friends, and
laid on my bed; where I lay in pain till some time in
the evening; and then was able to sit up and discourse
with friends. O how was this day spent in prayers
and praises among my dear people! One might hear
them, all the morning before public worship, and in
the evening, till near midnight, praying and singing
praises to God, in one or other of their houses. My
soul was refreshed, though my body was weak.

Oct. 11.—" Toward night was seized with an ague,
which was followed with a hard fever and considerable pain; was treated with great kindness; and was
ashamed to see so much concern about so unworthy a
creature as I knew myself to be. Was in a comfortable frame of mind, wholly submissive, with regard to
life or death. It was indeed a peculiar satisfaction to
me, to think that it was not *my* concern or business to
determine whether I should live or die. I likewise
felt peculiarly satisfied, while under this uncommon
degree of disorder; being now fully convinced of my
being really weak, and unable to perform my work.
Whereas, at other times, my mind was perplexed with
fears that I was a misimprover of time, by conceiving
I was sick, when I was not in reality so. O how precious is time! And how guilty it makes me feel, when
I think that I have trifled away and misimproved it

or neglected to fill up each part of it with duty, to the utmost of my ability and capacity!

Lord's day, Oct. 19.—" Was scarcely able to do any thing at all in the week past, except that on Thursday I rode out about four miles; at which time I took cold. As I was able to do little or nothing, so I enjoyed not much spirituality, or lively religious affection; though at some times I longed much to be more fruitful and full of heavenly affection; and was grieved to see the hours slide away, while I could do nothing for God.— Was able this week to attend public worship. Was composed and comfortable, willing either to die or live; but found it hard to be reconciled to the thoughts of living *useless.* Oh that I might never live to be a burden to God's creation; but that I might be allowed to repair *home*, when my *sojourning* work is done!"

This week, he went back to his Indians at Cranberry, to take some care of their spiritual and temporal concerns; and was much spent with riding, though he rode but a little way in a day.

Oct. 23.—" Went to my own house, and set things in order. Was very weak, and somewhat melancholy; labored to do something, but had no strehgth; and was forced to lie down on my bed, very solitary.

Oct. 24.—" Spent the day in overseeing and directing my people, about mending their fence and securing their wheat. Found that all their concerns of a secular nature depended upon me. Was somewhat refreshed in the evening, having been able to do something valuable in the day-time. O how it pains me to see time pass away, when I can do nothing to any purpose!

Lord's day, Oct. 26.—" In the morning was exceedingly weak. Spent the day, till near night, in pain, to

see my poor people wandering 'as sheep not having
a shepherd,' waiting and hoping to see me able to
preach to them before night. It could not but distress
me to see them in this case, and to find myself unable
to attempt any thing for their spiritual benefit. But
toward night, finding myself a little better, I called
them together to my house, and sat down, and read
and expounded Matthew, 5 : 1—16. This discourse,
though delivered in much weakness, was attended with
power to many of the hearers; especially what was
spoken upon the last of these verses; where I insisted
on the infinite wrong done to religion, by having our
light become darkness, instead of shining before men.
Many in the congregation were now deeply affected
with a sense of their deficiency with respect to a spiritual conversation which might recommend religion
to others, and a spirit of concern and watchfulness
seemed to be excited in them. One, in particular, who
had fallen in the sin of drunkenness some time before,
was now deeply convinced of his sin, and the great
dishonor done to religion by his misconduct, and
discovered a great degree of grief and concern on that
account. My soul was refreshed to see this; and
though I had no strength to speak so much as I would
have done, but was obliged to lie down on the bed, yet
I rejoiced to see such an humble melting in the congregation, and that divine truths, though faintly delivered, were attended with so much efficacy upon the
auditory.

Oct. 27.—" Spent the day in overseeing and directing the Indians about mending the fence round their
wheat: was able to walk with them, and contrive their
business, all the forenoon. In the afternoon, was visited by two dear friends, and spent some time in con-

versation with them. Toward night I was able to
walk out, and take care of the Indians again. In the
evening, enjoyed a very peaceful frame.

Oct. 28.—" Rode to Princeton in a very weak state,
had such a violent fever by the way, that I was forced
to alight at a friend's house, and lie down for some
time. Near night, was visited by Mr. Treat, Mr. Beaty
and his wife, and another friend. My spirits were refreshed to see them; but I was surprised, and even
ashamed, that they had taken so much pains as to ride
thirty or forty miles to see me. Was able to sit up
most of the evening; and spent the time in a very
comfortable manner with my friends.

Oct. 29.—" Rode about ten miles with my friends
who came yesterday to see me; and then parted with
them all but one, who stayed on purpose to keep me
company, and cheer my spirits.

Lord's day, Nov. 2.—" Was unable to preach, and
scarcely able to sit up the whole day. Was grieved,
and almost sunk, to see my poor people destitute of the
means of grace; especially as they could not read, and
so were under great disadvantages for spending the
Sabbath comfortably. O, methought, I could be contented to be sick, if my poor flock had a faithful pastor
to feed them with spiritual knowledge! A view of
their want of this was more afflictive to me than all my
bodily illness.

Nov. 3.—" Being now in so weak and low a state
that I was utterly incapable of performing my work,
and having little hope of recovery, unless by much
riding, I thought it my duty to take a journey into
New-England, and to divert myself among my friends,
whom I had not now seen for a long time. Accordingly I took leave of my congregation this day. Be-

fore I left my people, I visited them all in their respective houses, and discoursed to each one, as I thought most proper and suitable for their circumstances, and found great freedom in so doing. I scarcely left one house but some were in tears; and many were not only affected with my being about to leave them, but with the solemn addresses I made them upon divine things; for I was helped to be fervent in spirit while I discoursed to them. When I had thus gone through my congregation, which took me most of the day, and had taken leave of them, and of the school, I left home, and rode about two miles, to the house where I lived in the summer past, and there lodged. Was refreshed this evening, because I had left my congregation so well disposed and affected, and had been so much assisted in making my farewell addresses to them.

Nov. 5.—" Rode to Elizabethtown; intending, as soon as possible, to prosecute my journey into New England; but was, in an hour or two after my arrival, taken much worse. For near a week I was confined to my chamber, and most of the time to my bed; and then so far revived as to be able to walk about the house; but was still confined within doors.

" In the beginning of this extraordinary turn of disorder after my coming to Elizabethtown, I was enabled, through mercy, to maintain a calm, composed, and patient spirit, as I had been before from the beginning of my weakness. After I had been in Elizabethtown about a fortnight, and had so far recovered that I was able to walk about the house, upon a day of thanksgiving kept in this place, I was enabled to recal the mercies of God in such a manner as greatly affected me, and filled me with thankfulness and praise. Especially my soul praised God for his work of grace among the Indians, and the enlargement of his dear kingdom. My soul blessed God for what he is in himself, and adored him, that he ever would display himself to creatures. I rejoiced that he was God, and longed that all should know it, and feel it, and rejoice in it. 'Lord, glorify thyself,' was the desire and cry of my soul. O that all people might love and praise the blessed God; that he might have all possible honor and glory from the intelligent world!

"After this comfortable thanksgiving season, I frequently enjoyed freedom, enlargement, and engagedness of soul in prayer; and was enabled to intercede with God for my dear congregation, very often for every family, and every person in particular. It was often a great comfort to me, that I could pray heartily to God for those to whom I could not speak, and whom I was not allowed to see. But, at other times, my spirits were so low, and my bodily vigor so much wasted, that I had scarce any affections at all.

"In December, I had revived so far as to be able to walk abroad and visit my friends, and seemed to be gaining health, in the main, until Lord's day, December 21, when I attended public worship, and labored much, at the Lord's table, to bring forth a certain corruption, and have it slain, as being an enemy to God and my own soul; and could not but hope that I had gained some strength against this, as well as other corruptions; and felt some brokenness of heart for my sin.

"After this, having perhaps taken some cold, I began to decline as to bodily health; and continued to do so till the latter end of January, 1747. Having a violent cough, a considerable fever, an asthmatic disorder, and no appetite for any manner of food, nor any power of digestion, I was reduced to so low a state, that my

friends, I believe, generally despaired of my life; and
some of them, for a considerable time, thought I could
scarce live a day. I could then think of nothing with
any application of mind, and seemed to be in a great
measure void of all affection, and was exercised with
great temptations; but yet was not, ordinarily, afraid
of death.

Lord's day, Feb. 1.—"Though in a very weak and
low state, I enjoyed a considerable degree of comfort
and sweetness in divine things; and was enabled to
plead and use arguments with God in prayer, I think,
with a child-like spirit. That passage of scripture oc-
curred to my mind, and gave me great assistance, 'If
ye, being evil, know how to give good gifts to your
children, how much more will your heavenly Father
give the Holy Spirit to them that ask him?' This text
I was helped to plead, and insist upon; and saw the divine faithfulness engaged for dealing with me better
than any earthly parent can do with his child. This
season so refreshed my soul, that my body seemed also
to be a gainer by it. From this time I began gradually
to amend. As I recovered some strength, vigor, and
spirit, I found at times some freedom and life in the exercises of devotion, and some longings after spirituality
and a life of usefulness to the interests of the great Redeemer. At other times, I was awfully barren and lifeless, and out of frame for the things of God; so that I
was ready often to cry out, 'O that it were with me as
in months past!' O that God had taken me away in
the midst of my usefulness, with a sudden stroke, that
I might not have been under a necessity of trifling away
time in diversions! O that I had never lived to spend
so much precious time in so poor a manner, and to so
little purpose! Thus I often reflected, was grieved,

ashamed, and even confounded, sunk, and discouraged.

Feb. 24.—"I was able to ride as far as Newark, (having been confined in Elizabethtown almost four months,) and the next day returned to Elizabethtown. My spirits were somewhat refreshed with the ride, though my body was weary.

Feb. 28.—Was visited by an Indian of my own congregation, who brought me letters, and good news of the sober and good behavior of my people in general. This refreshed my soul. I could not but retire and bless God for his goodness; and found, I trust, a truly thankful frame of spirit, that God seemed to be building up that congregation for himself.

March 4.—"I met with reproof from a friend, which, although I thought I did not deserve it from him, yet was, I trust, blessed of God to make me more tenderly afraid of sin, more jealous over myself, and more concerned to keep both heart and life pure and unblameable. It likewise caused me to reflect on my past deadness and want of spirituality, and to abhor myself, and look on myself as most unworthy. This frame of mind continued the next day; and for several days after, I grieved to think that in my necessary diversions I had not maintained more seriousness, solemnity, and heavenly affection and conversation. Thus my spirits were often depressed and sunk; and yet, I trust, that reproof was made to be beneficial to me.

"*March* 11, being kept in Elizabethtown as a day of fasting and prayer, I was able to attend public worship; which was the first time I had been able so to do since December 21. O how much weakness and distress did God carry me through in this space of time! But 'having obtained help from him,' I yet live. O that I could live more to his glory!

Lord's day, March 15.—"Was able again to attend public worship, and felt some earnest desires of being restored to the ministerial work: felt, I think, some spirit and life to speak for God.

March 18.—"Rode out with a design to visit my people, and the next day arrived among them; but was under great dejection in my journey.

"On *Friday* morning I rose early, walked about among my people, enquired into their state and concerns, and found an additional weight and burden on my spirits, upon hearing some things disagreeable. I endeavored to go to God with my distresses, and made some kind of lamentable complaint, and in a broken manner spread my difficulties before God; but notwithstanding, my mind continued very gloomy. About ten o'clock I called my people together, and after having explained and sung a psalm, I prayed with them. There was considerable affection among them; I doubt not, in some instances, that which was more than merely natural."

This was the last interview which he ever had with his people. About eleven o'clock the same day he left them, and the next day came to Elizabethtown.

March 28.—"Was taken this morning with violent griping pains. These pains were extreme and constant for several hours; so that it seemed impossible for me, without a miracle, to live twenty-four hours in such distress. I lay confined to my bed the whole day, and in distressing pain all the former part of it; but it pleased God to bless means for the abatement of my distress. Was exceedingly weakened by this pain, and continued so for several days following; being exercised with a fever, cough, and nocturnal sweats. In this distressed case, so long as my head was free of vapory confusions, *death* appeared agreeable to me. I looked on it as the end of toils, and an entrance into a place 'where the weary are at rest;' and think I had some relish for the entertainments of the heavenly state; so that by these I was allured and drawn, as well as driven by the fatigues of life. O how happy it is to be drawn by desires of a state of perfect holiness!

April 4.—"Was sunk and dejected, very restless and uneasy, by reason of the misimprovement of time; and yet knew not what to do. I longed to spend time in fasting and prayer, that I might be delivered from indolence and coldness in the things of God; but, alas, I had not bodily strength for these exercises! O how blessed a thing it is to enjoy peace of conscience! but how dreadful is a want of inward peace and composure of soul! It is impossible, I find, to enjoy this happiness without *redeeming time*, and maintaining a spiritual frame of mind.

Lord's day, April 5.—"It grieved me to find myself so inconceivably barren. My soul thirsted for grace; but, alas, how far was I from obtaining what appeared to me so exceeding excellent! I was ready to despair of ever being a holy creature, and yet my soul was desirous of 'following hard after God;' but never did I see myself so far from 'having apprehended, or being already perfect,' as at this time. The Lord's supper being this day administered, I attended the ordinance; and though I saw in myself a dreadful emptiness and want of grace, and saw myself as it were at an infinite distance from that purity which becomes the gospel, yet at the communion, especially during the distribution of the bread, I enjoyed some warmth of affection, and felt a tender love to the brethren; and, I think, to the glorious Redeemer, the *first-born* among them. I endeavored then to bring forth mine and his 'enemies,' and 'slay them before him;' and found great freedom in begging deliverance from this spiritual death, as well as in asking divine favors for my friends and congregation, and the church of Christ in general.

April 10.—"This day my brother John arrived at Elizabethtown. Spent some time in conversation with him; but was extremely weak."

This brother had been sent for by the *Correspondents*, to take care of and instruct Brainerd's congregation of Indians; he being obliged by his illness to be absent from them. He continued to take care of them till Brainerd's death, and was soon after ordained his *successor* in his mission, and to the charge of his congregation.

April 17.—"In the evening, could not but think that God helped me to 'draw near to the throne of grace,' though most unworthy, and gave me a sense of his favor; which afforded me inexpressible support and encouragement. Though I scarcely dared to hope that the mercy was real, it appeared so great; yet could not but rejoice that ever God should discover his reconciled face to such a vile sinner. Shame and confusion, at times, covered me; and then hope, and joy, and admiration of divine goodness gained the ascendancy. Sometimes I could not but admire the divine goodness, that the Lord had not let me fall into all the grossest and vilest acts of sin.

April 20.—"Was in a very disordered state, and kept my bed most of the day. I enjoyed a little more comfort than in several of the preceding days. *This day I arrived at the age of twenty-nine years.*

April 21.—"I set out on my journey for New-Eng-

land, in order (if it might be the will of God) to recover
my health by riding."

This proved his final departure from New-Jersey.
He travelled slowly, and arrived among his friends at
East-Haddam, about the beginning of May. There is
very little account in his diary, of the time that passed
from his setting out on his journey to May 10. He
speaks of his sometimes finding his heart rejoicing in
the glorious perfections of God, and longing to live to
him; but complains of the unfixedness of his thoughts,
and their being easily diverted from divine subjects,
and cries out of his leanness, as testifying against him,
in the loudest manner. Concerning those *diversions*
which he was obliged to use for his health, he says,
that he sometimes found he could use diversions with
" singleness of heart," aiming at the glory of God; but
that he also found there was a necessity of great care
and watchfulness, lest he should lose that spiritual temper of mind in his diversions, and lest they should degenerate into what was merely selfish, without any
supreme aim at the glory of God in them.

Lord's day, May 10.—" I could not but feel some
measure of gratitude to God at this time, that he had
always disposed me, in my ministry, to insist on the
great doctrines of *regeneration,* the *new creature, faith
in Christ, progressive sanctification, supreme love to
God, living entirely to the glory of God, being not our
own,* and the like. God thus helped me to see, in the
surest manner, from time to time, that these, and the
like doctrines necessarily connected with them, are the
only foundation of safety and salvation for perishing
sinners and that those divine dispositions which are
consonant hereto, are that *holiness,* ' without which no
man shall see the Lord.' The exercise of these God-

like tempers—wherein the soul acts in a kind of concert with God, and would be and do every thing that is pleasing to him—I saw, would stand by the soul in a dying hour; for God must, I think, *deny himself*, if he cast away *his own image*, even the soul that is one in desires with himself.

Lord's day, May 17.—" Spent the forenoon at home, being unable to attend public worship. At this time, God gave me such an affecting sense of my own vileness, and the exceeding sinfulness of my heart, that there seemed to be nothing but sin and corruption within me. ' Innumerable evils compassed me about;' my want of spirituality and holy living, my neglect of God, and living to myself. All the abominations of my heart and life seemed to be open to my view; and I had nothing to say, but, 'God be merciful to me a sinner.' Toward noon, I saw that the grace of God in Christ is infinitely free toward sinners, such sinners as I was. I also saw that God is the supreme good; that in his presence is life; and I began to long to die, that I might be with him, in a state of freedom from all sin. O how a small glimpse of his excellency refreshed my soul! O how worthy is the blessed God to be loved, adored, and delighted in, for himself, for his own divine excellencies!

"Though I felt much dulness, and want of a spirit of prayer this week, yet I had some glimpses of the excellency of divine things; and especially one morning, in secret meditation and prayer, the excellency and beauty of holiness, as a likeness to the glorious God, was so discovered to me, that I began to long earnestly to be in that world where holiness dwells in perfection. I seemed to long for this perfect holiness, not so much for the sake of my own happiness, although I saw clearly that this was the greatest, yea, the only happiness of the soul, as that I might please God, live entirely to him, and glorify him to the utmost stretch of my rational powers and capacities.

Lord's day, May 24.—" (At Long-Meadow, in Massachusetts.) Could not but think, as I have often remarked to others, that much more of *true religion* consists in *deep humility, brokenness of heart, and an abasing sense of barrenness and want of grace and holiness,* than most who are called Christians imagine; especially those who have been esteemed the converts of the late day. Many seem to know of no other religion but elevated joys and affections, arising only from some flights of imagination, or some suggestion made to their mind, of Christ being their's, God loving them, and the like."

On Thursday, May 28, he came from Long-Meadow to Northampton, appearing vastly better than, by his account, he had been in the winter—indeed so well, that he was able to ride twenty-five miles in a day, and to walk half a mile; and appeared cheerful, and free from melancholy; but yet he was undoubtedly, at that time, in a confirmed, incurable consumption.

I had had much opportunity, before this, of particular information concerning him, from many who were well acquainted with him; and had enjoyed a personal interview with him, at New-Haven, near four years before, as has been already mentioned; but now I had opportunity for a more full acquaintance. I found him remarkably sociable, pleasant, and entertaining in his conversation; yet solid, savory, spiritual, and very profitable. He appeared meek, modest, and humble; far from any stiffness, moroseness, or affected singularity in speech or behavior, and seeming to dislike all such

things. We enjoyed not only the benefit of his conversation, but had the comfort and advantage of joining with him in family prayer, from time to time. His
manner of praying was very agreeable, most becoming a worm of the dust and a disciple of Christ, addressing an infinitely great and holy God, the Father
of mercies; not with florid expressions, or a studied
eloquence; not with any intemperate vehemence, or
indecent boldness. It was at the greatest distance from
any appearance of ostentation, and from every thing
that might look as though he meant to recommend
himself to those that were about him, or set himself off to
their acceptance. It was free also from vain repetitions;
without impertinent excursions, or needless multiply-
ing of words. He expressed himself with the strictest
propriety, with weight and pungency; and yet, what
his lips uttered seemed to flow from the *fulness of his
heart*, as deeply impressed with a great and solemn
sense of our necessities, unworthiness, and dependence,
and of God's infinite greatness, excellency and sufficiency, rather than merely from a warm and fruitful
brain, pouring out good expressions. I know not that
I ever heard him so much as ask a blessing or return
thanks at table, but there was something remarkable to
be observed both in the matter and manner of the performance. In his prayers, he insisted much on the
prosperity of Zion, the advancement of Christ's kingdom in the world, and the flourishing and propagation
of religion among the Indians. And he generally made
it one petition in his prayer, "that we might not outlive
our usefulness."

Lord's day, May 31.—"(At Northampton.) I had
little inward sweetness in religion most of the week
past; not realizing and beholding spiritually the glory

of God and the blessed Redeemer; from whence always arise my comforts and joys in religion, if I have any at all; and if I cannot so behold the excellencies and perfections of God, as to cause me to rejoice in him for what he is in himself, I have no solid foundation for joy. To rejoice, only because I apprehend I have an interest in Christ, and shall be finally saved, is a poor mean business indeed."

This week he consulted Dr. Mather, at my house, concerning his illness; who plainly told him, that there were great evidences of his being in a confirmed *consumption*, and that he could give him no encouragement that he would ever recover. But it seemed not to occasion the least discomposure in him, nor to make any manner of alteration as to the cheerfulness and serenity of his mind, or the freedom or pleasantness of his conversation.

Lord's day, June 7.—"My attention was greatly engaged, and my soul so drawn forth this day, by what I heard of the 'exceeding preciousness of the saving grace of God's Spirit,' that it almost overcame my body, in my weak state. I saw that true grace is exceedingly precious indeed; that it is very rare; and that there is but a very small degree of it, even where the reality of it is to be found; at least I saw this to be *my* case.

"In the preceding week, I enjoyed some comfortable seasons of meditation. One morning, the cause of God appeared exceedingly precious to me. The Redeemer's kingdom is all that is valuable in the earth, and I could not but long for the promotion of it in the world. I saw also, that this cause is God's; that he has an infinitely greater regard and concern for it than I could possibly have; that if I have any true love to this blessed interest, it is only a drop derived from that ocean. Hence I was ready to 'lift up my head with joy,' and conclude, 'Well, if God's cause be so dear and precious to him, he will promote it.' Thus I did, as it were, rest on God that he would surely promote that which was so agreeable to his own will; though the time when, must still be left to his sovereign pleasure."

He was advised by physicians still to continue riding, as what would tend, above any other means, to prolong his life. He was at a loss, for some time, which way to bend his course; but finally determined to ride from hence to Boston; we having concluded that one of our family should go with him, and be helpful to him in his weak and low state.

June 9.—" I set out on a journey from Northampton to Boston. Travelled slowly, and got some acquaintance with a number of ministers on the road.

"Having now continued to ride for a considerable time, I felt much better than I had formerly done, and found, that in proportion to the prospect I had of being restored to a state of usefulness, I desired the continuance of life; but now *death* appeared inconceivably more desirable to me than a useless life; yet, blessed be God, I found my heart, at times, fully resigned and reconciled to this greatest of afflictions, if God saw fit thus to deal with me.

June 12.—" I arrived in Boston this day, somewhat fatigued with my journey. Observed that there is no *rest* but in God; fatigues of body, and anxieties of mind, attend us both in town and country: no place is exempt.

Lord's day, June 14.—" I enjoyed some enlargement and sweetness in family prayer, as well as in secret exercises; God appeared excellent, his ways full of pleasure and peace, and all I wanted was a spirit of holy fervency to live to him.

June 17.—"This and the two preceding days I spent mainly in visiting the ministers of the town, and was treated with great respect by them.

June 18.—"I was taken exceedingly ill, and brought to the gates of death, by the breaking of small ulcers in my lungs, as my physician supposed. In this extremely weak state I continued for several weeks; and was frequently reduced so low as to be utterly speechless, and not so much as to whisper a word. Even after I had so far revived as to walk about the house, and to step out of doors, I was exercised every day with a faint turn, which continued usually four or five hours; at which times, though I was not so utterly speechless but that I could say yes or no, yet I could not converse at all, nor speak one sentence, without making stops for breath; and a number of times my friends gathered round my bed, to see me breathe my last, which they expected every moment, as I myself also did.

"How I was, the first day or two of my illness, with regard to the exercise of reason, I scarcely know. I believe I was somewhat shattered with the violence of the fever at times; but the third day of my illness, and constantly afterward, for four or five weeks together, I enjoyed as much serenity of mind, and clearness of thought, as perhaps ever in my life. I think that my mind never penetrated with so much ease and freedom into divine things, as at this time; and I never felt so capable of demonstrating the truth of many important doctrines of the Gospel as now. As I saw clearly the truth of those great doctrines, which are justly styled the *doctrines of grace;* so I saw with no less clearness, that the *essence of religion* consisted in the soul's *conformity to God*, and acting above all selfish views for his *glory*, longing to be *for him*, to live *to him*, and please and honor *him* in all things: and this from a clear view of his infinite excellency and worthiness in himself, to be loved, adored, worshipped, and served by all intelligent creatures. Thus I saw, that when a soul *loves* God with a supreme love, he therein acts like the blessed God himself, who most justly loves himself in that manner. So when God's interest and his are become one, and he longs that God should be *glorified*, and rejoices to think that he is unchangeably possessed of the highest glory and blessedness, herein also he acts in conformity to God. In like manner, when the soul is fully resigned to, and rests satisfied and content with the divine will, here it is also *conformed* to God.

" I saw farther, that as this divine temper, by which the soul exalts God, and treads self in the dust, is wrought in the soul by God's discovering his own glorious perfections *in the face of Jesus Christ* to it by the special influences of the Holy Spirit, so he cannot but have *regard to it* as his own work ; and as it is his image in his soul, he cannot but take *delight* in it. Then I saw again, that if God should slight and reject his own *moral image*, he must needs *deny himself;* which he cannot do. And thus I saw the *stability* and *infallibility* of this religion ; and that those who are truly possessed of it, have the most complete and satisfying evidence of their being interested in all the benefits of Christ's redemption, having their hearts conformed to him ; and that these, and these only, are qualified for the employments and entertainments of God's kingdom of glory ; as none but these have any relish for the business of heaven, which is to ascribe glory to

God, and not to themselves; and that God (though I would speak it with great reverence of his name and perfection) cannot, without denying himself, finally cast such away.

"The next thing I had then to do, was to inquire whether *this* was *my* religion; and here God was pleased to help me to the most easy remembrance and critical review of what had passed in course, of a religious nature, through several of the latter years of my life. Although I could discover much corruption attending my best duties, many selfish views and carnal ends, much spiritual pride and self-exaltation, and innumerable other evils which compassed me about, yet God was pleased, as I was reviewing, quickly to put this question out of doubt, by showing me that I had, from time to time, acted above the utmost influence of mere self-love; that I had longed to please and glorify him, as my highest happiness, &c. This review was, through grace, attended with a present feeling of the same divine temper of mind. I felt now pleased to think of the glory of God, and longed for heaven, as a state wherein I might glorify him perfectly, rather than a place of happiness for myself. This feeling of the love of God in my heart, which I trust the Spirit of God excited in me afresh, was sufficient to give me a full satisfaction, and make me long, as I had many times before done, to be with Christ.

"As God was pleased to afford me clearness of thought, and composure of mind, almost continually for several weeks, under my great weakness; so he enabled me, in some measure, to improve my time, as I hope, to valuable purposes. I was enabled to write a number of important letters to friends in remote places; and sometimes I wrote when I was speechless,

i. e. unable to maintain conversation with any body;
though perhaps I was able to speak a word or two so
as to be heard.

"At this season also, while I was confined at Boston,
I read with care and attention some papers of old Mr.
Shepard, lately come to light, and designed for the
press; and, as I was desired and greatly urged, made
some corrections where the sense was left dark for
want of a word or two. Beside this, I had many vi-
sitants, with whom, when I was able to speak, I always
conversed of the things of religion, and was peculiarly
assisted in distinguishing between the *true* and *false*
religion of the times. There is scarcely any subject
which has been matter of controversy of late, but I was
at one time or other compelled to discuss and show my
opinion respecting it, and that frequently before numbers of people. Especially, I discoursed repeatedly on
the nature and necessity of that *humiliation, self-emp-
tiness,* or full conviction of a person's being utterly
undone in himself, which is necessary in order to a
saving faith; and the extreme difficulty of being brought
to this, and the great danger there is of persons taking
up with some self-righteous appearances of it. The
danger of this I especially dwelt upon, being persuaded
that multitudes perish in this hidden way; and because
so little is said from most pulpits to discover any danger here; so that persons being never effectually brought
to *die in themselves,* are never truly *united to Christ,*
and so perish. I also discoursed much on what I take
to be the essence of true religion; endeavoring plainly
to describe that god-like temper and disposition of soul,
and that holy conversation and behavior, which may
justly claim the honor of having God for its original
and patron. I have reason to hope God blessed my

way of discoursing and distinguishing to some, both. ministers and people; so that my time was not wholly lost."

He was visited while in Boston by many, who showed him uncommon respect, and appeared highly pleased and entertained with his conversation. Beside being honored with the company and respect of ministers of the town, he was visited by several ministers from various parts of the country. He took all opportunities to discourse on the peculiar nature and distinguishing characteristics of true, spiritual, and vital religion; and to bear his testimony against the various false appearances of it, consisting in, or arising from impressions on the *imagination*, sudden and supposed immediate *suggestions* of truth not contained in the Scripture, and that faith which consists *primarily* in a person's believing that Christ died for him in particular, &c. What he said was, for the most part, heard with uncommon attention and regard; and his discourses and reasonings appeared manifestly to have great weight and influence with many with whom he conversed, both ministers and others.

The Commissioners in Boston, of the Society in London for propagating the Gospel in New-England and parts adjacent, having received a legacy of the late Rev. Dr. Daniel Williams, of London, for the support of two missionaries to the heathen, were pleased, while he was in Boston, to consult him about a mission to those Indians called the Six Nations, particularly respecting the qualifications requisite in a missionary to those Indians. They were so satisfied with his sentiments on this head, and had such confidence in his faithfulness, his judgment and discretion in things of this nature, that they desired him to undertake to find and recommend two persons fit to be employed in this business; and very much left the matter with him.

BRAINERD's restoration from his extremely low state in Boston, so as to go abroad again, and to travel, was very unexpected to him and his friends. My daughter, who was with him, writes thus concerning him, in a letter dated June 23:

"On Thursday, he was very ill with a violent fever, and extreme pain in his head and breast, and at turns delirious. So he remained till Saturday evening, when he seemed to be in the agonies of death; the family was up with him till one or two o'clock, expecting that every hour would be his last. On Sabbath day he was a little revived, his head was better, but he was very full of pain, exceeding sore at his breast, and had great difficulty in breathing. Yesterday he was better. Last night he slept but little. This morning he was much worse. Dr. Pynchon says, he has no hope of his life; nor does he think it likely that he will ever come out of the chamber; though he says he *may* be able to come to Northampton."

In another letter, dated June 29, she says:—"Mr. BRAINERD has not so much pain, nor fever, since I last wrote, as before; yet he is extremely weak and low, and very faint, expecting every day will be his last. He says it is impossible for him to live, for he has hardly vigor enough to draw his breath. I went this morning into town, and when I came home, Mr. Bromfield said he never expected I should see him alive, for he lay two hours, as they thought, dying; one could scarcely tell whether he was alive or not; he was not able to speak for some time; but now is much as he was before. The doctor thinks he will drop away in such a turn. Mr. BRAINERD says, he never felt any thing so much like *dissolution* as that he felt to-day; and says, he never had any conception of its being possible for any creature to be alive, and yet so weak as he is from day to day. Dr. Pynchon says, he should not be surprised if he should so recover as to live half a year; nor would it surprise him if he should die in half a day. Since I began to write, he is not so well, having had a faint turn again : yet he is patient and resigned, having no distressing fears, but the contrary."

He expressed himself to one of my neighbors, who at that time saw him in Boston, that he was as certainly a dead man, as if he was shot through the heart. But so it was ordered in divine Providence, that the strength of nature held out, and he revived, to the astonishment of all who knew his case.

After he began to revive, he was visited by his youngest brother, ISRAEL, a student at Yale College; who having heard of his extreme illness, went from thence to Boston, in order to see him; if he might find him alive, which he but little expected. BRAINERD greatly rejoiced to see his brother, especially because he had desired an opportunity of some religious conversation with him before he died. But this meeting was attended with sorrow, as his brother brought to him the tidings of his sister Spencer's death, at Haddam; a sister, between whom and him had long subsisted a peculiarly dear affection, and much intimacy in spiritual things, and whose house he used to make his own when he went to Haddam, his native place. But he had a confidence of her being gone to heaven, and an expectation of soon meeting her there. His brother continued with him till he left the town, and came with him from thence to Northampton. Concerning the last Sabbath Brainerd spent in Boston, he writes in his diary as follows :

Lord's day, July 19.—" I was just able to attend public worship, being carried to the house of God in a chaise. Heard Dr. Sewall preach in the forenoon: partook of the Lord's supper at this time. In this ordinance I saw astonishing divine *wisdom* displayed, such wisdom as clearly required the tongues of angels and glorified saints to celebrate. It seemed to me that I never should do any thing at adoring the infinite wisdom of God, discovered in the contrivance of man's redemption, until I arrived at a world of perfection; yet I could not help striving ' to call upon my soul, and all within me, to bless the name of God.' In the afternoon, heard Mr. Prince preach. I saw more of God in the *wisdom* discovered in the plan of man's redemption, than I saw of any other of his perfections, through the whole day."

The next day, having bid an affectionate farewell to his friends, he set out in the cool of the afternoon, on his journey to Northampton, attended by his brother and my daughter, who went with him to Boston; and would have been accompanied out of the town by a number of gentlemen, besides the respected person who gave him his company for some miles on that occasion, as a testimony of their esteem and respect, had not his aversion to any thing of pomp and show prevented it.

July 25.—" I arrived here, at Northampton; having set out from Boston on Monday, about 4 o'clock P. M. In this journey I usually rode about sixteen miles a day. Was sometimes extremely tired and faint on the road, so that it seemed impossible for me to proceed any further; at other times I was considerably better, and felt some freedom both of body and mind.

Lord's day, July 26.—" This day I saw clearly that

I should never be happy; yea, that God himself could not make me happy, unless I could be in a capacity to 'please and glorify him for ever.' Take away this, and admit me in all the fine heavens that can be conceived of by men or angels, and I should still be miserable for ever."

Though he had so revived as to be able to travel thus far, yet he manifested no expectation of recovery. He supposed, as his physician did, that his being brought so near to death at Boston, was owing to the breaking of ulcers in his lungs. He told me that he had several such ill turns before, only not to so high a degree, but, as he supposed, owing to the same cause, viz. the breaking of ulcers; that he was brought lower and lower every time; that it appeared to him, that in his last sickness he was brought as low as he could be, and yet live; and that he had not the least expectation of surviving the next return of this breaking of ulcers: he still appeared perfectly calm in the prospect of death.

On *Wednesday* morning, the week after he came to Northampton, his brother Israel left us for New-Haven, and he took leave of him, never expecting to see him again in this world.

When BRAINERD came hither, he had so much strength as to be able, from day to day, to ride out two or three miles, and sometimes to pray in the family; but from this time he gradually decayed, becoming weaker and weaker. As long as he lived, he spoke much of that *future prosperity of Zion* which is so often foretold and promised in the Scriptures; it was a theme upon which he delighted to dwell; and his mind seemed to be carried forth with earnest concern about it, and intense desires that religion might speedily and abundantly re-

vive and flourish; yea, the nearer death advanced, and
the more the symptoms of its approach increased, still
the more did his mind seem to be taken up with this
subject. He told me, when near his end, that "he
never, in all his life, had his mind so led forth in desires and earnest prayers for the flourishing of Christ's
kingdom on earth, as since he was brought so exceeding low at Boston." He seemed much to wonder that
there appeared no more of a disposition in ministers
and people to *pray* for the flourishing of religion
through the world; that so little a part of their prayers
was generally taken up about it, in their families and
elsewhere. Particularly, he several times expressed
his wonder that there appeared no more forwardness
to comply with the proposal lately made, in a Memo-
rial from a number of ministers in Scotland, and sent
over into America, for united extraordinary prayer,
amongst Christ's ministers and people, for the coming
of Christ's kingdom: and sent it as his dying advice to
his own congregation, that they should practise agreeably to that proposal.

Though he was constantly exceeding weak, yet
there appeared in him a continual care well to improve
time, and fill it up with something that might be profitable, and in some respect for the glory of God or the
good of men; either profitable conversation, or writing
letters to absent friends; or noting something in his
diary; or looking over his former writings, correcting
them, and preparing them to be left in the hands of
others at his death; or giving some directions concerning the future management of his people; or in secret
devotions. He seemed never to be easy, however ill,
if he was not doing something for God, or in his service. After he came hither, he wrote a *preface* to a

diary of Mr. Shepard, contained in the papers above mentioned, which has since been published.

In his diary for *Lord's day*, August 9, he speaks of longing desires after death, through a sense of the excellency of a state of *perfection*. In his diary for *Lord's day*, August 16, he speaks of his having so much refreshment of *soul* in the house of God, that it seemed also to refresh his *body*. And this is not only noted in his diary, but was very observable to others; it was apparent, not only that his mind was exhilarated with inward consolation, but also that his animal spirits and bodily strength seemed to be remarkably restored, as though he had forgot his illness. But this was the last time that ever he attended public worship on the Sabbath.

On *Tuesday* morning that week, as I was absent on a journey, he prayed with my family, but not without much difficulty, for want of bodily strength; and this was the last family prayer that he ever made. He had been wont, till now, frequently to ride out, two or three miles: but this week, on Thursday, was the last time he ever did so.

Lord's day, Aug. 23.—" This morning I was considerably refreshed with the thought, yea, the hope and expectation of the *enlargement of Christ's kingdom;* and I could not but hope that the time was at hand, when Babylon the great would fall, and ' rise no more.' This led me to some spiritual meditations, which were very refreshing to me. I was unable to attend public worship either part of the day; but God was pleased to afford me fixedness and satisfaction in divine thoughts. Nothing so refreshes my soul, as when I can go to God, yea, ' to God my exceeding joy.'

When he is such to my soul, O how unspeakably delightful is this !

" In the week past I had divers turns of inward refreshing, though my body was inexpressibly weak, followed continually with agues and fevers. Sometimes my soul centered in God, as my only portion; and I felt that I should be for ever unhappy, if He did not reign. I saw the sweetness and happiness of being his subject, at his disposal. This made all my difficulties quickly vanish."

Till this week he had been wont to lodge in a room above stairs, but he now grew so weak, that he was no longer able to go up stairs and down. *Friday, August* 28, was the last time he ever went above stairs; henceforward he betook himself to a lower room.

On *Wednesday, Sept.* 2, being the day of our public lecture, he seemed to be refreshed with seeing the neighboring ministers who came hither to the lecture, and expressed a great desire once more to go to the house of God on that day; and accordingly rode to the meeting, and attended divine service, while the Rev. Mr. Woodbridge, of Hatfield, preached. He signified that he supposed it to be the last time he should ever attend public worship; as it proved. Indeed it was the last time that he ever went out of our gate.

On the Saturday evening next following, he was unexpectedly visited by his brother, Mr. JOHN BRAINERD, who came to see him from New-Jersey. He was much refreshed by this unexpected visit, this brother being peculiarly dear to him; and he seemed to rejoice in a devout and solemn manner, to see him, and to hear the comfortable tidings which he brought concerning the state of his dear congregation of Christian Indians. A circumstance of this visit, of which he was exceedingly glad, was, that his brother brought him some of his *private writings* from New-Jersey, and particularly his *diary*, which he had kept for many years past.

Lord's day, Sept. 6.—" I began to read some of my private writings which my brother brought me, and was considerably refreshed with what I found in them.

Sept. 7.—" I proceeded further in reading my old private writings, and found that they had the same effect upon me as before. I could not but rejoice and bless God for what passed long ago, which, without writing, had been entirely lost.

" This evening, when I was in great distress of body, my soul longed that *God should be glorified.* O that I could for ever live to God ! The day, I trust, is at hand, the perfect day. O the day of deliverance from all sin !

Lord's day, Sept. 13.—" I was much refreshed and engaged in meditation and writing, and found a heart to act for God. My spirits were refreshed, and my soul delighted to do something for God."

On the evening of that Lord's day, his feet began to swell; and thenceforward swelled more and more : a symptom of his dissolution coming on. The next day, his brother John left him, being obliged to return to New-Jersey on some business of great importance and necessity ; intending to return again with all possible speed, hoping to see his brother yet once more in the land of the living.

BRAINERD having now, with much deliberation, considered the subject referred to him by the commissioners of the Society for propagating the Gospel in New-England and parts adjacent, wrote them about this time, recommending two young gentlemen of his acquaintance, Mr. Elihu Spencer, of East Haddam, and Mr.

Job Strong, of Northampton, as suitable missionaries to the Six Nations. The commissioners, on the receipt of this letter, cheerfully and unanimously agreed to accept of and employ the persons whom he had recommended.

On *Wednesday, Sept.* 16, he wrote to some charitable gentlemen in Boston in behalf of the Indian school, showing the need of another schoolmaster, or some person to assist the schoolmaster in instructing the Indian children. These gentlemen, on the receipt of his letter, had a meeting, and agreed with great cheerfulness to give £200 (in bills of the old tenor) for the support of another schoolmaster; and desired the Rev. Mr. Pemberton, of New-York, (who was then at Poston, and was also at their desire, present at the meeting,) as soon as possible to procure a suitable person for that service; and also agreed, in accordance with an intimation from BRAINERD, to allow £75 to defray some special charges which were requisite to encourage the mission to the Six Nations.

BRAINERD spent himself much in writing those letters, being exceedingly weak; but it seemed to be much to his satisfaction that he had been enabled to do it, hoping that it was something done for God, and which might be for the advancement of Christ's kingdom and glory. In writing the last of these letters, he was obliged to use the hand of another.

On Thursday of this week, (Sept. 17,) when he went out of his lodging-room for the last time, he was again visited by his brother ISRAEL, who continued with him till his death. On that evening he was taken with something of a diarrhea, which he looked upon as another sign of his approaching death; whereupon he expressed himself thus: " Oh, the glorious time is now coming'

I have longed to serve God perfectly: now God will gratify those desires!" And from time to time, at the several steps and new symptoms of the sensible approach of his dissolution, he was so far from being sunk or depressed in spirits, that he seemed to be *animated* and made more cheerful, as being glad at the appearance of death's approach. He often used the epithet *glorious*, when speaking of the day of his death. calling it that *glorious day*. And as he saw his dissolution gradually approaching, he talked much about it; and with perfect calmness spoke of a future state. He also settled all his affairs, giving directions very particularly and minutely concerning what he would have done in one respect and another after his decease. And the nearer death approached, the more desirous he seemed to be to depart. He several times spoke of the different kinds of willingness to die; and represented it as an ignoble, mean kind, to be willing to leave the body only to get rid of pain; or to go to heaven only to get honor and advancement there.

Sept. 19.—"Near night, while I attempted to walk a little, my thoughts turned thus: ' How infinitely sweet to love God, and be all for him!' Upon which it was suggested to me, ' You are not an angel, not lively and active.' To which my whole soul immediately replied, 'I as sincerely desire to love and glorify God as any angel in heaven.' Upon which it was suggested again, ' But you are filthy, not fit for heaven.' Hereupon instantly appeared the blessed robes of Christ's *righteousness*, in which I could not but exult and triumph; and I viewed the infinite excellency of God, and my soul even broke with longings that God should be glorified. I thought of dignity in heaven, but instantly the thought returned, 'I do not go to heaven to get

honor, but to give all possible glory and praise.' O
how I longed that God should be glorified on *earth*
also! O I was *made* for eternity, if God might be
glorified! Bodily pains I cared not for; though I was
then in extremity, I never felt easier. I felt willing to
glorify God in that state of bodily distress as long as
he pleased I should continue in it. The grave appeared really sweet, and I longed to lodge my weary bones
in it; but O that God might be glorified! this was the
burden of all my cry. O I knew that I should be active as an angel in heaven, and that I should be stripped of my filthy garments! so that there was no objection. But, O to love and praise God more, to please
him for ever! this my soul panted after, and even now
pants for, while I write. Oh that God might be glorified in the whole earth! ' Lord let thy kingdom come.'
I longed for a spirit of preaching to descend and rest
on ministers, that they might address the consciences
of men with closeness and power. I saw that God
had the residue of the Spirit, and my soul longed that
it should be ' poured from on high.' I could not but
plead with God for my dear congregation, that he
would preserve it, and not suffer his great name to lose
its glory in that work; my soul still longing that God
might be glorified."

The extraordinary frame he was in that evening
could not be hid. "His mouth spake out of the abun-
dance of his heart," expressing in a very affecting manner much the same things as are written in his diary.
Among very many other extraordinary expressions
which he then uttered, were such as these: "My
heaven is to please God, and glorify him, and to give all
to him, and to be wholly devoted to his glory; that is
the heaven I long for; that is my religion, and that is

my happiness, and always was, ever since I suppose I had any true religion; and all those that are of that religion shall meet me in heaven. I do not go to heaven to be advanced, but to give honor to God. It is no matter where I shall be stationed in heaven, whether I have a high or low seat there; but to love, and please, and glorify God is all. Had I a thousand souls, if they were worth any thing, I would give them all to God; but I have nothing to give when all is done. It is impossible for any rational creature to be happy without acting all *for God;* God himself could not make him happy any other way. I long to be in heaven, praising and glorifying God with the holy angels; all my desire is to glorify God. My heart goes out to the burying place; it seems to me a desirable place: but O to glorify God! that is it; that is above all. It is a great comfort to me to think that I have done a little for God in the world; Oh! it is but a very small matter, yet I have done a little, and I lament that I have not done more for him. There is nothing in the world worth living for, but doing good, and finishing God's work, doing the work that Christ did. I see nothing else in the world that can yield any satisfaction besides living to God, pleasing him, and doing his whole will. My greatest joy and comfort has been to do something for promoting the interest of religion and the souls of particular persons; and now, in my illness, while I am full of pain and distress from day to day, all the comfort I have is in being able to do some little service for God, either by something I say, or by writing, or in some other way."

He intermingled with these, and other like expressions, many pathetical counsels to those who were about him, particularly to my children and servants.

He applied nimself to some of my younger children at this time; calling them to him, and speaking to them one by one; setting before them, in a very plain manner, the nature and essence of true piety, and its great importance and necessity; earnestly warning them not to rest in any thing short of a true and thorough change of heart, and a life devoted to God. He counselled them not to be slack in the great business of religion, nor in the least to delay it; enforcing his counsels with this, that his words were the words of a *dying man*. Said he, "I shall die here, and here I shall be buried, and here you will see my grave, and I wish you to remember what I have said to you. I am going into eternity; and it is sweet for me to think of eternity; the endlessness of it makes it sweet: but O what shall I say of the eternity of the wicked! I cannot mention it, nor think of it; the thought is too dreadful. When you see my grave, then remember what I said to you while I was alive; then think how the man who lies in that grave counselled and warned you to prepare for death."

His *body* seemed to be marvellously strengthened, through the inward vigor and refreshment of his mind; so that, although before he was so weak that he could hardly utter a sentence, yet now he continued his most affecting and profitable discourse to us for more than an hour, with scarce any intermission; and said of it when he had done, "it was the last sermon that ever he should preach." This extraordinary frame of mind continued the next day, of which he speaks in his diary as follows:

Lord's day, Sept. 20.—"Was still in a sweet and comfortable frame, and was again melted with desires that God might be glorified, and with longings to love and live to him. Longed for the influences of the divine Spirit to descend on *ministers* in an especial manner. And O I longed to be with God, to behold his glory, and to bow in his presence."

It appears by what is noted in his diary, both of this day and the evening preceding, that his mind at this time was much impressed with a sense of the importance of the work of the *ministry*, and the need of the grace of God, and his special spiritual assistance in this work; it also appeared in what he expressed in conversation, particularly in his discourse to his brother Israel, who was then a member of Yale College at New-Haven, prosecuting his studies for the work of the ministry.* He now, and from time to time, in this his dying state, recommended to his brother a life of self-denial, of weanedness from the world and devotedness to God, and an earnest endeavor to obtain much of the grace of God's Spirit, and God's gracious influences on his heart; representing the great need in which ministers stand of them, and the unspeakable benefit of them, from his own experience. Among many other expressions, he said thus: "When ministers feel these special gracious influences on their hearts, it wonderfully assists them to come at the consciences of men, and as it were to handle them with hands; whereas, without them, whatever reason and

* This brother was ingenious, serious, studious, and hopefully pious; there appeared in him many qualities giving hope of his being a great blessing in his day. But it pleased God, soon after the death of his brother, to take him away also. He died that winter at New-Haven, January 6, 1748, of a nervous fever, after about a fortnight's illness.

oratory we make use of, we do but make use of stumps, instead of hands."

Sept. 21.—"I began to correct a little volume of my private writings. God, I believe, remarkably helped me in it; my strength was surprisingly lengthened out, my thoughts were quick and lively, and my soul refreshed, hoping it might be a work for God. O how good, how sweet it is to labor for God!

Sept. 22.—"Was again employed in reading and correcting, and had the same success as the day before. I was exceeding weak, but it seemed to refresh my soul thus to spend time.

Sept. 23.—"I finished my corrections of the little piece before mentioned, and felt uncommonly peaceful; it seemed as if I had now done all my work in this world, and stood ready for my call to a better. As long as I see any thing to be done for God, life is worth having; but O how vain and unworthy it is to live for any lower end! This day I indited a letter, I think, of great importance, to the Rev. Mr. Byram, in New-Jersey. Oh that God would bless and succeed that letter, which was written for the benefit of *his* church !* Oh that God would 'purify the sons of Levi,' that his glory may be advanced! This night I endured a dreadful turn, wherein my life was expected scarce an hour or minute. But, blessed be God, I have enjoyed considerable sweetness in divine things this week, both by night and day.

Sept. 24.—"My strength began to fail exceedingly; which looked, further, as if I had done all my work:

---

* It was concerning the qualifications of ministers, and the examination and licensing of candidates for the work of the ministry.

however, I had strength to fold and superscribe my
letter. About two I went to bed, being weak and much
disordered, and lay in a burning fever till night, without any proper rest. In the evening I got up, having
fain down in some of my clothes; but was in the greatest distress, having an uncommon kind of hiccough;
which either strangled me, or threw me into a strain-
ing to vomit, accompanied with other griping pains.
O the distress of this evening! I had little expectation
of living the night through, nor indeed had any about
me; and I longed for the finishing moment! I was
obliged to repair to bed by six o'clock; and through
mercy enjoyed some rest; but was grievously distressed at turns with the hiccough. My soul breathed
after God, 'When shall I come to God, even to God,
my exceeding joy?' Oh for his blessed likeness!

Sept. 25.—" I was unspeakably weak, and little better than speechless all the day; however, I was able to
write a little, and some part of the day was comfortable. O it refreshed my soul to think of former things,
of desires to glorify God, of the pleasures of living to
him! O, blessed God, I am speedily coming to thee,
I hope. Hasten the day, O Lord, if it be thy blessed
will. O come, Lord Jesus, come quickly. Amen.†

Sept. 26.—" I felt the sweetness of divine things this
forenoon, and had the consolation of a consciousness
that I was doing something for God.

Lord's day, Sept. 27.—" This was a very comfortable
day to my soul; I think, I awoke with God. I was enabled to lift up my soul to God, early this morning;

† This was the last time that ever he wrote in his diary with
his own hand; though it is continued a little farther, in a broken
manner; written by his brother Israel, but indited by his mouth,
in this his weak and dying state.

and while I had little bodily strength, I found freedom to lift up my heart to God for myself and others. Afterward, was pleased with the thoughts of speedily entering into the unseen world."

He felt this morning an unusual appetite for food, with which his mind seemed to be exhilarated, looking on it as a sign of the very near approach of death. At this time he also said, "I was *born* on a *Sabbath-day*, and I have reason to think I was *new-born* on a *Sabbath-day*; and I hope I shall *die* on this *Sabbath-day*. I shall look upon it as a favor, if it may be the will of God that it should be so: I long for the time. O, why is his chariot so long in coming? why tarry the wheels of his chariot? I am very willing to part with all: I am willing to part with my dear brother John, and never to see him again, to go to be for ever with the Lord.* O, when I go there, how will God's dear church on earth be upon my mind!"

Afterward, the same morning, being asked how he did, he answered, "I am almost in eternity; I long to be there. My work is done; I have done with all my friends: all the world is nothing to me. I long to be in heaven, praising and glorifying God with the holy angels. *All my desire is to glorify God.*"

During the whole of these last two weeks of his life, he seemed to continue in this frame of heart, as having finished his work, and done with all things here below. He had now nothing to do but to die, and to abide in an

* He had, before this, expressed a desire, if it might be the will of God, to live till his brother returned from New-Jersey: who, when he went away, intended, if possible, to perform his journey, and return in a fortnight; hoping once more to meet his brother in the land of the living. The fortnight was now nearly expired.

President Edwards' House, Northampton, Massachusetts, 1717.

earnest desire and expectation of the happy moment,
when his soul should take its flight to a state of perfect
holiness, in which he should be found perfectly glorifying and enjoying God. He said, "the consideration
of the day of death, and the day of judgment, had a long
time been peculiarly sweet to him." From time to
time he spake of his being willing to leave the body
and the world immediately—that day, that night, that
moment—if it was the will of God. He also was much
engaged in expressing his longings that the Church of
Christ on earth might flourish, and Christ's kingdom
here be advanced, notwithstanding he was about to
leave the earth, and should not with his eyes behold
the desirable event, nor be instrumental in promoting
it. He said to me, one morning, as I came into his
room, "My thoughts have been employed on the old
dear theme, the prosperity of God's church on earth.
As I waked out of sleep, I was led to cry for the pouring out of God's Spirit, and the advancement of Christ's
kingdom, for which the Redeemer did and suffered so
much. It is that especially which makes me long for
it." He expressed much hope that a glorious advancement of Christ's kingdom was near at hand.

He once told me, that "he had formerly longed for
the outpouring of the Spirit of God, and the glorious
times of the church, and hoped they were coming; and
that he should have been willing to live to promote religion at that time if that had been the will of God: but,"
says he, "I am willing it should be as it is; I would not
have the choice to make for myself, for ten thousand
worlds." He expressed on his death-bed a full persua-
sion that he should in heaven see the prosperity of the
church on earth, and should rejoice with Christ there

in; and the consideration of it seemed to be highly pleasing and satisfying to his mind.

He also still dwelt much on the great importance of the work of gospel ministers, and expressed his longings that they might be *filled with the Spirit of God.* He manifested much desire to see some of the neighboring ministers with whom he had some acquaintance, and of whose sincere friendship he was confident, that he might converse freely with them on that subject before he died. And it so happened, that he had opportunity with some of them according to his desire.

Another thing that lay much on his heart from time to time, in these near approaches of death, was the spiritual prosperity of his own congregation of Christian Indians in New-Jersey; when he spake of them, it was with peculiar tenderness, so that his speech would be presently interrupted and drowned with tears.

He also expressed much satisfaction in the disposal of Providence with regard to the circumstances of his *death;* particularly that God had before his death given him an opportunity in Boston, with so many considerable persons, ministers and others, to give in his testimony for God against false religion, and many mistakes that lead to it and promote it. He was much pleased that he had had an opportunity there to lay before pious and charitable gentlemen the state of the Indians, and their necessities, to so good effect; and that God had since enabled him to write to them further concerning these affairs; and to write other letters of importance, which he hoped might be of good influence with regard to the state of religion among the Indians, and elsewhere, after his death. He expressed great thankfulness to God for his mercy in these things.

He also mentioned it as what he accounted a merciful circumstance of his death, that he should die *here.* Speaking of these things, he said, "God had granted him all his desire;" and signified that now he could joyfully leave the world.

Sept. 28.—"I was able to read and make some few corrections in my private writings, but found I could not write as I had done; I found myself sensibly declined in all respects. It has been only from a little while before noon till about one or two o'clock, that I have been able to do any thing for some time past; yet it refreshed my heart that I could do any thing, either public or private, that I hoped was for God."

This evening he was supposed to be dying, both by himself and by those about him. He seemed glad at the appearance of the near approach of death. He was almost speechless, but his lips appeared to move, and one that sat very near him heard him utter such expressions as these: "Come, Lord Jesus, come quickly. O why is his chariot so long in coming?" After he revived, he blamed himself for having been too eager to be gone. And in expressing what was the frame of his mind at that time, he said he then found an inexpressibly sweet love to those whom he looked upon as belonging to Christ, beyond almost all that ever he felt before; so that it seemed, to use his own words, "like a little piece of heaven to have one of them near him." And being asked whether he heard the prayer that was, at his desire, made with him, he said, "Yes, he heard every word, and had an uncommon sense of the things that were uttered in that prayer, and that every word reached his heart."

On the evening of *Tuesday, Sept.* 29, as he lay on his bed, he seemed to be in an extraordinary frame; his

mind greatly engaged in sweet meditations concerning
the prosperity of Zion.   There being present here, at
that time, two young gentlemen of his acquaintance,
who were candidates for the ministry, he desired us
all to unite in singing a psalm on that subject, even
Zion's prosperity.   And on his desire we sung a part
of the 102d psalm.   This seemed much to refresh and
revive him, and gave him new strength; so that though
before, he could scarcely speak at all, now he proceeded, with some freedom of speech, to give his dying
counsels to these young gentlemen relative to their preparation for the great work of the ministry; and in
particular, earnestly recommended to them frequen*
secret fasting and prayer; and enforced his counse*
with regard to this, from his own experience of the
great comfort and benefit of it; "which," said he, "I
should not mention, were it not that I am a dying per
son."   After he had finished his counsel, he made a
prayer in the audience of us all; wherein, besides pray
ing for this family, for his brethren, and those candidates
for the ministry, and for his own congregation, he earnestly prayed for the reviving and flourishing of reli
gion in the world.—Till now, he had every day sat up
part of the day; but after this he never rose from his bed.

Sept. 30.—"I was obliged to keep my bed the whole
day, through weakness.   However, redeemed a little
time, and, with the help of my brother, read and cor-
rected about a dozen pages in my manuscript, giving
an account of my conversion.

Oct. 1.—"I endeavored again to do something by
way of writing, but soon found my powers of body
and mind utterly fail.   Felt not so sweetly as when I
was able to do something which I hoped would do some
good.   In the evening, was discomposed and wholly

delirious; but it was not long before God was pleased to give me some sleep, and fully compose my mind.* O blessed be God for his great goodness to me, since I was so low at Mr. Bloomfield's on *Thursday, June* 18. He has, except those few minutes, given me the clear exercise of my reason, and enabled me to labor much for him in things both of a public and private nature, and perhaps to do more good than I should have done if I had been well; besides the comfortable influences of his blessed Spirit, with which he has been pleased to refresh my soul. May his name have all the glory for ever and ever. Amen.

Oct. 2.—"My soul was this day, at turns, sweetly set on God: I longed to be *with him,* that I might *behold his glory.* I felt sweetly disposed to commit all to him, even my dearest friends, my dearest flock, my absent brother, and all my concerns for time and eternity. O that *his kingdom* might come in the world; that they might all love and glorify him for what he is in himself; and that the blessed Redeemer might 'see of the travail of his soul, and be satisfied!' O come, Lord Jesus, come quickly! Amen."

Here ends his diary. These are the *last words* which are written in it, either by his own hand, or by any other from his mouth.

The next evening we very much expected his brother John from New-Jersey; it being about a week after the time that he proposed for his return, when he went away. Though our expectations were still disappointed, yet Brainerd seemed to continue unmoved, in the same calm and peaceful frame which he had before

---

* From this time forward he had the free use of his reason till the day before his death; except that at some times he appeared a little lost for a moment when first waking out of sleep.

manifested; as having resigned all to God, and having done with his friends, and with all things here below.

On the morning of the next day, being *Lord's day*, Oct. 4, as my daughter Jerusha, who chiefly attended him, came into the room, he looked on her very pleasantly, and said, " Dear Jerusha, are you willing to part with me ?"—"I am quite willing to part with you: I am willing to part with all my friends: I am willing to part with my dear brother John, although I love him the best of any creature living: I have committed him and all my friends to God, and can leave them with God. Though, if I thought I should not see you, and be happy with you in another world, I could not bear to part with you. But we shall spend an happy eternity together !"* In the evening, as one came into the room with a Bible in her hand, he expressed himself thus: "O that dear book—that lovely book! I shall soon see it opened! The mysteries that are in it, and

* In about four months, it pleased a holy and sovereign God to take away this my dear child by death, on the 14th of February, after a short illness of five days, in the eighteenth year of her age. She was a person of much the same spirit with BRAINERD. She had constantly taken care of, and attended him in his sickness, for nineteen weeks before his death; devoting herself to him with great delight, because she looked on him as an eminent servant of Jesus Christ. In this time he had much conversation with her on the things of religion; and in his dying state, often expressed to us, her parents, his great satisfaction concerning her true piety, and his confidence that he should meet her in heaven. She had manifested a heart uncommonly devoted to God; and said on her death-bed, that " she had seen no time for several years, when she desired to live one minute longer, for the sake of any other good in life, but doing good, living to God, and doing what might be for his glory."

the mysteries of God's providence, will be all un-
folded!"

On *Tuesday*, Oct. 6, he lay for a considerable time
as if he were dying; at which time he was heard to
utter, in broken whispers, such expressions as these:
"He will come, he will not tarry. I shall soon be in
glory. I shall soon glorify God with the angels."—But
after some time he revived.

The next day, *Wednesday*, Oct. 7, his brother John
arrived from New-Jersey; where he had been detained
much longer than he intended, by a mortal sickness
prevailing among the christian Indians, and by some
other circumstances that made his stay with them necessary. BRAINERD was affected and refreshed with
seeing him, and appeared fully satisfied with the reasons of his delay; seeing the interest of religion and
the souls of his people required it.

The next day, *Thursday*, Oct. 8, he was in great distress and agonies of body; and for the greater part of
the day was much disordered as to the exercise of his
reason. In the evening he was composed, and had
the use of his reason; but the pain of his body continued and increased. He told me that it was impossible 'for any one to conceive of the distress he felt in
his breast. He manifested much concern lest he should
dishonor God by impatience under his extreme agony;
which was such, that he said the thought of enduring
it one moment longer was almost insupportable. He
desired that others would be much in lifting up their
hearts continually to God for him, that God would support him, and give him patience. He signified that he
expected to die that night; but seemed to fear a longer
delay; and the disposition of his mind with regard to
death, appeared still the same that it had been all along.

And notwithstanding his bodily agonies, yet the interest of Zion lay still with great weight on his mind. On that evening he had considerable discourse with the Rev. Mr. Billing, one of the neighboring ministers, concerning the great importance of the work of the ministry. Afterward, late in the night, he had much very proper and profitable discourse with his brother John, concerning his congregation in New-Jersey, and the interest of religion among the Indians. In the latter part of the night his bodily distress seemed to rise to a greater height than ever. Toward day his eyes became fixed; and he continued lying immovable till about six o'clock on Friday, Oct. 9, 1747, when his soul, as we may well conclude, was received by his dear Lord and Master into that state of perfection of holiness, and fruition of God, for which he had so often and so ardently longed; and was welcomed by the glorious assembly in the upper world, as one peculiarly fitted to join them in their blessed employ and enjoyment.

Much respect was shown to his memory at his *funeral;* which was on the Monday following, after a sermon preached on that solemn occasion. His funeral was attended by eight of the neighboring ministers, and a great concourse of people.

CHAPTER X

Reflections on the preceding Memoirs.

REFLECTION I

In the life of BRAINERD we may see, as I apprehend *the nature of true religion, and the manner of its ope ration*, when exemplified in a *high degree* and in *powerful exercise.* Particularly it may be worthy to be observed :

1. How greatly BRAINERD'S religion *differed* from that of some pretenders to the experience of a *clear work* of saving *conversion* wrought on their hearts ; who, depending and living on that, settle in a *cold, careless,* and *carnal* frame of mind, and in a neglect of a thorough, earnest religion, in the stated practice of it.   Although his convictions and conversion were in all respects exceedingly clear, and very remarkable ; yet how far was he from acting as though he thought he had *got through his work,* when once he had obtained comfort, and satisfaction of his interest in Christ and a title to heaven ! On the contrary, that work on his heart, by which he was brought to this, was with him evidently but the *beginning of his work ;* his first entering on the great business of religion, and the service of God ; his first setting out in his race.   His work was not finished, nor his race ended, till life was ended.

As his conversion was not the end of *his work,* or of the course of his diligence and strivings in religion, so neither was it the end of the *work of the Spirit* of God on his heart.   On the contrary, it was the first dawning of the light, which thenceforth increased more and more ; the beginning of his holy affections, his sorrow for sin, his love to God, his rejoicing in Jesus Christ, his longing after holiness.   There are many, who, after the effect of novelty is over, soon find their situation and feelings very much the same as before their supposed conversion, with respect to any present thirstings for God, or ardent out-goings of their souls after divine objects. Now and then, indeed, they have a comfortable reflection on the past, and are somewhat affected with the remembrance, and so rest easy, thinking that it is *safe ;* and they doubt not but they shall go to heaven when they die. Far otherwise was it with BRAINERD. His experiences, instead of dying away, were evidently of an increasing nature. His first love, and other holy affections, even at the beginning, were very great ; but, after the lapse of months and years, became much greater and more remarkable.

2. His religion apparently and greatly *differed* from that of many high pretenders to religion, who are frequently actuated by *vehement emotions* of mind, and are carried on in a course of *sudden and strong impressions*, and supposed high *illuminations and immediate discoveries ;* and at the same time are persons of a virulent " zeal, not according to knowledge." If we look through the whole series of his experience, from his conversion to his death, we shall find none of this kind—no imaginary sight of Christ hanging on the cross with his blood streaming from his wounds; or with a countenance smiling on him; or arms open to embrace him : no sight of the book of life opened, with his name written in it; no hearing God or Christ speaking to him; nor any sudden suggestions of words or sentences, either of Scripture or any other, as then immediately spoken or sent to him; no new revelations; no sudden strong suggestions of secret facts. Nor do I find any one instance in all the records which he has left of his own life, from beginning to end, of joy excited from a supposed *immediate* witness of the Spirit; or inward immediate suggestion, that his state was surely good. But the way in which he was satisfied of his own good estate, even to the entire abolishing of

fear, was by feeling within himself the lively actings of a holy temper and heavenly disposition, the vigorous exercises of that divine "love which casteth out fear."

3. BRAINERD's religion was not *selfish* and *mercenary;* his love to God was primarily and principally for the supreme excellency of his *own nature*, and not built on a preconceived notion that God loved *him*, had received him into favor, and had done great things for him, or promised great things to him. His joy was joy in *God*, and not in *himself.* We see by his diary how, from time to time, through the course of his life, his soul was filled with ineffable sweetness and comfort. The affecting considerations and lively ideas of *God's infinite glory*, his unchangeable blessedness, his sovereignty and universal dominion; together with the sweet exercises of love to God, giving himself up to him, abasing himself before him, denying himself for him, depending upon him, acting for his glory, diligently serving him; and the pleasing prospects or hopes he had of the future advancement of the kingdom of Christ, were the grounds of his strong and abiding consolation.

It appears plainly and abundantly all along, from his conversion to his death, that the sort of good which was the great object of the new relish and appetite given him in conversion, and thenceforward maintained and increased in his heart, was HOLINESS, conformity to God, living to God, and glorifying him. This was what drew his heart; this was the centre of his soul; this was the ocean to which all the streams of his religious affections tended; this was the object which engaged his eager thirsting desires and earnest pursuits. He knew no true excellency or happiness but this; this was what he longed for most vehemently and constantly on *earth;* and this was with him the beauty and blessedness of *heaven.* This made him so much and so often long for that world of glory. It was to be perfectly holy, and perfectly exercised in the holy employments of heaven; and thus " to glorify God and enjoy him for ever."

His religious illuminations, affections, and comfort, seemed, to a great degree, to be attended with *evangelical humiliation;* consisting in a sense of his own utter insufficiency, despicableness, and odiousness; with an answerable disposition and frame of heart. How deeply affected was he almost continually with his great defects in religion; with his vast distance from that spirituality and holy frame of mind that became him; with his ignorance, pride, deadness, unsteadiness, barrenness! He was not only affected with the remembrance of his *former* sinfulness before his conversion, but with the sense of his *present* vileness and pollution. He was not only disposed to think meanly of himself as *before God,* and in comparison of him; but *among men,* and as compared with them. He was apt to think other saints better than himself; yea, to look on himself as the meanest and least of saints; yea, very often, as the vilest and worst of mankind. And notwithstanding his great attainments in *spiritual knowledge,* yet we find there is scarcely any thing, with a sense of which he is more frequently affected and abased, than his *ignorance.*

How eminently did he appear to be of a *meek* and *quiet* spirit, resembling the lamb-like, dove-like spirit of Jesus Christ! How full of love, meekness, quietness, forgiveness, and mercy! His love was not merely a fondness and zeal for a party, but an universal benevolence; very often exercised in the most sensible and ardent love to his greatest opposers and enemies.

Of how *soft* and *tender* a spirit was he! How far were his experiences, hopes, and joys, from a tendency finally to stupify and harden him, to lessen convictions and tenderness of conscience, to cause him to be less affected with present and past sins, and less conscientious with respect to future sins! How far were they from making him more easy in neglect of duties which are troublesome and inconvenient, more slow and partial in complying with difficult commands, less apt to be alarmed at the appearance of his own defects and transgressions, more easily induced to a compliance with carnal appetites! On the contrary, how tender was his conscience! how apt was his heart to smite him! how easily and greatly was he alarmed at the appearance of moral evil! how great and constant was his jealousy over his own heart! how strict his care and watchfulness against sin! how deep and sensible were the wounds that sin made in his conscience! Those evils which are generally accounted small, were almost an insupportable burden to him; such as his inward deficiencies, his having no more love to God, finding within himself any slackness or dullness in religion, any unsteadiness or wandering frame of mind. How did the consideration of such things as these oppress and abase him, and fill him with inward shame and confusion! His love and hope, though they were such as cast out a servile fear of hell, yet were attended with, and abundantly cherished and promoted a reverential filial fear of God, a dread of sin and of God's holy displeasure. His joy seemed truly to be a rejoicing with trembling. His assurance and comfort differed greatly from a false enthusiastic confidence and joy, in that it promoted and maintained mourning for sin. He did not, after he received comfort and full satisfaction of the safety of his state, forget his past sins, whether committed before or after his conversion; but the remembrance of them, from time to time, revived in his heart with renewed grief. That passage was evidently fulfilled in him, " That thou mayest remember, and be confounded, and never open thy mouth any more, because of thy shame; when I am pacified toward thee for all that thou hast done." Ezek. 16 : 63

His religious affections and joys were not like those of some, who have rapture and mighty emotions from time to time in *company;* but have very litt'e affection in *retirement* and secret places. Though he was of a very sociable temper, and loved the company of saints, and delighted very much in religious conversation, and in social worship; yet his warmest affections, and their greatest effects on his animal nature, and his sweetest joys, were in his closet devotions, and solitary transactions between God and his own soul: as is very observable through his whole course, from his conversion to his death. He delighted greatly in sacred retirements; and loved to get quite away from all the world, to converse with God alone, in secret duties.

Brainerd's experiences and comforts were very far from being like those of some persons, which are attended with *a spiritual satiety,* and which put an end to their religious desires and longings, at least to the edge and ardency of them; resting satisfied in their own attainments and comforts, as having obtained their chief end, which is to extinguish their fears of hell, and give them confidence of the favor of God. On the contrary, they were always attended with longings and thirstings after greater degrees of conformity to God! The greater and sweeter his comforts were, the more vehement were his desires after holiness.

His longings were not so much after joyful discoveries of God's love, and clear views of his own title to future advancement and eternal honors in heaven; as after more of present holiness, greater spirituality, an heart more engaged for God, to love, and exalt, and depend on him. He earnestly wished to serve God better, to do more for his glory, to do all that he did with more of a regard to Christ as his righteousness and strength, and to behold the enlargement and advancement of his kingdom on earth. His desires were not idle wishes, but such as were powerful and effectual, to animate him to the earnest, eager pursuit of these things, with the utmost diligence and unfainting labor and self-denial. His *comforts* never put an end to his seeking after God, and striving to obtain his grace; but, on the contrary, greatly engaged him therein.

4. His religion did not consist in *experience* without *practice.* All his inward illuminations, affections, and comforts, seemed to have a direct tendency to practice, and to issue in it: and this, not merely a practice *negatively* good, free from gross acts of irreligion and immorality; but a practice *positively* holy and Christian, in a serious, devout, humble, meek, merciful, charitable, and beneficent conversation; making the service of God and our Lord Jesus Christ the great business of life, to which he was devoted, and which he pursued with the greatest earnestness and diligence to the end of his days, through all trials. In him was to be seen the right way of being lively in religion. His liveliness in religion did not consist merely, or mainly, in his being lively with the *tongue,* but in *deed;* not in being forward in profession and outward show, and abundant in declaring his own experiences; but chiefly in being active and abundant in the labors and

duties of religion; "not slothful in business, but fervent in spirit, serving the Lord, and serving his generation, according to the will of God."

REFLECTION II

The foregoing account of BRAINERD's life may convince us, that there is indeed such a thing as true *experimental religion*, arising from an immediate divine influence, supernaturally enlightening and convincing the mind, and powerfully impressing, quickening, sanctifying, and governing the heart.

If any insist that BRAINERD's religion was mere *enthusiasm*, the result of a heated imagination, I would ask, What were the FRUITS of his enthusiasm? In him we behold a great degree of honesty and simplicity; sincere and earnest desires and endeavors to know and do whatever is right, and to avoid every thing that is wrong; a high degree of love to God; delight in the perfections of his nature, placing the happiness of life in him, not only in contemplating him, but in being active in pleasing and serving him; a firm and undoubting belief in the Messiah, as the Savior of the world, the great Prophet of God, and King of the church, together with great love to him, delight and complacence in the way of salvation by him, and longing for the enlargement of his kingdom; earnest desires that God may be glorified and the Messiah's kingdom advanced, whatever instruments are employed; uncommon resignation to the will of God, and that under vast trials; and great and universal benevolence to mankind, reaching all sorts of persons without distinction, manifested in sweetness of speech and behavior, kind treatment, mercy, liberality, and earnestly seeking the good of the

souls and bodies of men. All this we behold attended
with extraordinary humility, meekness, forgiveness
of injuries, and love to enemies. In him we see a
modest, discreet, and decent deportment, among supe-
riors, inferiors, and equals; a most diligent improvement of time; earnest care to lose no part of it; and
great watchfulness against all sorts of sin, of heart,
speech, and action. This example and these endeavors we see attended with most happy fruits, and
blessed effects on *others*, in humanizing, civilizing, and
wonderfully reforming and transforming some of the
most brutish savages; idle, immoral drunkards, mur-
derers, gross idolaters, and wizards; bringing them to
permanent sobriety, diligence, devotion, honesty, con-
scientiousness, and charity. The foregoing virtues and
successful labors all end at last in a marvellous peace,
immovable stability, calmness, and resignation, in the
sensible approaches of death; with longing for the
heavenly state; not only for the honors and circum-
stantial advantages of it, but above all, for the *moral
perfection* and holy and blessed employments of it.
These things are seen in a person indisputably of good
understanding and judgment. I therefore say, if all
these things are the fruits of *enthusiasm*, why should
not *enthusiasm* be thought a desirable and excellent
thing? For what can true religion, what can the best
philosophy, do more?

REFLECTION III

The preceding history serves to confirm *the doctrines
of grace.* For if it be allowed that there is truth, substance, or value in the main of BRAINERD'S religion, it
will undoubtedly follow, that those doctrines are di-

vine; since it is evident that the whole of it, from beginning to end, accords with them.   He was brought, by
doctrines of this kind, to his awakening and deep concern about things of a spiritual and eternal nature; by
these doctrines his convictions were maintained and
carried on; and his conversion was evidently altogether agreeable to them.   His conversion was no con-
firming and perfecting of moral principles and habits,
by use, and practice, and industrious discipline, together with the concurring suggestions and conspiring
aids of God's Spirit; but entirely a supernatural work,
at once turning him from darkness to marvellous light,
and from the power of sin to the dominion of divine
and holy principles.   It was an effect, in no respect
produced by *his* strength or labor, or obtained by *his*
virtue; and not accomplished till he was first brought
to a full conviction, that all his own virtue, strength,
labors and endeavors, could never avail any thing toward producing or procuring this effect.

If ever BRAINERD was truly turned from sin to God
at all, or ever became truly religious, none can reasonably doubt but that his conversion was at the time
when he supposed it to be. The change which he then
met with, was evidently the greatest moral change
that he ever experienced; and he was then apparently
first brought to that kind of religion, that remarkable
new habit and temper of mind, which he held all his
life after. The narration shows it to be different, in
nature and *kind*, from all of which he was ever the
subject before. It was evidently wrought at once
without fitting and preparing his mind, by gradually
convincing it more and more of the same truths, and
bringing it nearer and nearer to such a temper: it was
soon after his mind had been remarkably full of blas-

phemy, and a vehement exercise of sensible enmity against God, and great opposition to those truths which he was now brought with his whole soul to embrace, and rest in as divine and glorious; truths, in the contemplation and improvement of which he placed his happiness. He himself, who was surely best able to judge, declares, that the dispositions and affections which were then given him, and thenceforward maintained in him, were, most sensibly and certainly, altogether different in their *nature* from all of which he was ever the subject before, or of which he ever had any conception.

Hence it is very evident that BRAINERD's religion was the effect of the doctrines of grace applied to his heart: and certainly it cannot be denied that the effect was good, unless we turn atheists or deists. I would ask whether there be any such thing, in reality, as *Christian devotion?* If there be, what is it? what is its nature? and what its just measure? Should it not be in a great *degree?* We read abundantly in Scripture of "*loving* God with all the heart, with all the soul, with all the mind, and with all the strength; of *delighting* in God, of *rejoicing* in the Lord, rejoicing with joy unspeakable and full of glory; the soul magnifying the Lord, thirsting for God, hungering and thirsting after righteousness; the soul breaking for the longing it hath to God's judgments, praying to God with groanings that cannot be uttered, mourning for sin with a broken heart and contrite spirit," &c. How full are the Psalms, and other parts of Scripture, of such things as these! Now wherein do these things, as expressed by and appearing in BRAINERD, either the things themselves, or their effects and fruits, differ from the Scripture representations? To these things he was brought by that strange and wonderful transformation of the man, which he called *his conversion*. Does not this well agree with what is so often said in the Old Testament and the New, concerning "giving a new heart. creating a right spirit, being renewed in the spirit of the mind, being sanctified throughout, becoming a new creature?"

REFLECTION IV

Is there not much in the preceding memoirs of BRAINERD to teach, and excite to duty, us who are called to the work of the *ministry*, and all who are *candidates* for that great work? What a deep sense did he seem to have of the greatness and importance of that work, and with what weight did it lie on his mind! How sensible was he of his own insufficiency for this work; and how great was his dependence on God's sufficiency! How solicitous that he might be fitted for it! and to this end, how much time did he spend in prayer and fasting, as well as reading and meditation; *giving himself to these things!* How did he dedicate his whole life, all his powers and talents to God; and forsake and renounce the world, with all its pleasing and ensnaring enjoyments, that he might be wholly at liberty to serve Christ in this work, and to "please him who had chosen him to be a soldier under the Captain of our salvation!" With what solicitude, solemnity and diligence did he devote himself to God our Savior, and seek his presence and blessing in secret, at the time of his *ordination!* and how did his whole heart appear to be constantly engaged, his whole time employed, and his whole strength spent in the business he then solemnly undertook, and to which he was publicly set apart. His history shows us the right way to *success* in the work of the ministry. He sought it, as a resolute soldier seeks victory in a siege or battle; or as a man who runs a race, seeks a great prize. Animated with love to Christ and the souls of men, how did he "labor always fervently," not only in word and doctrine, in public and private, but in *prayers* day and night, "wrestling with God" in secret, and "travailing in birth," with unutterable groans and agonies, "until Christ were formed" in the hearts of the people to whom he was sent! How did he thirst for a blessing on his ministry, and "watch for souls, as one that must give account!" How did he "go forth in the strength of the Lord God," seeking and depending on a special influence of the *Spirit* to assist and succeed him! What was the happy fruit at last, though after long waiting, and many dark and discouraging appearances? Like a true son of Jacob, he persevered in wrestling, through all the darkness of the night, until the breaking of the day.

To *Missionaries* in particular, may his example of laboring, praying, denying himself, and enduring hardness with unfainting resolution and patience, and his faithful, vigilant, and prudent conduct in many other respects, afford instruction.

REFLECTION V

The foregoing account of BRAINERD's life may afford instruction to *Christians in general;* as it shows, in many respects, the right way of *practising* religion, in order to obtain the *ends*, and receive the *benefits* of it; or how Christians should "run the race set before them," if they would not "run in vain, or run as uncertainly,"[*] but would honor God in the world, adorn their profession, be serviceable to mankind, have the comforts of religion while they live, be free from disquieting doubts and dark apprehensions about the state of their souls, enjoy peace in the approaches of death, and " finish their course with joy." In general, he much recommended, for this purpose, the *redemption of time*, great *diligence* in the business of the Christian life, *watchfulness*, &c. and he very remarkably exemplified these things.

Particularly, his example and success with regard to one duty, in an especial manner, may be of great use to both ministers and private Christians; I mean the duty of *secret fasting*. The reader has seen how much BRAINERD recommends this duty, and how frequently he exercised himself in it; nor can it well have escaped observation, how much he was owned and blessed in it, and of what great benefit it evidently was to his soul. Among all the many days he spent in secret fasting and prayer, of which he gives an account in his *diary*, there is scarcely an instance of one which was not either attended or soon followed with apparent success, and a remarkable blessing, in special influences and consolations of God's Spirit; and very often before the day was ended. But it must be observed, that when he set about this duty, he did it in good earnest; " stirring up himself to take hold of God," and " continuing instant in prayer," with much of the spirit of Jacob, who said to the angel, " I will not let thee go, except thou bless me."

REFLECTION VI

There is much in the preceding account to excite and encourage God's people to earnest prayers and endeavors for the *advancement and enlargement of the kingdom of Christ in the world.* BRAINERD set us an excellent example in this respect. He sought the prosperity of Zion with all his might; and preferred Jerusalem above his chief joy. How did his soul long for it, and pant after it! how earnestly and often did he wrestle with God for it! and how far did he in these desires and prayers seem to be carried beyond all private and selfish views! being animated by a pure love to Christ, an earnest desire of his glory, and a disinterested affection to the souls of mankind.

The consideration of this, not only ought to be an *incitement* to the people of God, but may also be a just *encouragement* to them, to be much in seeking and praying for a general outpouring of the Spirit of God, and an extensive revival of religion. I confess, that God's giving so much of a spirit of prayer for this mercy to so eminent a servant of his, and exciting him in so extraordinary a manner, and with such vehement thirstings of soul, to agonize in prayer for it, from time to time, through the course of his life, is one thing, among others, which gives me great hope that God has a design of accomplishing something very glorious for the interest of his church before long. One such instance as this, I conceive, gives more encouragement than the common, cold, formal prayers of thousands. As BRAINERD's desires and prayers for the coming of Christ's kingdom were very *special* and *extraordinary;* so I think we may reasonably hope, that the God who excited those desires and prayers, will answer them with something *special* and *extraordinary.* And in a particular manner do I think it worthy of notice for our encouragement, that he had his heart unusually drawn out in longings and prayers for

the flourishing of Christ's kingdom on earth when he
was in the approaches of *death;* and that with his dying breath he breathed out his departing soul into the
bosom of his Redeemer, in prayers and pantings after
the glorious event; expiring in very great hope that
it would soon begin to be fulfilled.

I would not conclude these reflections without a
grateful acknowledgment of the mercy of God in the
circumstances of BRAINERD's death, and especially the
gracious dispensation of Providence to me and my
family, in so ordering that he, though the ordinary
place of his abode was more than two hundred miles
distant, should be brought to my house in his last sickness, and should die here. Thus we had opportunity
for much acquaintance and conversation with him, to
show him kindness in such circumstances, to see his
dying *behavior*, to hear his dying *speeches*, to receive
his dying *counsels*, and to have the benefit of his dying
prayers. May God in infinite mercy grant, that we
may ever retain a proper remembrance of these things,
and make a due improvement of the advantages we
have had in these respects! The Lord grant also, that
the foregoing account of BRAINERD's life and death may
be for the great spiritual benefit of all who shall read it,
and prove a happy means of promoting the revival of
true religion! *Amen.*